Praise for *On the* [Rez]

"[Frazier] is a writer to be prized, and his new book...is a book to admire."
—Andrew Ferguson, *Fortune* magazine

"[A] continuously rich and rewarding read."
—John McCormick, *LA Weekly*

"The best book on the Indian in American life...since Evan S. Connell's *Son of the Morning Star*."
—David Walton, *The Plain Dealer* (Cleveland)

"This is a meticulously observed, eloquently written book."
—Sam Coale, *Providence Journal*

"With warmth, humor, and poignancy, he creates a portrait of a people with a rich living heritage."
—Lynn Harnett, *Herald Sunday* (New Hampshire)

"Frazier brings to life a great tribe, through its hard times and its glorious history."
—Lisa Shea, *Elle* magazine

"[Frazier] is always trying to understand the Sioux, which leads him to all kinds of fascinating facts. He is straightforward about the problems the Sioux face—jealousy, alcoholism, violence. He admires them but does not romanticize them."
—Anthony Brandt, *Men's Journal*

"A serious but never somber chronicler of the American heartland."
—Paul Gray, *Time* magazine

"Probably no book since Evan S. Connell's *Son of the Morning Star* has so imaginatively evoked the spirit of the American Indian in American life.... Funny and sad, but never bleak."
—*Publishers Weekly* (starred review)

Also by Ian Frazier
Coyote v. Acme (1996)
Family (1994)
Great Plains (1989)
Nobody Better, Better Than Nobody (1987)
Dating Your Mom (1986)

On the Rez

• • •

Ian Frazier

Picador

Farrar, Straus and Giroux

New York

Picador® is a U.S. registered trademark and is used by Farrar, Straus
and Giroux under license from Pan Books Limited.

For information on Picador USA Reading Group Guides, as well as
ordering, please contact the Trade Marketing department at St.
Martin's Press.
Phone: 1-800-221-7945 extension 763
Fax: 212-677-7456
E-mail: trademarketing@stmartins.com

Designed by Jonathan D. Lippincott

Parts of this book first appeared in *The Atlantic Monthly*.

Library of Congress Cataloging-in-Publication Data
Frazier, Ian.
    On the rez / Ian Frazier.
        p. cm.
    ISBN 0-312-27859-4
    1. Oglala Indians. 2. Pine Ridge Indian Reservation (S.D.)
    3. War Lance, Le. 4. Indians of North America—Great Plains.
    5. Big Crow, SuAnne.   I. Title.
    E99.03F73 2000
    978.3'66—dc21   99-28353
                                                       CIP

First published in the United States by Farrar, Straus and Giroux

14 13 12

For Cora and Thomas

Contents

On the Rez

CHAPTER

1

This book is about Indians, particularly the Oglala Sioux who live on the Pine Ridge Reservation in southwestern South Dakota, in the plains and badlands in the middle of the United States. People want to know what a book is about right up front, I have found. They feel this way even if the book does not yet exist, if it is only planned. When I describe the subject to non-Indians, they often reply that it sounds bleak. "Bleak" is the word attached in many people's minds to the idea of certain Indian reservations, of which the Oglala's reservation is perhaps the best example. Oddly, it is a word I have never heard used by Indians themselves. Many thousands of people—not just Americans, but German and French and English people, and more—visit the reservations every year, and the prevailing opinion among the Indians is not that they come for the bleakness. The Indians understand that the vistors are there out of curiosity and out of an admiration which sometimes even reaches such a point that the visitors wish they could be Indians, too. I am a middle-aged non-Indian who wears his hair in a thinning ponytail copied originally from the traditional-style long hair of the leaders of the American Indian Movement of the 1970s, because I thought it looked cool. When I'm driving across a field near the town of Oglala on the Pine Ridge Reservation and I see my friend Floyd John walking across it the other way, I stop, and he comes over to the car and leans in the window and smiles a big-tooth grin and says, "How ya' doin', wannabe?"

I kind of resent the term "wannabe"—what's wrong with wanting to be something, anyway?—but in my case there's some truth to it. I don't want to participate in traditional Indian religious ceremonies, dance in a sun dance or pray in a sweat lodge or go on a vision quest with the help of a medicine man. The power of these ceremonies has an appeal, but I'm content with what little religion I already have. I think Indians dress better than anyone, but I don't want to imitate more than a detail or two; I prefer my clothes humdrum and inconspicuous, and a cowboy hat just doesn't work for me. I don't want to collect Indian art, though pots and beadwork and blankets made by Indians remain the most beautiful art objects in the American West, in my opinion. I don't want to be adopted into a tribe, be wrapped in a star quilt and given a new name, honor though that would be. I don't want to stand in the dimness under the shelter at the powwow grounds in the group around the circle of men beating the drums and singing ancient songs and lose myself in that moment when all the breaths and all the heartbeats become one. What I want is just as "Indian," just as traditional, but harder to pin down.

In 1608, the newly arrived Englishmen at Jamestown colony in Virginia proposed to give the most powerful Indian in the vicinity, Chief Powhatan, a crown. Their idea was to coronate him a sub-emperor of Indians, and vassal to the English King. Powhatan found the offer insulting. "I also am a King," he said, "and this is my land." Joseph Brant, a Mohawk of the Iroquois Confederacy between eastern New York and the Great Lakes, was received as a celebrity when he went to England with a delegation from his tribe in 1785. Taken to St. James's Palace for a royal audience, he refused to kneel and kiss the hand of George III; he told the King that he would, however, gladly kiss the hand of the Queen. Almost a century later, the U.S. government gave Red Cloud, victorious war leader of the Oglala, the fanciest reception it knew how, with a dinner party at the White House featuring lighted chandeliers and wine and a dessert of strawberries and ice cream. The next day Red Cloud parleyed with the government officials just as he was accustomed to on the prairie—sitting on the floor. To a member of a Senate select committee who had delivered a tirade against Sitting Bull, the Hunkpapa

Sioux leader carelessly replied, "I have grown to be a very independent man, and consider myself a very great man."

That self-possessed sense of freedom is closer to what I want; I want to be an uncaught Indian like them.

Another remark which non-Indians often make on the subject of Indians is "Why can't they get with the program?" Anyone who talks about Indians in public will be asked that question, or variations on it; over and over: Why don't Indians forget all this tribal nonsense and become ordinary Americans like the rest of us? Why do they insist on living in the past? Why don't they accept the fact that we won and they lost? Why won't they stop, finally, being Indians and join the modern world? I have a variety of answers handy. Sometimes I say that in former days "the program" called for the eradication of Indian languages, and children in Indian boarding schools were beaten for speaking them and forced to speak English, so they would fit in; time passed, cultural fashions changed, and Hollywood made a feature film about Indians in which for the sake of authenticity the Sioux characters spoke Sioux (with English subtitles), and the movie became a hit, and lots of people decided they wanted to learn Sioux, and those who still knew the language, those who had somehow managed to avoid "the program" in the first place, were suddenly the ones in demand. Now, I think it's better not to answer the question but to ask a question in return: What program, exactly, do you have in mind?

We live in a craven time. I am not the first to point out that capitalism, having defeated Communism, now seems to be about to do the same to democracy. The market is doing splendidly, yet we are not, somehow. Americans today no longer work mostly in manufacturing or agriculture but in the newly risen service economy. That means that most of us make our living by being nice. And if we can't be nice, we'd better at least be neutral. In the service economy, anyone who sat where he pleased in the presence of power or who expatiated on his own greatness would soon be out the door. "Who does he think he is?" is how the dismissal is usually framed. The dream of many of us is that someday we might miraculously have enough money that we could quit being nice, and everybody would then have to be nice to us, and niceness would surround us like a warm dome. Certain speeches we would love to make accompany this dream, glorious, blistering tellings-off of those to whom we usually hold our tongue. The eleven people who actually have enough money to do that are icons to us. What we read in newsprint and see on television always reminds us how great they are, and we can't disagree. Unlike the rest of us, they can deliver those speeches with no fear. The freedom that inhered in Powhatan, that Red Cloud carried with him from the plains to Washington as easily as air—freedom to be and to say, whenever, regardless of disapproval—has become a luxury most of us can't afford.

From a historical perspective, this looks a lot like where America came in. When Columbus landed, there were about eleven people in Europe who could do whatever they felt like doing. Part of the exhilaration of the age was the rumored freedom explorers like Columbus found. Suddenly imagination was given a whole continent full of people who had never heard of Charlemagne, or Pope Leo X, or quitrents, or the laws of entail, and who were doing fine. Amerigo Vespucci, the explorer whose name and the continent's would be the same, brought back news that in this land "every one is his own master." If this land new to Europeans was the setting, the lives of these untrammeled people suggested the plot: we could drop anchor in the bay, paddle up the river, wade up the creek, meet a band of Indians, and with them disappear forever into the country's deepest green. No tyranny could hold us; if Indians could live as they liked, so could we.

The popular refrain about Indians nowadays is that they and their culture were cruelly destroyed. It's a breast-beatingly comfortable idea, from the destroyers' point of view. In the nineteenth century, with white people firmly established on the continent, common wisdom had it that the Indian must eventually die out. That meant die, literally, and give way in a Darwinian sense to the superiority of the Anglo-Saxon. "Adieu, red brother! You are going to join the Mastodon and the Scthysaurus," wrote humorist Bill Nye in 1891, shortly after the massacre at Wounded Knee. In the twentieth century, stories of the Indians' destruction, set mostly in the past tense, made a follow-up to this comfortable idea. From one century to the next, the destruction of the Indians was such a common theme that if they did not die out in fact, by the sound of it they might as well have. But beyond the sphere of

rhetoric, the Indians as a people did not die out, awful though the suffering was. Killing people is one thing, killing them off is another. The
Sand Creek Massacre, one of the bloodiest episodes on the Western
frontier and a permanent scar on the history of the state of Colorado,
killed at least two hundred, mostly women and children, of Chief Black
Kettle's band of Southern Cheyenne in 1864. Today there are more
than four thousand descendants of Sand Creek Massacre survivors; they
hope for restitution and a reservation of their own. New England's Pe-
quots, a tribe "extinct as the ancient Medes," according to Herman
Melville, rebounded from a recent time when just two members were
still living on the reservation and now run a gambling casino which
takes in x billion dollars a year. The Mohicans, of whom we were supposed to have seen the last in the 1750s, recently prevented Wal-Mart
from building a multiacre discount store on land they consider sacred in
upstate New York. In 1900, there were fewer than a quarter of a million
Indians in the United States. Today there are two million or more. The
population of those claiming Indian descent on the census forms has
been growing four times as fast as the population as a whole, making Native Americans one of the fastest-growing ethnic groups in the country.

Like many comfortable stories, the story of the Indians' destruction
hides other stories that are less so. For starters, it leaves out that the destruction was and is actually worse than can be easily described. A well-
informed person probably knows of the bigger and more famous
massacres, but big and small massacres took place in many states over
the years. Killing Indians was once the official policy of the state of California, which spent a million dollars reimbursing Indian-hunters for
the ammunition they used. Helen Hunt Jackson's history of Indian-
white relations, A Century of Dishonor, published in 1881, recounted
episodes of killing and mistreatment which have long faded into the
past. Its modern reader can weep at descriptions of massacres he has
never heard of—does anyone besides those who live in the town of
Gnadenhutten, Ohio, know of the slaughter in 1780 of the peaceful Indians at the Moravian mission there? Jackson's book could be revised
and reissued today, with another hundred years added to the title. After
the frontier gunfire died down, violence and untimely death found
other means. The Indian was supposed to be heading off to join his ancestors in the Happy Hunting Ground, and the path he might take to

get there (alcoholism? pneumonia? car wreck? the flu epidemic of 1918?) apparently did not need to be too closely explained. The violence continued, and continues today. Among the Navajo, the largest tribe in the United States, car accidents are the leading cause of death. Especially in Western towns that border big reservations, stabbings and fights and car wrecks are a depressingly regular part of life.

Also, the destruction story gives the flattering and wrong impression that European culture showed up in the Americas and simply mowed down whatever was in its way. In fact, the European arrivals were often hungry and stunned in their new settlements, and what they did to Indian culture was more than matched for years by what encounters with Indians did to theirs. Via the settlers, Indian crops previously unknown outside the Americas crossed the Atlantic and changed Europe. Indian farmers were the first to domesticate corn, peanuts, tomatoes, pumpkins, and many kinds of beans. Russia and Ireland grew no potatoes before travelers found the plant in Indian gardens in South America; throughout Europe, the introduction of the potato caused a rise in the standard of living and a population boom. Before Indians, no one in the world had ever smoked tobacco. No one in the Bible (or in any other pre-Columbian text, for that matter) ever has a cigarette, dips snuff, or smokes a pipe. The novelty of breathing in tobacco smoke or chewing the dried leaves caught on so fast in Europe that early colonists made fortunes growing tobacco; it was America's first cash crop. That the United States should now be so determined to stamp out all smoking seems historically revisionist and strange.

Surrounded as we are today by pavement, we assume that Indians have had to adapt to us. But for a long time much of the adapting went the other way. In the land of the free, Indians were the original "free"; early America was European culture reset in an Indian frame. Europeans who survived here became a mixture of identities in which the Indian part was what made them American and different than they had been before. Influence is harder to document than corn and beans, but as real. We know that Iroquois Indians attended meetings of the colonists in the years before the American Revolution and advised them to unite in a scheme for self-government based on the confederacy that ruled the six Iroquois nations; and that Benjamin Franklin said, at a gathering of delegates from the colonies in Albany in 1754, "It would be a strange thing if six nations of ignorant savages should be capable of forming a scheme for such a union and be able to execute it in such a manner as that it has subsisted for ages and appears indissoluble, and yet that a like union should be impracticable for ten or a dozen English colonies." His use of the term "ignorant savages" is thought to have been ironical; he admired the Iroquois plan, and it formed one of the models for the U.S. Constitution. We know, too, that Thomas Jefferson thought that American government should follow what he imagined to be the Indian way. He wrote: ". . . were it made a question, whether no law, as among the savage Americans, or too much law, as among the civilized Europeans, submits man to the greatest evil, one who has seen both conditions of existence would pronounce it to be the last . . . It will be said, that great societies cannot exist without government. The savages, therefore, break them into small ones."

Indian people today sometimes talk about the need to guard their culture carefully, so that it won't be stolen from them. But what is best (and worst) about any culture can be as contagious as a cold germ; the least contact passes it on. In colonial times, Indians were known for their disregard of titles and for a deep egalitarianism that made them not necessarily defer even to the leading men of their tribes. The route this trait took as it passed from Indian to white was invisible. Probably, contagion occurred during official gatherings, as when an exalted person arrived at a frontier place from the governor's palace or across the sea. The Indians spoke to the exalted person directly, equals addressing an equal, with no bowing or scraping or bending of the knee. Then, when their white neighbors got up to speak, perhaps ordinary self-consciousness made it hard to act any differently—to do the full routine of obeisance customary back in England—with the Indians looking on. Or maybe it was even simpler, a demonstration of the principle that informal behavior tends to drive out formal, given time. However the transfer happened, in a few generations it was complete; the American character had become thoroughly Indian in its outspokenness and all-around skepticism on the subject of who was and was not great.

We often hear that Indians traditionally believed in the Great Circle of Being, the connectedness of all creation, and the sacredness of every blade of grass. That the example of individual freedom among the Indians of the Americas inspired writers from Thomas More to Locke to

Shakespeare to Voltaire is seldom mentioned these days. (None of those writers, for their part, seem to have heard of the Great Circle of Being.) The Indians' love of independence and freedom has dwindled in description in recent years to the lone adjective "proud." Any time the Apache, for example, or the Comanche, or a noted Indian leader is described, that adjective is likely to be someplace close by. We are told that the Comanche or the Apache were or are "a proud people," and we get used to hearing it, and we forget what it means: centuries of resistance to authority, intractibility and independent-mindedness have won them only that brief epithet. The excitement of new discoveries in the Americas fired all sorts of fantasies about Indians in the minds of Europeans, and Indians remain the objects of fantasy today. The current fantasy might be summed up: American Indians were a proud people who believed in the Great Circle of Being and were cruelly destroyed.

I don't doubt that Indians in general saw all parts of creation as holy; references to such beliefs come up often in translated and transcribed speeches of Indians from years ago. At a treaty council between General Oliver O. Howard and the Nez Perce in 1877, Howard got tired of what he called "the oft-repeated dreamer nonsense" of the Indians, and told them, "Twenty times over I hear that the earth is your mother, and about the chieftainship of the earth. I want to hear it no more." What strikes me as fishy is that white people, having had no apparent interest in the Great Circle of Being for centuries, should find it so compelling now. I think its appeal has partly to do with its vague and unthreatening environmentalism, the genial Earth Day sort that leaves larger problems aside. Beyond that, I think the idea of connectedness is its key selling point. It reminds me of an advertisement for a telephone company, the one that used to say, "We're all connected." That statement could be further from the truth, but not much; no matter how many wires we thread into our homes, no matter the increasing complexity of the machines we hook them to, we are getting more disconnected all the time. People with money and without, people of different races and sexual identities, people in tinier and tinier areas of specialization, people in various categories off in gated communities by themselves—we are divided and a scattered every which way. Whiskey-trading forts on the Western frontier had special entrance enclosures where goods could be exchanged under guard, with escape doors at the other end for the traders in case negotiations got out of hand. That's essentially the connectedness the modern "we're-all-connected" world provides.

The Indian inclination toward personal freedom, no matter the consequences, made for endless division and redivision among tribes. Social problems often were solved geographically: you and I don't get along, so you stay here and my family and friends and I will move over there. Also, of course, splitting up into smaller groups was an efficient way to use the wild resources of the land. To give an accurate picture of any tribe, you need not just an identifying name or two but plenty of subcategories as well. For example, the Sioux, a populous and powerful tribe west of the Great Lakes when white men arrived, got that name apparently from a French corruption of the word *nadowesioux,* which was said to mean "little snakes" in the language of their enemies the Chippewa. Among themselves, the Sioux used (and use) the name Lakota, or variations of it, to indicate the tribe as a whole. Lakota means "allies." Setting aside the Assiniboine Sioux, a more northerly tribe, the Sioux in the United States were of three kinds: the Eastern, or Santee Sioux, who lived near the Mississippi in and around what is now Minnesota; the Yankton Sioux, a central branch, who lived between them and the Missouri; and the Western, or Teton Sioux, who lived farther to the west, on the Great Plains. The Santee were divided into a number of tribes, including the Sisseton, the Wahpekute, and the Mdewakanton. The Yankton had two subgroups—the Yankton and the Yanktonai. The Teton Sioux were of seven tribes, also called the seven council fires. They were the Sicangu, the Minnecojou, the Oohenumpa, the Itazipcho, the Sihasapa, the Hunkpapa, and the Oglala. Each name has a Lakota meaning whose origin is more or less obscure. One translation of Oglala is "dust scatterers." It may have come from a time when members of that tribe tried unsuccessfully to farm in the unwatered soil of the plains. After the Western Sioux got horses, they thrived as buffalo hunters on the plains. The Oglala tribe grew in numbers, and spread out and divided into bands. Important moments in Oglala history involved a conflict between a band of Oglala called the Bad Faces and a band called the Cut Off People. There were other bands of Oglala as well.

Historians have said that this kind of social division was a reason for the Indians' defeat. Inability to unite in common interest ruined the conspiracy of Pontiac, and the alliance Tecumseh tried to create among tribes resisting white encroachment in 1811. Indians lost battles because they couldn't keep together and attack all at the same time, like the white soldiers. Indian leaders often worried more about enemies within the tribe than about threats from outside, and survived wars with the whites only to die at the hands of Indian rivals. Certainly, pursuit of individual freedom among Indians has had a dreadful downside in quarreling and jealousy. Some Indians say that jealousy is a bigger problem for their people than alcohol. On Indian reservations nationwide, it is hard to find one that has no ongoing intratribal dispute.

Any smugness at the thought of this urge to division in Indian society ignores how powerful it has been in the United States at large. From a certain perspective, the history of the United States has been the history of schism. Whether we would be one nation or many has perplexed us from the start. The Civil War seemed to decide the question in favor of unity. Many Northerners who cared nothing for the fate of enslaved blacks had been persuaded to fight to preserve the union; "Union!" was the wartime rallying cry that echoed in the names of national companies like the Western Union Telegraph Company and the Union Pacific Railroad that prospered after the war. As a plot device, union proved ideal. It gave the American story a clarity of outcome and a vista of happily-ever-after. Out of many, so we were told, we had become one.

Disunion, on the other hand, is complicated and ambiguous and inconclusive, and more difficult to describe. In our history whose winner is union, disunion is the bad guy, the loser. Its story is less often told. But it holds there, right below the surface of American history, threatening to turn the story of our union into countless numbers of stories too complicated to follow or tell. We know, for example, that the United States has been a Protestant-majority nation since it began. That fact seems simple, white-bread, monochrome. But the origin of Protestantism was protest and argument. Especially in the early nineteenth century the Protestants in America argued and disagreed and divided into factions so prolifically as to make the Indian tribes seem unanimous by comparison. A glance into the can of worms that is the Baptist sects, the Hard-Shell and Foot-Washing and Six Principle and Free

Will and Primitive and so on, or at the multiplicity of Presbyterian sects strewn across the range of opinion on the doctrine of predestination, suggests why there is not yet any comprehensive and coherent account of the Protestant Churches of America. Like Indian tribes, Protestant Churches split up into smaller groups, solved disputes geographically, and took advantage of the immensity and variety of the land. America was resettled by Protestant division, as it had been settled by Indian division before. Confidently *unum*, we looked down on the Indian *pluribus*; but we have always been at least as *pluribus* as they.

So, to the question "Why can't Indians get with the program?" one might reply that we have already gotten with theirs. Immigrants did not simply reproduce in America the life they had left behind overseas. They adapted instead to the culture they found here, a native culture that was immeasurably old and that still survives today. The latest version of American history tends to describe the meeting of white and Indian in terms of despoilment, with the Indian getting the worst of it, as indeed occurred. But such accounts can't do justice to the thrilling spark of freedom in the encounter—the freedom the Indians had, the freedom that white people found. As surely as Indians gave the world corn and tobacco and potatoes, they gave it a revolutionary new idea of what a human being could be. Thanks to Indians, we learned we didn't have to kneel to George III. In the droning sameness of history, this was front-page, glorious news: we could walk the earth the equal of anyone we met, no princeling's inferior, unobliged to kiss anyone's hand in subjugation or to have anyone kiss ours. As with other inventions, this one succeeded because it met people who were ready for it, and Enlightenment-era Europeans in particular were. Generations of thought about the right relationship of people to God and to each other had already moved Europeans away from the oppressions of feudalism; but the example of freedom and equality among Indians provided a resounding real-life confirmation of theory. The pursuit of freedom drove the social revolutions that occupied much of the world over the last two centuries, and reform in the name of equality produced great improvements and disasters.

Now, in America, we have gotten used to freedom. We heard about it in school, we know we have it, theoretically; and so what? With regard to its original thrill, we are like frequent fliers grown so used to the routine of modern air travel that we've lost the heart-lifting joy people felt at the sight of Wilbur Wright flying past the New York skyline and circling the Statue of Liberty in his homemade biplane back in 1909. But like the principles of flight, the idea of freedom still survives. It is what makes people all over the world still want to come to America, and still have hopes for what America can be and do. It is part of the allure in American advertising, and in American popular music, and in the images we export of gangsters and bikers and heavily armed lone-wolf fighters of evil. Freedom illuminates the cheapest made-in-Taiwan feathers in the toy-store Indian costume and provides the theme of every Western movie, in which the irresponsible and too-free freedom of wild Indians and outlaws yields inevitably to the more responsible, less-free freedom which we townsfolk understand.

And now we look out upon the traffic jam and wonder, "Is this the land of the free?" We turn on the television along with the rest of America every evening and wonder whether this is the equality the Founders had in mind. Yes, we do kiss a hand now and then, the boss's or the loan officer's or the preferred customer's—it's just part of life, no big deal—and we take a certain pleasure in having our own hand kissed as well. (Though our kissing metaphor, like the rest of our culture, has moved a bit lower down.) The day after tomorrow the earth will be so crowded you won't be able to turn around without stepping on someone's toes, and what will be the purpose of freedom then? In our spare moments we worry about what the world's coming to, and our worry breeds proposals: one expert reveals that the solution is all in education, in improving the public schools and in hiring more teachers to reduce the number of students per classroom. Another says the solution requires the perfection of the electric car. Others talk of changing the policies of the Federal Reserve Bank, of campaign-finance reform, of making new laws or getting rid of laws we already have. Not long ago I read in the newspaper about new kinds of bioengineered trees that will produce nearly thirty times the annual growth of ordinary trees, thereby supposedly saving the rain forests and providing us with lumber and protecting the ozone until kingdom come.

But even if we somehow do all the experts say we should, and even if the solutions work better than we could expect, will we be free? Will the question even be mentioned at all? Will anything remain of that urge to freedom that drove people across oceans and continents, and caused them to struggle and die, and inspired them to speechify in such high-flown terms? In our smaller public school classes, at the wheels of our electric cars, in control of our bank policies and our politicians' campaign spending, listening to the rustling of our frantically photosynthesizing trees, what kind of people will we be? Will we be a free people, will that idea have meaning anymore?

When I go to Indian reservations in the West, and especially to the Pine Ridge Reservation, I sometimes feel unsure where to put my foot when I open the car door. The very ground is different from where I usually stand. There are fewer curbs, fewer sidewalks, and almost no street signs, mailboxes, or leashed dogs. The earth here is just the earth, unadorned, and the places people walk are made not by machinery but by feet. Those smooth acres of asphalt marked with lines to tell you where to park and drive which cover so much of America are harder to find on the reservations. If the Iroquois hadn't resisted the French in the 1600s, the Northeast would be speaking French today; if the Comanche hadn't opposed the Spanish, the American Southwest would now be Mexico. The Oglala Sioux reservation, actively or otherwise, continues to resist the modern American paving machine. Walking on Pine Ridge, I feel as if I am in actual America, the original version that was here before and will still be here after we're gone. There are windblown figures crossing the road in the distance who might be drunk, and a scattering of window-glass fragments in the weeds that might be from a car accident, and a baby naked except for a disposable diaper playing in a bare-dirt yard, and an acrid smell of burning trash—all the elements that usually evoke the description "bleak." But there is greatness here, too, and an ancient glory endures in the dust and the weeds. The way I look at it, this is the American bedrock upon which the society outside its borders is only a later addition. It's the surviving piece of country where "the program" has not yet completely taken hold.

Of course I want to be like Indians. I've looked up to them all my life. When I was a young man my number-one hero was the Oglala leader Crazy Horse. I read every source I could find about him, went to many places of importance in his life, and studied his history as an example of what a person should be. I discovered many others who felt as strongly about Crazy Horse as I did. Crazy Horse was born about 1840 into the Bad Faces band of Oglala at Bear Butte, near where Sturgis, South Dakota, is today. He grew up in the neighborhood of Fort Laramie on the prairie in what is now southeastern Wyoming, made his reputation as a young man in battles with the Crow and other tribes, and won his greatest fame for his part in Indian victories over the Army, most notably the killing of General Custer and others of his command at the battle of the Little Bighorn. The following spring Crazy Horse agreed to stop fighting and come in to the Red Cloud Agency—the early version of the Pine Ridge Reservation, located then in western Nebraska. The Army put him under arrest and killed him, under confused and shameful circumstances, that fall. A large plaque erected in 1964 on the reservation just off Highway 18 by the turnoff to the village of Wounded Knee recounts his biography in some detail. As a rule, historical markers on the reservation get hit pretty hard by vandalism. Almost any unattended point of interest, it seems, will attract a scrawl of spray paint or a hurled Budweiser bottle sooner or later. But I have never seen a speck of graffiti or a sliver of glass on the marker commemorating Crazy Horse. Evidently, even the most hell-bent drunks leave it alone. When its lettering begins to age, someone carefully paints it in again.

I wrote a lot about Crazy Horse in a book I published in 1989, and I continued to refer to his example when wondering how I should act in certain situations. I had decided that Crazy Horse's one mistake was in coming into the agency, where his halfhearted efforts at accommodation led only to intrigue, jealousy, and death. When faced with a possibly compromising decision, I would ask myself, "Is this 'coming into the agency'?" Having lunch with certain people in the magazine business or applying for an arts grant was 'coming into the agency,' I believed. My wife and I bought a cooperative apartment in Brooklyn, and it had a shabby kitchen, and my wife decided to remodel it. She went to a remodeling firm, then sat down with me to go over the estimates. I asked myself, "Would Crazy Horse have spent this much to remodel a kitchen?"

Crazy Horse's recent popularity dates from the years of the Vietnam War, when a lot of people began to see the sense in his resistance to the

U.S. government. The political activists who made up the American Indian Movement loved Crazy Horse. AIM leaders often repeated the few quotations attributed to him—"One does not sell the earth on which the people walk"; "Today is a good day to die!"—and took inspiration from his warlike determination to be himself no matter what. Watching AIM leaders on the news in those days, I sometimes found them scary, with their improvised protest demonstrations and violent talk. But I admired them, too. Most of them were of the same age as the older guys I had looked up to in school. AIM guys—and AIM was very much a "guy" organization—usually came from city-Indian backgrounds and dressed in an eclectic combination of street tough and Indian traditional that no one had seen before. To a press conference, an AIM leader might wear a beaded black leather vest, black chinos, and black boots, with his hair in waist-length braids wrapped in strips of red felt and otter fur. Violence and dissension and FBI informers did in AIM eventually, and its members ended up scattered, more than a few in jail. But AIM changed the way people regarded Indians in this country, and the way Indians regarded themselves; in an assimilationist America, they showed that a powerful Indian identity remained. A while ago I was reminded of my admiration for Clyde Bellecourt, a Chippewa from Minnesota and one of the founders of AIM. Back in 1973, as a result of a long-standing dispute between AIM factions, an AIM member named Carter Camp shot Clyde Bellecourt in the stomach on the Rosebud Reservation in South Dakota. Clyde Bellecourt survived the shooting and refused to press charges, and Carter Camp went free. What reminded me was a recent item in an Indian newspaper saying that Clyde Bellecourt's daughter Mary, a tenth-grader, was about to receive a high award in her Girl Scout troop. To have survived a shooting *and* to have a daughter who wins a high award in Girl Scouts—how much cooler can a middle-aged father be?

I'd like to be a hero myself, especially for dramatic, action-hero exploits of some kind. Riding the subway from Brooklyn to Manhattan, I used to daydream of rescuing a helpless person from armed muggers, of knocking guns to the subway floor and subduing criminals and turning them over nonchalantly to the Transit Police. Other fantasies, even more far-fetched and Walter Mittyish than that, sometimes ran through my mind; a few scenarios I now know so well I have them nearly memorized and could direct the film versions to the smallest detail. In reality, I've never performed any heroic feat, and I'm glad that no mugging has ever taken place in front of me to reveal what I would actually do. On a subway train I often rode, but at a time when I was not there, someone once set off a firebomb in a car filled with rush-hour passengers. The bomb burned forty-seven people, some of them critically. A passenger who survived the blast ran back into the burning car to rescue a number of injured people who were still on fire. In news stories that followed, when reporters asked the rescuer about his deed he always said, "I'm no hero." This, I have found, is a constant in modern-day news stories in which heroic acts are involved. You will meet the disclaimer by the third paragraph, almost without fail. Regardless of the courageous, dangerous, lifesaving thing the person has done, he or she always insists, "I'm no hero."

Most everybody wants to be rich, millions want to be famous, but no one today wants to be mistaken for a hero. This recent change in our psychology is baffling to me. It is also profoundly un-Indian. Indians who were heroes generally came out and said so. For many tribes, life revolved around heroism. Young men dreamed of setting off from camp alone and on foot, and of returning days or weeks later on a fine mount with eight other ponies captured from the Snakes; the old women would cry their praises, the drummers would compose songs in their honor, the chiefs would hold feasts and giveaways, and the young women would look at them over the tops of their shawls. For many Indians, autobiography was just a series of brave exploits strung together over years. Naturally, Indian culture produced heroes of all sizes in plentiful supply. Bil Gilbert, biographer of Tecumseh, says that the Indians of North America resembled the ancient Greeks in their ability to produce heroes, and that both societies considered heroism more important than wealth or power. In American history, the names of Sequoyah and Osceola and Black Hawk and Roman Nose and Chief Joseph and Looking Glass and Satank and Quanah Parker and Cochise and Geronimo ring like names of heroes out of Homer.

The Western Sioux, who never numbered more than seventy thousand souls in all, have given America and the rest of the world heroes in quantity far out of proportion to the size of the tribe. Sitting Bull, the Hunkpapa warrior and medicine man, became one of the most famous

Americans of all time. Spotted Tail, of the Sicangu or Brule Sioux, was perhaps the greatest Indian diplomat and negotiator. Other Sioux, like Rain in the Face and Gall and Pawnee Killer, were known mainly for deeds in battle. Among the Oglala, the number of heroes is unusually high. Besides Crazy Horse, the Oglala included Red Cloud, who spoke to power in Washington and New York as no Indian had done before. Oglala chiefs like Little Wound and Red Dog and American Horse and He Dog and Young Man Afraid of His Horses attained eminence within the tribe and beyond. One of the greatest Oglala heroes was a holy man, Nicholas Black Elk, who held on to his people's ancient religion during a time when it was actively suppressed. Toward the end of his life he conveyed some of the holy teachings in print, most notably in the book *Black Elk Speaks,* written with the help of Nebraska poet John G. Neihardt. *Black Elk Speaks*, published in 1932, became a classic of religious literature, familiar to readers around the world.

A surprising amount of Oglala culture is the same today as it was in pre-reservation times. The Oglala still produce heroes, despite the fact that the wider market for them seems to have waned. If you want to see a lot of combat veterans in one place, go to a Veterans' Powwow in Pine Ridge village on an August afternoon. There's probably more foreign shrapnel walking around the small towns of the reservation than there is in similar towns anywhere in America; some Oglala families can give you a genealogy of warriors that begins at Operation Desert Storm and continues back to the Little Bighorn and before. The Oglala have always honored warriors, and they honor children as well. The Lakota word for child, *wakanyeja,* translates literally as "the child is also holy." An Oglala hero of recent history was a girl athlete who died just before she turned eighteen. She starred for the Lady Thorpes, the girls' basketball team at Pine Ridge High School, from 1987 through 1991. I have only heard about her and read local news stories about her, but words fail me when I try to say how much I admire her. Her name was SuAnne Big Crow.

CHAPTER

2

So Le War Lance and I became friends. I mentioned him in a book, the same one in which I wrote about Crazy Horse, and in the same chapter; I said that I had noticed an Indian waiting to cross the street in front of my apartment in New York City, that I had asked on impulse if he was Sioux, and that he had replied, "I'm an Oglala Sioux Indian from Oglala, South Dakota." I described a conversation Le War Lance and I had on the subject of Crazy Horse and how he had told me, "Crazy Horse was my gran'father!" Le War Lance liked what I wrote about him; he said that I told the truth. I included a photograph of him in the book, and for a while he was carrying a paperback copy around in his back pocket so he could show the photo to people from time to time. He said he even used it for a picture ID once or twice. I kept running into him in various parts of the city: by the statue of Garibaldi in Washington Square Park at two in the morning as I was returning from some party, or on a park bench in Columbus Circle in the middle of the afternoon. He wrote down his phone number for me and added mine to the long list of phone numbers he keeps in his head. He called me often, and he still does. I've known Le War Lance now for going on twenty years. All my other friends I met in school, at work, or through connections from work. Le War Lance is the only friend I have who I met originally on the street.

Le's appearance has varied over those years. He is about six feet tall, and he has a broad face rather like the actor Jack Palance's. Le's eyes can be merry and flat as a smile button, or deep and glittering with malice or slyness or something he knows and I never will. He is fifty-seven years old. I have seen his hair, which is black streaked with gray, when it was over two feet long and held with beaded ponytail holders a foot or so apart, and I have seen it much shorter, after he had shaved his head in mourning for a friend who had died. He has big hands which can grip a basketball as easily as I can hold a softball, and long arms. He is almost never able to find shirts or coats with long-enough sleeves. I've seen him in fancy tooled cowboy boots, in oversize Italian loafers with metal buckles, and in running shoes; in many different cowboy hats, in an orange-and-white knit ski cap bearing the name of an insurance company, and in snowmobiler caps with fur earflaps. I've seen him fat and thin. For a while he was about 260 pounds, a pro-football heft. Then he became slim and rangy-looking. He told me he was losing weight because he had cancer. I asked what kind of cancer he had and he replied, "Generic." He told me he would be dead in six weeks, and even gave the date on which he would die, which he said had been revealed to him in a dream. That was about eight years ago. He has gained back a lot of the weight since then.

Le and I have fallings-out from time to time. He often is not a very nice guy. If he has done only a few of the things he says he has done, it's amazing he isn't in jail. (Evidently he did go to prison for car theft and writing bad checks back in the early sixties.) When he's drinking, which is frequently, he tells me all kinds of stories. I don't completely disbelieve any of them. For years I thought his story about jumping off the Space Needle in Seattle attached by just a Band-Aid to the end of a bungee cord in a promotional stunt for the Johnson & Johnson company might have a grain of truth to it somewhere. When I reminded him of it recently, he laughed and said if he had told me that he was just having fun with me. Other stories that are only slightly less wild have turned out to be true.

He calls me every few weeks, it seems, to ask for money. It's good that he does, I suppose, to keep me from getting sentimental when I think of him. Even now I can feel my words want to pull him in a wrong direction, toward a portrait that is rose-tinted and larger than life, while he is pulling the other way, toward reality. Sometimes when he calls, his voice is small and clear, like neat printed handwriting; other times, depending on his mood and how much he's had to drink, his voice is sprawling and enlarged, like a tall cursive signature with flourishes on the tail letters and ink blots and splatters alongside. I have wired him money many times, for more purposes than I can remember—to help a friend who was stranded at a Micmac Indian reserve in Canada, to resole a pair of boots, to fix a heater, to buy any number of car parts and tanks of gas, to provide a wreath on a coffin, to provide a suit of clothes for a relative who had just died, to buy a used mobile home, to buy steamer trunks to hold the presents at a giveaway ceremony, to pay a DWI fine. After a while the wire-transfer company sent me a good-customer card that lets me take a dollar or so off the service charge. I get a satisfaction from these transactions which would be complicated to explain. Of course, I also often get annoyed. Once when I said I had no money to send, Le became angry and told me he would not be seeing me again, that he expected soon to die. Then he told me to "suck on a banana and make it real," and hung up. I didn't hear from him for a year or more after that, and I began to worry that maybe he actually had died. At Christmas I sent a card to his girlfriend's address and inquired about him. Four or five days after I mailed the card, I found a message on my answering machine: Le's voice, the extra-large version, in a rising volume: "Hey—Little Brother—I hear you forgot my NAME!" I played it over several times. I was delighted to hear from him again.

One Sunday morning I was lying in my bed in lower Manhattan when I got a call from Le. He said he had been partying the night before with Jimmy Page of Led Zeppelin and had just gotten home. He planned to take a nap, he said, and after that he wanted me to come by his apartment for a visit. Then he told me he was going to buy an Appaloosa mare and asked if I would like to have one of her colts. He said he would raise the colts on land he owned on the reservation. He said he planned to go back to the reservation that spring and trap an eagle there. He said he trapped eagles by going up on a butte and burying himself in the earth and covering his face with sagebrush and holding a live rabbit on the sagebrush. When the eagle came down for the rabbit, he said, he grabbed the eagle by the leg. The last one he had caught, he said, beat its wings so hard it pulled him out of the earth. I said that I would not want to try that, that I would be afraid the eagle would peck my eye out. Le said, "Nothing eats me."

I told him I would be there about one o'clock. Le was living in Washington Heights at the time. The A train, which stopped below my apartment, took me right there. Washington Heights is at the far northern end of Manhattan, where the island is so rocky it's almost mountainous. I rode an elevator many stories from the subway up through the rock, walked around some hilly streets, and finally found his building, Cabrini Terrace, on 191 Street. A Hasidic man all in black with side curls pointed it out to me. I climbed the stairs to Apartment 5K and knocked on the door. Le opened it, shirtless, barefoot, in brown pegged pants rolled up at the cuffs and curled under at the waistline, where his stomach overhung. He had his hair piled high on his head and held with elastic bands so that it fanned out above in sort of a delta shape; it looked like a nineteenth-century hairstyle of a Plains Indian in a portrait by Catlin or Bodmer. The room was full of the smell of stew cooking. Light came from a lamp or two and from the blue glow of a large TV against one wall. There was no daylight; all the windows were covered completely with aluminum foil. Le saw me notice the foil. "My girlfriend's paranoid. She just discovered she was an orphan," he explained.

Le was drinking a sixteen-ounce can of Budweiser beer. He asked me to sit, and he offered me one. As I got accustomed to the light, I saw sixteen-ounce Budweiser cans everywhere—not scattered around carelessly, but set upright neatly among the furniture, on the end table, in the shelves of the bookcase, under the television, in the corners; it was like a brain-teaser drawing: "How many beer cans can you find in this picture?" He introduced me to his cat, Hey Baby, and to Coyote, his dog. Coyote was small and waggy and blind in one eye. A painting of an eagle with wings spread covered an entire wall. It was done in sketchy strokes of brown on the wall itself, and one of the legs in particular was so detailed and eagle-like, with careful feathering and sickle-shaped claws, that I thought it possible he had gotten as close to a real eagle leg as he said he had. In the middle of the eagle he had pasted a poster advertising the Longest Walk, a demonstration organized by the American

Indian Movement in 1978 to protest anti-tribal legislation then before Congress. Le said he had participated in the walk, which began in California and ended in Washington, D.C., and that he had worn out four pairs of boots, three pairs of tennis shoes, and two pairs of other shoes along the way. He said concrete just eats shoes up. Then he told me to look at the ceiling; a sketch of a buffalo head done in carpenter's pencil, full face, stared down. He walked to different parts of the room and pointed up. "Here is his horns . . . here is his eyes . . . here is his nose . . . here is his beard." The ceiling was white; this was a sacred white buffalo, he said.

He said, "I want to tell you my movie," and for the next forty minutes or so, he did, almost frame by frame. He said that Howard Hughes's lawyer either had given him money to make it or was about to give him money to make it. The plot involved a woman who wakes up in the morning ("The sun comes up and kisses the sky and paints Mother Earth in all the colors of the day . . ."), rummages in a cupboard, makes herself some tea, drinks it, and drives into town. She goes into a café and sits down. Everybody knows her. She's a model. She's beautiful. She looks out the window of the café and sees an Indian painting a picture. She gets up and goes out and looks at it. It's a picture of an old Indian. Suddenly she's reminded of a time when she was at the café and the café was robbed and the robbers took her away in an airplane and the airplane crashed and she was the only one who survived and she slid down the wing with a broken leg, broken ribs, two broken arms, and a concussion. When she came to, she saw this old Indian—the same one as in the picture—on an Appaloosa horse looking down at her. (Here Le did an imitation of a man sitting on horseback with the reins in two hands resting one atop the other on the saddlehorn.) The Indian took her and made a sweat bath for her and took off all her clothes except her slip and put red-hot rocks in the sweat lodge, and the woman picked up one of them, and suddenly she was sitting outside the lodge in the middle of nowhere. Then she put the rock down and she was back in the sweat lodge. Then she picked up some sage and suddenly she's in her own garden smelling a flower. She put it down and she's back in the sweat lodge again. The old Indian cured her and took her back to the highway, where somebody could pick her up, and as she's about to get in the car she turns around and he has disappeared. But nobody can explain the buffalo-hide splints on her arms and legs. She remembers all this, and she asks the Indian painting the picture who the man in it is, and the Indian says, "That was my grandfather." So she goes in and finishes eating and comes out and gets in her car, and in her rearview mirror as she drives away you see the old Indian sitting on his horse looking after her.

Le put on a shirt and pulled on some boots, and we went out for more beer. He had a cheerful word for the doorman in the lobby, a woman watching two children on the sidewalk out front, and the man behind the deli counter. He took two six-packs of sixteen-ounce Budweisers from the cooler; I paid. As we came back down his hall, he pointed to the door next to his and said, "The lady who lives there is a Holocaust survivor." Angling for approval, I said that he was kind of a holocaust survivor, too. He said, "You got that right, bro."

The stew was ready. Le called it soup and a Lakota word I didn't catch. He took me into the kitchen and showed it to me, ladling through it with a big spoon. Its main ingredients were pieces of cow stomach and intestines and Indian corn. The long boiling had caused the individual kernels to expand to the size of pieces of popcorn. I had only seen this kind of corn on colorful dried corncobs in autumn displays on suburban front doors; I had never realized it was a food. Le filled a big bowl for me, and I cleared away some magazines and Budweiser cans on a small table and set it down. The soup was good, hot and strong-tasting; but when I looked close up at the intricacies of a piece of stomach wall, for a second I blanched. After that I ate without looking, keeping my eyes instead on the television, which had never been off since I arrived. Le looked at the television, too. After a moment he said, "I've seen this movie before. It's called *Body Heat*—it's a pretty raunchy movie. That woman is Kathleen Turner."

"No, it isn't," I said. "I've seen this movie, too. That's an actress named Kim Zimmer. I know, because she's married to a guy who used to live across the street from me in Ohio. She plays Reva Lewis in the soap opera *Guiding Light*."

Le leaned forward to the screen and examined it. Then he turned back to me. "You're right," he said. "That *is* Kim Zimmer."

We each had another bowl of soup, and more cold Budweiser to go with it. Then we sat back, content. "I see you like the soup," Le said, using the Lakota word for it. I agreed it was very good. Again shirtless, Le began to point out his scars to me and tell the stories he said were behind them. On one arm and shoulder he said he had 250 scars the size of a matchhead, from flesh offerings he had made at sun dances. On the other shoulder, a more visible pale zipper of a scar he identified as the result of a rotator cuff operation. He had been a minor league pitcher, he said, and once pitched against fastballer Nolan Ryan. After his arm blew up he couldn't pitch again, despite the operation, and had to switch to his left arm when he went back to riding bulls in the rodeo. He held on with his left hand and used his injured right arm for balance when he rode. He was once fourth in the world championship rodeo in bull riding, he said.

He told me that he had worked sorting potatoes and sewing potato bags shut in a field near Hemingford, Nebraska, for three dollars an hour; that he had worked as a gandy dancer fixing the Northern Pacific tracks from Gillette, Wyoming, clear across the state for twelve hundred dollars a week; that he had once helped a shady guy on the reservation rustle cattle for a flat fee of two hundred dollars and no questions asked. He said he had played professional basketball for the Denver Truckers in the Amateur Athletic Union, had driven stunt cars in the movies, and had driven an Oppenheimer Lotus racing car in a race in Antwerp, Belgium, at a clocked speed at 190.280 miles per hour. He said he was a good friend of Scottish racer Jim Clark, and had given up racing for good after Clark died in a crash at Indianapolis. He described, by my count, seven or eight guys he had killed—all in self-defense. The telephone rang. He picked it up, said "Yo!" into the receiver, and slammed it down. He said it was his girlfriend checking in from Montclair, New Jersey, where she was taking care of her mother. How that squared with her being an orphan puzzled me, but I did not ask.

Occasionally he sang Lakota songs. His voice went from deep and throaty to wavery and high in a song whose words he translated as "Young Lakota man, come into the center of the circle, so the young women can see your pheasant dance!" Another song he said was an old one that had been sung first by Red Cloud. Its words went:

You ask me to be a Lakota,
And that is the hardest thing in the world to be.
I am a Lakota,
So I suffer for my people.

Sometimes he idly leaned forward and turned the TV channels, never finding anything that held his attention for long. Suddenly the Winter Olympics was on, and he stopped talking. The announcer said the next event would be the Women's Figure Skating. Le said, "I have to see this. I want Katarina Witt to win. She'll be skating the compulsory figures. I told everybody, 'If Katarina Witt finishes any higher than fifth in the compulsories, she's got the whole thing sewed up.'"

"Why is that?" I asked.

"Because she *hates* the compulsories—it's her worst event. All she has to do is place fourth or higher." He sat with his elbows on his knees and watched, his piled-up hair silhouetted against the screen.

For a while I was seeing Le every few weeks. When he happened to be downtown he stopped by my apartment, and on weekend afternoons I sometimes made the trip up to Washington Heights. Most visits were like my first one: we sat around and drank beer and talked and watched TV. Though I didn't meet Le's girlfriend, I met a number of his Lakota friends and relatives who were staying in his apartment. There was a skinny guy with glasses named Will, who Le introduced as his brother; they looked so unlike that I asked Will if he really was Le's brother, and Will said, "Well, that's what he introduces me as." Another guy, Thomas Yellow Hair, I recognized right away. He was the marcher featured prominently in the Last Walk photograph in the poster hanging on Le's wall. A guy in a Western shirt and blue jeans who was so thin his beaded belt seemed to go around him twice Le also introduced as his brother. In this case, he really was a brother—Floyd John, born five years and five days after Le. Floyd John said little the first time I saw him. Le told me that Floyd John was a veteran who had served two tours in Vietnam, and that after he had signed up for the second tour, their uncle had given him his own name, Loves War. To make conversation, I asked Floyd John which branch of the service he had been in. Floyd

John said, "Army." He said nothing else to me the rest of the afternoon.

I usually showed up with beer. Once I brought a six-pack of a beer called Moosehead, which I happened to have in my refrigerator because a guest had left it. It was not a brand I would have bought myself. When I pulled it out of the shopping bag, the shouts of derision from Le and Floyd John (who had begun talking to me by then) were something to hear. I might as well have pulled an actual moosehead out of the sack. How could I have been so peculiar as to bring this extremely non-Budweiser, off-brand beer? Le and Floyd John never got over it. They still remind me of that Moosehead incident to this day. If this were 150 years ago and I were an eccentric white traveler passing through the Oglala camps, I have no doubt what my Indian name would be.

With other people around, Le did not tell yarns the way he did the first time I visited. Mostly we all sat in Le's living room and watched television. Le's TV got the cable channels, and one of them showed old Western movies. Generally Le and the others preferred Westerns to anything else that was on. I did, too. My TV didn't get cable, and the other channels in New York didn't seem to care about Westerns at all. When I first moved to the city I had complained about this, and pointlessly told people that the only movie I ever could find on television in New York was *Daddy Long Legs,* starring Fred Astaire. Most of my favorite movies are Westerns. That sound of Indians screaming and yipping and firing guns as they circle the wagon train was the basic TV background noise of my childhood.

Perhaps it should have occurred to me that those TV and movie war cries were made by actual people with names. It didn't, though, until I watched Westerns in Le's living room. Often an Indian would cross the screen to tomahawk a soldier or catch a bullet and fall, and (depending on the movie) Le or Floyd John would say, "That's Burgess Red Cloud."

"No," the other would reply, "that's what's-his-name, Kills Enemy. Lived over there with Mildred? Was it Bob? Bob Kills Enemy?"

"No, not Bob."

"Burgess Red Cloud was the guy in the buffalo-horn hat in *How the West Was Won.*"

"No, man—Burgess wasn't in that movie."

"That guy—*there*—that's Marvin Thin Elk."

"Yeah, that's Marvin."

"That's Vince LaDuke. He played the Indian guy on *Bonanza*."

"That guy that just got shot off the roof—I forget his name—wasn't he the guy the Mennonites gave a trailer house to over by Manderson? Died of alcoholism?"

"I don't know. Now that guy right there, that's Matthew Two Bulls as a younger man. You can't hardly recognize him. He's the greatest Lakota drummer and singer of all time. Of course, they had to get Victor Mature to play Crazy Horse."

"Victor Mature as Crazy Horse! It's insane!"

One time a face appeared and Le said, "There's Lot Cheyenne! Hang on, Lot!" and both he and Floyd John began to laugh. Le said to me, "Lot Cheyenne lives near where we used to over by Oglala on the reservation, and he told us about this movie or maybe it was another one—anyway, him and these other Indians was supposed to attack a wagon train, and they all had it in their contracts that they was gonna get twenty-five dollars a day, and if any of them fell off his horse he'd get a bonus of fifty dollars. So Lot and them went riding and hollering up to the wagon train, and a cowboy sticks his head out and fires one shot with a pistol, and immediately all thirty Indians go sprawling off their horses onto the ground!"

A footnote:

Thousands of Indians have been in movies. They appeared in some of the first movie footage ever made; starting in 1894, Thomas Edison filmed documentary scenes of Indian life and Indian performers in Buffalo Bill Cody's Wild West Show. The first American hit movie was a ten-minute-long Western called *The Great Train Robbery,* made in 1903. It had no Indians, but many films that imitated it did, as the Western became the basic American movie genre. As in the Wild West Shows, some movie directors preferred to use "real" Indians. By that they generally meant Plains Indians like Sioux or Cheyenne. Around 1910, a moviemaker named Thomas Ince brought a group of Sioux to his studio near Los Angeles and set them up in a village there so as to have a ready supply. To the many categories of Sioux, a new one was added: the Inceville Sioux, as these movie-actor Indians were sometimes called.

Buffalo Bill Cody had his own moviemaking company, and in 1913 he went to the Pine Ridge Reservation and places nearby to film a movie about the Plains Indian wars of forty years before. The federal bureaucracy that ran the reservations let over a thousand Sioux be in the movie. Some were old men who had fought in the actual battles portrayed. Short Bull, one of two Indians listed by name in the credits, was the same man who had been among the leaders of the Ghost Dance on the reservation back in 1890 and 1891. After Wounded Knee, and after the Army had suppressed the dance and imprisoned him and others, he had gone on to become a performer for Buffalo Bill.

Westerns tended to use actors who didn't look even remotely Indian in Indian roles, but Indian actors like William Eagleshirt and Chief Thundercloud and Chief Big Tree and Lois Red Elk and Jay Silverheels played those parts, too. Generally their names were pretty far down in the credits, their characters called simply "Indian" or "Indian Brave." John Ford, perhaps the greatest director of Westerns, often used the dramatic landscape of Arizona's Monument Valley for the setting of his films. Monument Valley is on the Navajo Reservation, and the Indian actors in John Ford Westerns are usually Navajo. In one movie they play Comanche, in another Arapahoe, in another Cheyenne; whenever background dialogue was required, they spoke Navajo regardless. If you look closely at the Navajo in a John Ford Western—for example, when they are Apache waiting along a ridgetop for the approach of the unsuspecting cavalry in *Fort Apache*—sometimes they seem to be trying hard not to smile.

The real boom in Westerns came in the 1950s and early 1960s, when scores of Western TV shows filled the air. Many Indians had bit parts then; it's not uncommon to find that a Sioux of sixty-five or older has appeared briefly in a TV show or film. By the 1970s, eighty-one movies had been made about the Sioux alone. (Only the Apache, with 104, had more.) About that time the Western briefly died. It soon revived, and casting directors again returned to the reservations. As happened with Short Bull, Indians who had formerly scared white people seemed to have a theatrical advantage; AIM leaders Russell Means and Dennis Banks and John Trudell have all appeared in movie roles.

Despite the participation of Indians in American moviemaking from its very beginnings, Hollywood has never given them much credit or praise. Of the many Indians who have appeared in movies, only three have been nominated for Academy Awards: Dan George, for Best Supporting Actor in the movie *Little Big Man*; Graham Greene, for Best Supporting Actor in *Dances with Wolves*; and Buffy Sainte-Marie, for writing the theme song "Up Where We Belong" for *An Officer and a Gentleman*. The only Indian ever to win an Academy Award is Buffy Sainte-Marie.

After a few months, my visits to Le's apartment came to an end. One day I got a call from him saying that he and his girlfriend had moved to near the town of Monsey, in upstate New York. He and I made many arrangements to meet when he said he was coming to town, but usually he didn't show up. Once he called and said he would be at a performance of the American Indian Dance Theater on West Nineteenth Street, and I went and waited outside, on the off chance. He and his girlfriend were among the first through the door when the show was over. Le was wearing a red turtleneck pullover, a fringed leather jacket, a straw cowboy hat, baggy stonewashed jeans, and snakeskin cowboy boots. He introduced me to his girlfriend, Noelle, a short, dark-haired woman with glasses and slightly out-of-sync eyes. She had on a sweater that buttoned and a white blouse with a gold print. The three of us went to a restaurant by the theater. Le and I had Budweisers and mozzarella sticks, and Noelle had coffee. They said they had just been out to the Pine Ridge Reservation to attend the August powwow and an honoring ceremony for Le's ninety-year-old father, Asa, known as Ace. Noelle said the reservation was like a black hole to her, with all that drinking and driving around on bumpy dirt roads, and that she had been glad to leave. She said they had gotten lost in the middle of the night on a dirt road somewhere in the badlands, and Le was passed out in the back seat, and she turned to ask him where they were; he woke up, looked around, said, "The New Jersey Turnpike," and went back to sleep. Le told me that they had gone to Wounded Knee and had taken some photographs of the mass gravesite, but the film had come back blank. He said that always happens when you photograph there.

Another time, Le and a half-Sioux, half-Micmac friend of his named Sequoyah and a woman friend of Sequoyah's and the woman's eleven-year-old son stopped by my apartment one evening when I was away at an art opening. My wife and I had moved to Brooklyn by then, and our daughter was three years old. My wife was sick with the flu and didn't answer the buzzer, but Le persisted, showing our upstairs neighbor the picture of him in my book and telling the neighbor that he was dying. The neighbor held the front door for them, and Le and his friends slept for a while on the floor in the basement of our building, then came up and knocked at our door. They sat around the apartment for several hours, smoking and talking with my wife and playing with my daughter. Later, when I asked her what she thought of Le, she said he had a "rough, gruff voice," but she liked him.

Le and Sequoyah rang the buzzer again a few nights later, and I went down and met them in the vestibule. My wife was still sick, so I didn't ask them in. Instead, we sat in Sequoyah's car, Le and I in the front seat, Sequoyah in the back, all of us about waist-deep in a rubble of Budweiser cans. We watched the passersby on Tenth Street through windows streaked with dried beer foam as Le told about the spiritual advantages of eating dog. He said that a faithful, fat puppy was best for eating, and that if you ever got lost wandering in the spirit world, the dog's faithfulness would recall you to yourself. Le got out of the car for a moment just as a neighbor of mine passed by walking his dog. Le said to him, conversationally, "I don't eat those. I just eat little puppies." The neighbor hurried away up the sidewalk. Sequoyah and I got out, too, and Le opened the trunk. He said he had a present for me and pulled out a Western-style saddle and laid it in the street next to the car. Its stirrups stretched almost from one side of Tenth Street to the other. He said it was mine. I said I had no horse. He tried to persuade me to take it, then reluctantly put it back in the trunk, meanwhile asking me for $500. I said I didn't have $500 either, at the moment. Le said I would get it tomorrow, that he would call me in the morning and I would give it to him.

Then for a long while I didn't see him, only heard from him by phone. Misfortune became the theme of his calls. He had been in a car wreck on the New York Thruway. A car in which he was riding had skidded and crashed into a culvert, and a screw jack under the front seat had come loose and cracked his kneecap, and his face hit the metal dashboard three times, and he had to go to a special Indian hospital in

Omaha for plastic surgery. A house he and Noelle had bought turned out to be on land which had not belonged to the seller, and the owner of the land was trying to evict them. He had pleaded guilty to a drunk-driving charge due to the incompetence of his lawyer and had been sentenced to a year in state prison as a repeat offender. A highway patrolman had come to his house with drawn gun and had taken him away. A judge had released him. He needed money for a new lawyer. His attempts to avoid prison had failed, and he had been given a date to begin to serve his sentence. He told me he would rather be dead than go to prison again.

One afternoon he called me from the Port Authority Bus Terminal in Manhattan. I remembered that this was the day he was supposed to go to prison. I went downstairs and got on the subway and met him by the Greyhound ticket counter. He looked tired and hungover, but otherwise better than I expected; I would not have noticed the scars on his face from his car accident if he hadn't pointed them out. He said he was going back to South Dakota. I said becoming a fugitive was a bad idea. We argued about this for a while. Finally he agreed to go back upstate and report to jail. I bought him an Adirondack Trailways bus ticket using my credit card, so the ticket could not be refunded. Then we went to a nearby cash machine and I took out fifty dollars and gave it to him. He was wearing a gray felt cowboy hat with a tall, uncreased crown and an eagle feather hanging from the back on a buckskin thong. He took off the hat and untied the eagle feather and handed it to me. He said it was a present for my son, then only a month or two old. We shook hands, and I wished him luck. He said as soon as he had gotten himself some Chinese food he would catch the next bus home. On the subway back to Brooklyn, three people asked me about the eagle feather. A black man in an Indian-style choker necklace made of pipe beads asked if I would be interested in selling it. I smiled and said no.

Le did not take the next bus home, or the bus after that. Noelle and I exchanged several anxious phone calls. About a week later, he called from a truck stop just east of Rapid City, South Dakota. He said he needed money for carfare; he was going back to the reservation.

CHAPTER

3

A while later, my family and I moved to Montana. It was either there or Russia. I had finished writing a long book, I became restless, I wanted a change. I went to Moscow to check it out and stayed in the apartment of a friend of mine's mother who was visiting the United States. I got my daughter enrolled in the first grade at the American School on Leninsky Prospect without too much difficulty (although the high tuition I would have to pay surprised me). Finding an apartment proved more of a challenge. I asked around among friends of friends, but no one knew of anything in the size and price range I wanted. I went to Moscow University and copied some telephone numbers from apartment ads on a bulletin board there. When I called the numbers, however, the people who answered all spoke Russian. Even flipping quickly through my Russian-English dictionary I could not keep up. After I came back to Brooklyn, my wife and I talked it over and decided, with some relief, on Missoula, Montana, instead. Having already moved to Montana once before when restlessness overcame me, I felt a bit self-conscious about doing it again. A friend in Montana told me that it was nothing to worry about; he had moved to Missoula seven times already, he said.

We put our apartment on the market, we attended farewell parties, we packed up our stuff. One hot morning in August a moving van came, and five black moving men working hard emptied the apartment in a few hours, never commenting to us on the dozens of cardboard boxes labeled TOYS and the scores of heavy cardboard boxes labeled BOOKS. We took a final look around the apartment and locked the door for the last time. We had lived there for six and a half years. We stopped at the dry cleaners on the corner and picked up my poplin suit, drove up to my sister's husband's parents' place in Connecticut, stayed there with my sister's family for a day or two, and set out across the country in our rented car.

The moving company had told us that the van might take as long as seventeen days to get to Missoula, so we didn't hurry. We visited my brother in Cleveland and ancestral graves in Norwalk, Ohio. My daughter saw her first rainbow in Nappanee, Indiana. My wife took pictures of Amish laundry hanging on clotheslines because she liked how all the garments were black and the same. Rows of corn wound around hills in Iowa like threads on a screw; woodlots sat on the prairie horizon suspended on a shimmering, like hovercraft. In Nebraska, while I was driving and perversely defending a recent magazine column by George Will that said the late Jerry Garcia of the Grateful Dead was responsible for America's drug problem, a column I didn't even agree with, I was stopped by a highway patrolman barely out of puberty and given a ninety-dollar ticket for speeding. When I got back in the car, humbled, the children looked at me with fearful eyes. My wife, who had been angrily arguing the anti–George Will position, could not stop laughing. She couldn't have been happier if ninety dollars had just flown in the window, instead of out the other way.

We passed through western South Dakota not far from the Pine Ridge Reservation; I wanted to go there and visit Le, but we didn't, choosing by majority vote to go to a reptile garden instead. I sulked about that as we drove through the Black Hills. When we called in the evening to check with the moving company, they said there had been a change of schedule and the van would be in Missoula in two days. We hurried across Montana to beat them there. Our friends Bryan and Dee, who had found us a house to rent near theirs in town, met us when we arrived. Bryan had given the wooden frame of the swing in the back yard of our house a new coat of paint, bright blue. We slept on the floor that night, and the next morning the van arrived. Three moving men from Seattle carried our stuff in, making derisive note of all the boxes of toys and books. "Books and toys, toys and books," they kept saying. The van driver told me that the movers in New York who had loaded our stuff into the van had all been crackheads, and I told him that they definitely weren't crackheads and that he wasn't from New York and that he had no idea what he was talking about. After that he was disagreeably polite.

When the van had left and we had unpacked the essentials, I went around town looking at cars with FOR SALE signs in people's yards. I found a 1988 Chevy Blazer in good condition—owned by an optometrist—and I bought it. A few days later, I drove back 780 miles to Oglala, South Dakota, to visit Le.

I was on the road by 6:45 in the morning. Mist rose from the Clark Fork River and hung up in the bushes beside it like packing material; a man stood on the front of a log loader and wiped the mist off the windshield with full gestures of his arm. I took Interstate 90 almost all the way—up the Clark Fork valley to Butte, over the Continental Divide, over more ranges of mountains, then along the valley of the Yellowstone River to Billings. Beyond Billings the road headed south into Wyoming, past the site of the battle of the Little Bighorn, then across the creased and empty near-desert in the northeastern part of that state. At first I had the visor down against the sunrise. Five hundred miles later, the sun was way behind me, bouncing off my rearview mirror and tinting the buttes and strips of plowed ground a red like the red that runs along the gutter by a brownstone being sandblasted in Brooklyn.

Full dark had fallen by the time I reached Rapid City. I followed South Dakota Highway 79 heading through town and then south, toward Le's house on the reservation about eighty miles away. Just beyond the city's last lights, an Indian hitchhiker appeared suddenly on the roadside. The wind had come up, and his long hair flew in the headlights. I didn't stop. The sameness of the interstate seemed far behind me now. On the dark, narrow two-lane, the occasional cars coming the other way seemed to blast by at highest speed. In this part of the country, Indians have an average life expectancy about eleven years shorter than that of Americans as a whole. As I approached the reservation, I imagined I could feel the life expectancy drop, as palpable as a sudden drop in temperature. Just before the little town of Hermosa, South Dakota, my headlights picked out a group of the white reflecting-metal highway markers which South Dakota puts up at places where fatal car accidents have occurred. I counted eight markers—eight souls—set in a row that ascended from the ditch by the road and up the grassy incline beside it.

Over the next four years, I traveled back and forth to the reservation many times. Usually I went via the interstate and Highway 79, and I noted those markers whenever I passed. If I had the radio on, I turned it off, and I said a prayer. I wondered about the markers, so I called the South Dakota Department of Transportation, and a man in the accident records division found the accident report and sent it to me. The crash had happened at eight minutes after nine o'clock on the evening of Friday, June 27, 1986. A northbound car went out of control and collided with a southbound car, and both cars caught fire. Seven members of a Sioux family originally from the Rosebud Reservation died in the southbound car. Three of them were children under seven years old. The family's name was Dismounts Thrice. The northbound driver, who had a bottle of whiskey of a brand the highway patrol did not specify with only an inch left in it in his car, and whose blood alcohol content was three times the legal limit, also died. The Indian driver had no alcohol in his blood. The drunk driver was not an Indian. He worked for the Better Business Bureau.

I searched out local newspaper stories about the crash and read about the heat of its flames, the immense rising pillar of dark-black smoke, and the thunderstorm that poured down not long afterward. I pursued even further, found the apartments where the people in the southbound car had lived in the mostly Indian housing developments north of Rapid City and the convenience store where they had bought their last tank of gas. I went to the small Western city where the drunk driver had grown up and saw the ample brick house he had grown up in, his picture in his high school yearbook, the apartment where his parents lived. After a couple of years, it occurred to me that maybe by now God had granted some peace to the people who had died in the crash and to those who loved them, and that I should, too.

The first time I saw the markers, I decided I did not want to drive anymore. I had gone 720 miles since morning. I pulled over in Hermosa and parked in a shadowed place behind a gas station–convenience store–casino–restaurant. I picked a spot by the aluminum-can recycling Dumpster where I hoped my car wouldn't be too conspicuous, folded down the back seat, unrolled my sleeping bag, and went to sleep. At an unknown hour of the night, I came half awake in a flood of light from a brilliant source at my back window. In my sleep I thought I was dreaming of that floodlit moment in the movies when the alien spaceship descends. The light seemed to be coming from a giant vehicle parked behind me. I got up on one elbow. Someone rapped on the driver's-side window with something metal—a flashlight—and asked me to roll the window down. The flashlight was in the hand of a short, blond, crew-cut man in a blue denim coat and jeans with a big pistol in a black holster on his hip. He asked for my driver's license and I groggily fumbled it to him. He beamed the light on it, asking me quick questions all the while. Finally, looking at his denim outfit, I said, "Who are *you*?" He said, with a drawling flourish, "I'm the local law." Then he disappeared, the mothership ascended, and I went back to sleep.

At dawn, I took a back road from Hermosa to the reservation. There was no one else about. I had the radio tuned to KILI, the Pine Ridge radio station, which broadcasts from the reservation near the village of Porcupine. It was playing Lakota singing and drumming. Under an overcast sky, the prairie looked drained of color. Here and there I saw burned patches, the black extending in tongues where the wind had pushed it. In the middle of one burned patch was a car seat, also burned. A wheel rim with shreds of tire still on it hung from a fence-post. Two rows of tires lay flat on the roof of a turquoise-colored trailer, anchoring the roof against the wind. I followed the road into a wide valley, crossed a bridge over the Cheyenne River, and was on the reservation.

How many boundaries this reservation has had over the years! About a century and a half ago, the lands set aside for the Sioux by treaty stretched from the Powder River to the west, to the Heart River in the north, to the Missouri River in the east, to the North Platte River in the south—an immense expanse in the middle of the continent, covering parts of the present states of Montana, Wyoming, North Dakota, South Dakota, and Nebraska. Since then, Sioux lands have shrunk and shrunk again, leaving behind vestigial boundaries like a drying sea. In 1868, after the Sioux had won the Powder River war, a new treaty actually increased their lands somewhat, giving them hunting rights as far north as the Yellowstone River and as far west as the Bighorn Mountains. A provision of that treaty, which the Indians may have overlooked, however, required them to make their permanent homes only in a smaller part of their lands, in what was called the Great Sioux Reservation, most of which lay within the half of present South Dakota west of the Missouri River. After the Indian victory over Custer and the Seventh Cavalry at the Little Bighorn, a punitive spirit in the United States led to the so-called sell-or-starve agreement of 1876: the Sioux got a token land exchange for much of their original territory, and the Great Sioux Reservation was relieved of its westernmost part, which included the gold-rich Black Hills. If the Sioux refused to sign, the government commissioners told them, the food-ration payments which had begun with earlier treaties would be cut off. Even with this threat, the commissioners could not collect the signatures of three-fourths of the adult males of the tribe as required by law. Congress went ahead and ratified the agreement anyway the following year.

In 1889, the federal government unilaterally broke up what remained of the Great Sioux Reservation, and gave nine million acres of it to the new states of North Dakota and South Dakota. Again, the Sioux had no say. The Sioux tribes ended up with six reservations within the former Great Sioux Reservation's boundaries. The Oglala got a piece of land in southwestern South Dakota about ninety miles long and fifty-five miles wide at its widest point. Its southern boundary was the Nebraska state line. On paper, the Oglala reservation included almost three million acres; another act of Congress, however, had the long-term effect of removing much of that from Indian hands. The Dawes Act of 1887, called the Allotment Act, intended to make Indians full citizens through ownership of land. Tribal holdings were allotted to individual tribal members in parcels of 160 acres per head of household. Lands left over, called "surplus lands," were open for settlement by non-Indians. The people who wrote the act considered themselves friends of the Indian, and they put in various clauses and safeguards to see that Indians kept the land they received. In fact, the Dawes Act proved an efficient means for the further drastic reduction of Indian lands. Individual ownership of land, that notion imported from Europe, generally did not make much sense to Indians. White ranchers and farmers and speculators found taking land from Indians one at a time to be simpler and more legal than previous methods of taking it from the tribe as a whole.

By 1934, when another act of Congress ended the allotment program, Indian lands had decreased from 138 million acres to 47 million acres nationwide. On the Oglala reservation, about a million acres passed from Indian ownership. Perhaps believing the nineteenth-century dictum that the Indian must soon disappear, the authors of allotment did not provide for the possibility the Indian populations would expand. Indians often were not fond of making wills, and many died intestate, with many heirs, leaving allotted lands to be divided into equal shares. Over generations, this occurred again and again. Today, on Pine Ridge and other reservations, some Indians own parcels of original allotments which are measured not in acres but in square yards, feet, and inches.

Past the village of Red Shirt inside the border of the reservation, the road entered a piece of grassy tableland which descends steeply at its edges into badlands. Locals call this the Red Shirt Table Road. At certain places beside the road, the badlands are like an erosion carnival opening at your feet. Travelers on the Red Shirt Table Road, frustrated by its lack of public restrooms, sometimes pull over, step out, stroll a short distance away from the car, and accidentally plunge into the chasms below. Some of the pillars of rock still have a flat piece of prairie on top the size of a living-room rug, from which the eroded rock face complicatedly declines hundreds of feet to the canyon floor. Some of the monoliths are jagged on top, like newspaper torn against the grain. Others are rounded and smooth, and shiny as old pants. In places the ranks recede, one eroded gray-and-pink wall of rock behind the other, all the way to the horizon. The Red Shirt Table Road is the worst paved road I have ever driven. Even here on the flat, the badlands seem to want to make their point. Sinks afflict the road's asphalt, creating places where you drive down in and then up the other side. Plates of roadway lurch upward toward you, bumper-high. Potholes slurp and open wide. Not every road on Pine Ridge or in its vicinity is as bad as this, but anyone who visits the reservation more than twice learns that Pine Ridge is a difficult place to get to. No major thoroughfare or rail line runs to it, or even very close by. This may seem at first to be a coincidence of geography or bad planning. In fact, it is deliberate. To oversimplify only a little, it is the result of the bad conscience of General William Tecumseh Sherman.

The Oglala Sioux, pre-reservation, lived mostly west of here, in present Wyoming west and south of the Black Hills. If their nation had had a capital, it would have been there on the prairies in the valley of the North Platte River, perhaps near the fur-trading post at Fort Laramie. The Oglala liked to trade at the fort, then move into the Powder River country to the north, for the good buffalo hunting and the convenient raiding distance from the Crow. The Oregon Trail ran along the North Platte Valley, and the Oglala found the wagon trains interesting. After they had chased the Army out of Wyoming's Powder River country in 1868, they could not understand why General Sherman and the other treaty commissioners kept insisting that they move well away from the Platte, preferably to the northeast and out of Wyoming Territory entirely. Which is to say, they did not understand about the railroad. In 1868 the Union Pacific Railroad was building the first transcontinental line on a route that ran through southern Wyoming. The government had issued the railroad millions of dollars in bonds and needed to get the line completed fast. Nobody in the government or in the employ of the railroad wanted the warlike Oglala anywhere near the railroad line.

General Sherman, who led the government negotiators, no doubt had a more personal vision of what the Oglala might do to it; he had himself torn railroad lines to shreds all over the South during the Civil War just a few years earlier. He knew how easy it was to wreck a railroad, and maybe even how much fun it was. Still fighting the previous war, as generals do, Sherman thought first of securing the railroad. He and many others wanted to move the Oglala all the way back east to the shores of the Missouri River; steamboat contracts to supply them there had already been let. The struggle went on for ten years, Red Cloud and the Oglala pulling to stay in the West, the government pushing them east. This corner of South Dakota somewhere between each's desire became the final compromise. Red Cloud accepted it, but didn't like it. Sherman and the railroad builders were satisfied; no one was ever going to try to lay railroad tracks through those badlands anyway.

Within fifteen miles or so, the Red Shirt Table Road left the bumpiness of the tableland and became a good gravel surface running straight through an expanse of little bare-top clay hills like gray haystacks, then through rolling prairie with low buttes to the east and west. The road turned to asphalt again, this section smooth and newly paved. Up ahead a magpie flapped black and white across it like a checkered flag. Occasional dirt driveways to either side dwindled to house trailers, each one solitary in the distance, blue wood smoke rising from the stovepipes. Next to almost every lonesome trailer, you could see the silhouette of a basketball backboard and pole. James Naismith, who in 1891 invented the game of basketball, never made any money from it; but, he wrote, "I am sure that no man can derive more pleasure from money or power than I do from seeing a pair of basketball goals in some out of the way place." I crossed the bridge over the White River and soon saw a water tower on the horizon. When I came up to it, I could read the word LONEMAN in black letters on its silver side. It's in the little community of Loneman, uphill from a housing development and the Loneman Elementary School. Past Loneman I continued to the junction of Highway 18, turned left, and drove on a mile or so to the village of Oglala. A woman sorting mail in the gray cement post office told me how to find the house of a woman named Sarah Brave, who told me through her closed screen door how to find Le.

His house stood by a bend in the road with no other houses around, singular as a letter in an alphabet book. It was a standard government-built house of the kind often seen on military bases or Indian reservations. It was one-story, with faded brown siding and a yard run mostly to weeds. Six or eight cars and a pickup truck, in various stages of dilapidation, made a loose semicircle around one corner. I pulled into the rutted mud driveway, opened the door, and stepped out onto a flattened Budweiser can. Le was standing in the yard. We had not seen each other in a year and a half, since that time at the Port Authority Bus Terminal. He greeted me without surprise. We hugged each other and shook hands, and Le felt the pulse in my wrist with his thumb. He said, "*Hoka hey*, Little Brother. I am honored to be in your presence." His breath was Budweiser and a chemical I couldn't place. He was wearing cowboy boots, faded pegged blue jeans, a red cowboy shirt with buttons of blue imitation mother-of-pearl, and a neck brace in a color sometimes called "flesh" extending from his collarbone up to his ears. On the front of the neck brace, just above the collarbone, large raised letters said FRONT. He had his hair in the piled-high style I'd seen before. Combined with the brace, it gave him the look of a starched-collar lady from out of the past.

"I was in a car wreck three weeks ago," he explained. "Me and this guy named Archambault that I went to Indian boarding school with was drinking in White Clay, Nebraska, and in the afternoon we started hitchhiking back to Pine Ridge. We got picked up by Joe Red Star and Mark Goings, and me and Archambault got in the back seat, and I hadn't hardly got in when them guys floored it and we was flyin' up Highway 407, and then suddenly we was off the road on the right and I looked up and saw the light pole comin' at us. I was yellin', 'Hey, hey, hey!' and we took out the light pole and rolled four times. I went flyin' over the front seat and hit the windshield with the back of my head and shoulders, and I had the top of the car pressed right against my face. Man, there was a whole lot of moanin' and groanin' in that car. It took the emergency medical technician guys three and a half hours to cut us out. We backed up traffic on 407 for miles. It was *hot* in that car, too. I could hear people sayin', 'Why can't they get 'em *out*?' Finally they had the top cut off and one of the EMT guys took hold of my head to see if my neck was broken and I let out a bloodcurdling scream. They put a big plastic thing under my head and put me on a slab of wood and then onto a gurney and took me to Rapid City Regional Hospital. I was in surgery for about four hours. They fixed the broken vertebrae in my neck—I think they used some bone taken from my hip. Everybody came to the hospital to visit. Elliott Gould called to tell me to get better, and his daughter Molly called, too. David Carradine called, and Robert Altman, the movie director. My sister Norma sat by my bedside and prayed for me for eight straight hours. I was out of the hospital in a week. The other guys didn't have nothin' serious—broken ankle, broken nose, bruises and scrapes. Last week I ran into Archambault, and he said, 'If we'd known those guys was so drunk, we'd've waited for the next car.' "

Le invited me in, and we climbed the single cinder block he used for a doorstep. His door latch was a green-and-white plastic fish stringer, which he tied to a nail inside. He asked if I'd had breakfast and offered me a beer. I replied that I had quit drinking. He said, "That reminds me—I've got to take my pills again." He produced half a dozen pill bottles of various sizes and shook pills from them into his palm. Hospitably, he first offered a large orange capsule to me: "Want one?" I declined, with thanks. Then he washed them all down with a few swigs of beer. He sat on a stove log and I on the only chair. The amount of stuff in his house overthrew my attempt to take it in. There was a nonworking clock on the wall, and a brown hole near it where the oven pipe used to be, and a cast-iron woodstove, and a plastic milk crate full of silver tinsel Christmas wreaths, and a yellow hard hat, and a photograph of a statuesque Indian woman in a T-shirt smiling and holding a .357 Magnum revolver ("That's my nephew's wife, Deborah. She's a rowdy from the Fort Apache Reservation"), and a rolled-up section of snow fence, and a poster from the movie *Incident at Oglala,* and a copy of the collected short stories of Ernest Hemingway, and several sports trophies, and the paperwork from Le's recent hospital bills. A door just behind me opened into a room filled several feet deep with suitcases, plastic picnic coolers, backpacks, baby carriers, trunks, and heavyweight canvas tote bags. I remembered when Le had just moved from New York City up to Monsey, and I had commiserated with him, saying how hard it was to move. He had replied, "It's not hard for me. I'm nomadic."

I asked if this stuff was his. He said, "Most of it belongs to my sister Florence. She lived here for a while with her kids and grandkids, until the tribe gave her a new house in a development in Oglala on the other side of Highway 18. Before that, my dad lived here. It was his house originally, and they all moved in here with him. He needed a house close to the highway like this because he had cancer and had to get back and forth over to the clinic for treatment. He lost a quarter of his stomach and one and a half of his lungs, and he still was smokin' three packs a day. He didn't care what brand—any tobacco he could get, as long as he could blow smoke. The tribe or the BIA or someone moved this house here from the Army munitions depot over in Igloo, South Dakota. I think that at one time it might have been near to some nuclear weapons. A while ago they tested it and it was really radioactive. It still will get a Geiger counter going pretty good. It had a fire in '83, and when they fixed it up afterward they didn't put in no insulation, so when the temperature drops it can get pretty chilly in here. When winter comes I'll just get me a fat woman and let her sleep on the windy side."

Back in the yard, he led me on a brief tour of the accumulated cars. All of them, according to him, were much closer to being drivable than they appeared. He kept saying, "Oh, it'll run. Put a new battery and a windshield and a new set of tires and some gas in it, and it'll run." Then he said, "Let's go—I'll take you to see my mom and dad." We got in my car. He did not put on his seat belt, but I insisted that he put on his seat belt. We headed north, on the road I had driven from Red Shirt Table. I asked him if anyone on the reservation called him Le. I knew his birth name was Leonard Thomas Walks Out; Sarah Brave had referred to him as Leonard. "There's people here who call me Le or Laid-Back, but most call me Leonard," he said. "Or Lenny. And there's still a few real old-timers who remember when I was the baby of my family, before Floyd John was born. One old lady, Leonora Fast Horse, saw me at the post office the other day and said, 'Look! It's Baby Leo!' I mean, here I'm goin' on fifty-five years old!"

After about three miles Le directed me onto a grassy track leading off to the right. In the high weeds next to it were pieces of a broken guitar. The track led onto a low rise with a barbed-wire fence around a small plot of gravestones and crosses; set back from and above the road, it would be hard to spot if you didn't know it was there. Le braced his chest against the gatepost, reached around it with both arms, and pulled hard to free the gate end from the taut loop of barbed wire that latched it; then he dragged the gate open and laid it on the ground (not bad, I thought, for a person with a broken neck). I took off my baseball cap and walked quietly as we entered the cemetery grounds. The more Le talked, the quieter I became. On this little patch of earth, a vastness of suffering and disaster had converged. Among the murders, suicides, and car accidents the headstones could not describe, these three seemed central to Le's life:

Albert C. Walks Out; Feb. 23, 1933–Aug. 3, 1957. "This was my brother," Le said. "Albert was nine years older than me. He joined the Army during the Korean War. He had only an eighth-grade education, but he became a war hero and got a battlefield commission as a sergeant first class when he was only twenty years old. He was a really tough guy, and a lot of people around here were jealous of him. When he was home on leave, he stopped to help some guys whose car had a flat tire on the county road eight miles east of Oelrichs, South Dakota, and they beat him to death with a tire iron. I was fifteen years old at the time. The guys who killed him were Jonas and Franklin Belt and Charles Blind Man. They were drunk when they did it. They all went to prison, and they're all dead now. I believe one or two of them are buried in this cemetery, too."

Elizebith Walks Out; May 22, 1906–April 7, 1958. "This is my mom. She was born on the Cheyenne River Reservation, by Eagle Butte. We still have inheritance land over there. She and my dad got married in 1926, and they had eleven children. I'm the eighth. Her maiden name was Blacksmith, and I've got a lot of Blacksmith relatives around here and on Cheyenne River. Her grandfather Moses Blacksmith was a Canadian Frenchman with a light-colored, curly hairdo like George Washington's. Her dad had a ranch with racehorses and pigs and chickens and ducks on the Moreau River near Thunder Butte. But then her mom died and her dad moved over here and married Edna Loafer and became a member of the Oglala Tribe. After they moved here was when my mom met Asa Walks Out, my dad. She got killed in an accident on Highway 87 between Rushville and White Clay, Nebraska. She had gone over there shopping with Amos Red Paint and they ran out of gas and they were pushing the car by the side of the road when a bootlegger from White Clay with no headlights ran into them from behind. She got both her legs cut off and died seven days later. My dad lived to be ninety-one. He died just last summer. We buried him on top of her, but we don't have a marker for him yet."

Elda Asa Walks Out; March 7, 1935–Feb. 14, 1959. "My mom died eight months after Albert, and Elda—we called him Eldee—died ten months after my mom. Eldee was just out of the Army and he could kick anyone's ass. He didn't even care if he got his own ass kicked once in a while. He'd get back in the car with his nose all bloodied and say, 'Well, at least I got the anger out of me!' He was running my dad's spread near here, and me and him had gone up to Rapid to buy sixteen hundred pounds of cattle feed, and we were coming back in the pickup drinking whiskey and beer, and he started telling me that he'd made a terrible mistake. He said he had married too young and in a Catholic ceremony and now he couldn't get out of it, and he was in love with a fifteen-year-old girl. So we got back to his place and I was outside unloading the truck when one of his kids come running out of the house saying, 'Mommy and Daddy is fightin'.' So I picked the kid up and comforted him and went inside and asked what they were fightin' about, and Eldee said, 'We're not fightin', we're just talkin'.' Then he takes me out in the yard and says, 'She won't give me a divorce. I'm goin'.' I said, 'Where to? I'll go with you.' He says, 'Where I'm goin' you can't follow. Take care of my kids.' He gets a rifle out of the truck and I think, Whoa, I better get the kids back in the house. I go in and right away I hear BLAM—he shoots himself right in the head. I run out and he's flat on his back and blood is gushing from his forehead eighteen inches in the air. I ran to a white rancher's house and said, 'Call the fuckin' ambulance! My brother has shot himself in the head!' By the time I got back, there was blood all over the place but nobody there.

"After that I went crazy for a while, writing bad checks. I got caught, went to prison, got out, stole a government truck, ended up back in prison again. When Eldee shot himself I was sixteen years old."

As we walked back to my car, Le stopped by an unmarked grave near the middle of the cemetery. He said, "This is my grandfather James Walks Out. He was born in 1861, and he lived to be an old man. When I was a little boy, I lived with him for a few years. He raised me, more than my mom and dad. One of his Lakota names was Woz'aglai, which means Gatherer of the Spirits. He was a famous medicine man. He was really good at helping people to find stuff they had lost. He had special ceremonies for that; white people and Indians used to come to him from all around. He was a boy at Fort Robinson when Crazy Horse was killed, and he helped smuggle Crazy Horse's bones from a grave there. Him and a few other young guys took the bones at night to near Chadron Creek and met up with Crazy Horse's parents, and the parents carried them from there. Woz'aglai was one of the few people who knew where Crazy Horse was buried. Once my oldest brother, Hermus, asked him where that was. Hermus said he would go and dig the bones up and sell them and make a lot of money. Woz'aglai refused to tell, and after that he never talked about where Crazy Horse was buried anymore."

Le closed the cemetery gate, again pulling on it hard, and he latched it with the loop of wire. Then we drove back the way we had come. As we approached his house, Le said, "Floyd John ought to be awake by now. Let's go eat up his food." We drove on, and he directed me to turn onto a puddled road just past the Loneman School. The ruts were deep and the car jounced, and Le's neck caused him to wince with each jounce. The going got muddier and muddier. I stopped and shifted into four-wheel drive. The ruts then split up into an every-man-for-himself profusion across a mudflat, and I must have guessed wrong, because soon I was roaring across it at maximum rpms slewing back and forth, going nearly sideways sometimes, and hurling up flying mud around me like a magnetic field. Floyd John heard us coming—anyone would have—and he was standing outside his green tar-paper shack as we squished to a stop in his yard. The car had mud on the hood and the windshield and the side windows. I turned off the steaming engine. Floyd John walked to the car, looked me over, and asked, "Well, bro, are you likin' the rez as much as you liked New York?"

"Tell me, Floyd John—when are they going to finish building the subway out to your house?"

"Any day, any day. The bull snakes and the king snakes are workin' on it right now."

CHAPTER

4

Floyd John had put on some weight since I'd last seen him, and now he walked with a limp and used a cane. He began to tell me how he had been working on a modular home over at the air base by Rapid City and a wall had fallen on him and crushed his hip. Then he described which new benefits this entitled him to. The paperwork of it, between agencies of the state and the federal government and the tribe, was so complicated that I couldn't have kept up if he'd explained it to me five times. Le asked him if he had any red beans with hot sauce we could eat, and Floyd John said he had no food in the house. He wasn't due to pick up his commodities for a couple of days. He said that his girlfriend, Wanda Kindle, who worked for the tribal police, was due to get paid that afternoon. He climbed with difficulty into the back seat, and we roared and crawfished our way back to the paved road.

First we stopped at the Oglala post office so Le and Floyd John could check their mail. The postmaster usually has all the mail sorted and in the boxes by 10:30, a time known thereabouts as "mail": "I'll see you tomorrow morning after mail." Not many on the reservation get their mail brought to where they live; most people have to go in and pick it up, either from a post office box or by asking at the window for general delivery. In the later years of Red Cloud's life, his two-mile trip to the post office and back was the big event of his day. At 10:45 that morning, the rutted lot by the Oglala post office was full of idling cars, some of them making plenty of noise and smoke. Le and Floyd John got out and exchanged a few words with the woman in the station wagon next to us. Then they went into the building and came out again in a second, disappointed and blue. "Nothing," Le said. "A lot of days there's nothing. I usually check it anyway. You never know. A few weeks ago I got a letter from the Attorney General of New York saying that he wasn't gonna come after me and make me go to jail as long as I never set foot in New York State again. It was a pretty friendly letter, all in all."

Like many of the other cars, we then pulled out of the post office lot and headed for the village of Pine Ridge fifteen miles away. Pine Ridge is the largest town on the reservation. The center of tribal government is there, and the reservation headquarters of the U.S. Bureau of Indian Affairs, and the Indian Health Services hospital. Many days on the reservation include a trip to Pine Ridge. The road from Oglala follows the valley of White Clay Creek much of the way. For some distance the creek bottom and a reservoir are on one side, then the creek crosses to the other. To the north and south are uplands leading to low, chalk-colored buttes that rise from the prairie like molars from a gumline. Groups of the yellow pines that give Pine Ridge its name fit themselves into the upland creases and folds. On unsettled days, cumulus clouds pile up for miles above. We passed a tipi made of white canvas, a tipi made of weathered white plyboard, a Quonset hut, a Seventh-Day Adventist church. Trailer homes and one-story houses appeared here and there, mostly set far apart. Wherever their driveways met the road, deltas of muddy tire tracks spread across the pavement. Le made me retell for Floyd John the story about the policeman in Hermosa who had awakened me the night before. They said the cop was famous for giving a hard time to Indians on their way through town. He and Floyd John kept repeating, *"I'm the local law!"* and laughing.

A rise brought us in view of the Pine Ridge water towers—most towns on the reservation have a water tower fixing them in place, but Pine Ridge has four—and the rise after that showed a slow line of cars below us moving to the only traffic light on the reservation, at the intersection of Highways 18 and 407, in downtown Pine Ridge. The intersection has had a traffic light for only five years or so. Before, it was a four-way stop. People on the reservation called it "the four-way," and many still call it that today. The four-way is the main crossroads of the Oglala nation. On one corner is a wooden bench whose back is a square concrete planter containing weeds and a small pine tree. A large concrete pot full of earth nearby perhaps was once intended to grow flowers. People sit on the bench and cross their legs and talk for hours, just as old men used to do years ago, long before the bench and the flowerpot, telling about the time Queen Victoria kissed them when they were young children in England with Buffalo Bill. "Bullshit Corner" is this corner's unofficial name. On another corner is the Pine Ridge post office, which shares a large brick building with an auditorium called Billy Mills Hall, where most of the important indoor community gatherings are. On another corner is a two-story brick building containing tribal offices and the offices of the Oglala Department of Public Safety—the tribal police. Floyd John got out and went to look for Wanda there. On another corner is a convenience store–gas station which then was called Big Bat's Conoco and now is called Big Bat's Texaco. Le and I parked and went in.

In Pine Ridge, Big Bat's is the place you go. If you're just passing through or visiting, you go to Big Bat's because it's one of the few places on the reservation that look like what you're used to in paved America. Big Bat's has a big, highway-visible, red-and-white sign, and rows of pumps dispensing gasoline and diesel fuel, and full-color cardboard advertisements affixed to the top of the pumps, and country music playing from speakers in the canopies above; inside, it has the usual brightly lit shelves of products whose empty packages will end up on the floor of your car, and freezers and beverage coolers set into the wall, and a deli counter highlighted in blue neon and staffed by aproned young people who use disposable clear plastic gloves to put cold cuts on your six-inch or twelve-inch submarine sandwich, and video games, and TV monitors just below ceiling level showing CNN or country-music videos, and plastic tables and window booths where you can sit and eat or just sit, and a row of pay telephones. If you live on the reservation, if you're not just passing through, you go to Big Bat's because that's where everybody goes.

The original Big Bat was Baptiste "Bat" Pourier, a trader who married into the Sioux and who often served as an interpreter between them and government officials in the second half of the nineteenth century; he was called Big to distinguish him from another interpreter, Baptiste "Little Bat" Garnier. Big Bat's name comes up often in chronicles of the Plains Indian wars. The present Big Bat, also a Pourier, is the original Bat's four-greats grandson. He is a well-built man in his forties with a close-cropped head, a round, boyish face, and dark eyes that register minute changes in the progress of his enterprise. Often, they gleam with triumph; Big Bat's is always busy. No other small-town place I know of has such a plentiful and varied clientele. There are Indians, of course, of all blood degrees, full-blood as well as almost blond. Employees of the tribe and of the BIA and tribal politicos come in for breakfast and for coffee afterward, prolonging conversations that are elliptical and hard to eavesdrop on. Drunks who have been up all night nurse cups of coffee they have bought with change and use the john. There are truck drivers running overweight and avoiding the weigh stations on the main roads, Oglala teenagers in groups of four or five wearing the colors of Denver street gangs, Methodist ministers on their way to local volunteer jobs, college professors leading tours of historical sites, TV crews shooting documentary footage, Mormon missionary ladies in polyester raincoats and with scarves tied around their heads. In the summer, tourists multiply—mid-Americans wearing clothes so casual they might as well be pajamas and toting large video cameras, and fiftyish English couples having one of those bitter, silent arguments travelers have, and long-haired New Age people smelling of patchouli oil, and Australian guys with leather Aussie hats and lissome girlfriends, and college kids from Massachusetts singing in a fake-corny way songs they just heard on the radio in their van, and black families in bright sportswear, and strangely dressed people speaking Hungarian, and ash-blond German women backpackers in their early twenties effortlessly deflecting the attentions of various guys trying to talk to them, and Japanese people by the occasional busload, and once in a while a celebrity with an entourage. Observers who noted about a hundred years ago the disappearance of the American frontier have turned out to be wrong; America will always have its frontier places, and they will always look like Big Bat's.

Le and I each got twelve-inch club combo sandwiches with everything, including jalapeños, and medium sodas. Total cost: $10.62. The sandwiches lasted all day, because half was enough to fill us up, and we saved the rest for later. We sat at a table and ate, and Floyd John and Wanda joined us. Wanda was a short, unsmiling woman with long hair parted in the middle. She wore a heavy shirt unbuttoned like a jacket over a dark pullover and blue jeans. Her wary eyes took me in at a glance when Floyd John introduced us. He said she was the only person on the reservation who knew how to run the computer system for the police department. Wanda accepted this without comment; as we talked, she mostly listened, adding only a remark or two in a small, clear voice quieter than a whisper. Le made me tell for the third time the story about the cop in Hermosa, and when I finished Wanda just nodded, as if she'd heard it before.

Le turned to three guys seated at a table next to ours and began talking to them in Sioux. He stopped for a moment to introduce me to one of them, who he said was his cousin, but I didn't catch the name. Floyd John joined the discussion, which went back and forth and seemed to be verging on an argument. After the three guys had left, I asked Le what it had been about. "White guys dancing," he said. "My cousin was saying that there was too many white guys dancing at the sun dances on the reservation last summer. Him and his friends think letting white guys or any non-Indians in ruins the ceremonies. They don't think outsiders should be allowed even as helpers or water carriers. They say that you let white guys buy the food and the firewood, the way some sun dances do, and then you've gotta let 'em dance, and then pretty soon people who don't know anything are running the whole ceremony. And he's right that there was *hundreds* of white guys goin' to the sun dances last summer. But I say, If a person's heart is good, let him participate in a respectful way. There's non-Indian people that love the sun dance and are really sincere. You just have to be sure that you have elders and medicine men who run the ceremony as it's supposed to be."

Over the next summers, the question of white guys dancing would become one of the most controversial on the reservation. Some traditionalists wanted the tribal council to pass a law banning all non-Indians from sun dances held on Pine Ridge. People who favored open sun dances answered that they would use guns to defend their right to practice their religion with whomever they chose. At least one respected leader kept his sun dance strictly closed. Some dances were open, others were semi-open but had entrances with many checkpoints at which undesirables could be turned away, others were small and secret and held in remote places where passersby and tourists would never see. A hundred years ago Oglala who continued to practice their traditional ceremonies despite the government's ban did so in secret, for fear of white people finding out and shutting them down; today the fear is of white people finding out and wanting to join.

The first afternoon I spent on the reservation can stand for many: we went to Big Bat's, then gassed up, got supplies, and drove around. That day, Le and Floyd John wanted to show me around the reservation, which meant a lot of driving, but being on the reservation almost always does. Two 32-mile round trips between Oglala and Pine Ridge in a day were not uncommon. Then there were the longer drives up to Rapid City to see doctors or relatives, trips to Chadron, Nebraska, to take a television to a repair shop, trips to Hot Springs, South Dakota, to drop Floyd John off at the Veterans' Hospital, trips to see a medicine man who lives miles off the paved road. It seemed as if every time I looked at the gas gauge it was falling back to empty, and every time I checked the odometer I had added another 300 miles. The Oglala may have lost the prairie vastnesses they used to hunt, but they are still obliged to roam. The supplies we picked up beforehand were usually beer. Afternoons almost always began with a trip to the town of White Clay, Nebraska, a mile and three-quarters from the town of Pine Ridge and just across the Nebraska line. Selling alcohol is illegal on the reservation, but legal in Nebraska. I will say more about White Clay later. I dreaded going there.

The reservation landscape is dense with stories. As we drove around, Le told me some of them, and Floyd John occasionally joined in. In the valley of the White River northwest of Oglala, on paved roads and gravel roads near where they grew up, Le said:

"I was riding over this bridge one night with the He Crow boys when we saw a ghost. We heard the hoofs of a horse climbing out of the creek bottom, and then the sound came onto the road right in front of us, and there wasn't nothin' there. Then just for a second we saw the face and body of this Indian rider. The ghost said, 'Hey'—and man, did we go gallopin' hell for leather out of there! We didn't stop till we reached the ridgetop. I never laughed so hard.

"That flat ground above the creek over there is where Francis Slow Bear died. He was playin' cards one night at his brother's cabin back in the hills, and he decided to walk home, and everybody told him to stay till morning, but he went anyway. It was late November, and a blizzard hit. A cowboy found him the next morning froze to death just above his cabin. He had got lost in the blizzard, probably snow-blind. His tracks showed he had walked in circles before he died.

"All back there along the river is Earl Charging Thunder's land. Earl had a string of good buckin' horses he used to hire out to rodeos, and sometimes he let the kids around here practice on 'em. I learned to ride broncs at Earl's.

"Everybody around here used to have horses. Us kids used to ride up on those ridgetops and spread out along 'em just at dark, and then one of us would hold up a lighted kitchen match, and then pretty soon all of us would be holdin' up matches, and you could see the little lights in a line strung out for miles.

"One time me and some guys was huntin' along here, and Timothy Bear Nose said, 'I'm gonna shoot me a mule deer, and if I can't find a deer I'm gonna shoot me a cow.' So here we saw a deer grazin' about a hundred yards away. We roll down the window and Timothy Bear Nose sticks his rifle out and sights it and pulls the trigger and the gun goes off really loud, and there's a puff of dust in front of the deer and the deer trots away. And immediately a cow about three hundred yards on up the hill falls flat on its side! It was a freak shot—he'd been aimin' at the deer, but the bullet ricocheted and hit the cow. Of course, there was nothin' we could do but drive over there and butcher it out.

"I used to walk along here with a buddy of mine when I was about fifteen sniffin' that white-gas gasoline. We'd keep it in a gallon bleach bottle and sniff it out of a rubber tube. It will really get you high. We huffed regular gas sometimes, too. That was back before unleaded gas, though, and the lead was bad for you. There was some guys around here almost died of lead poisoning from it. I only did it for about three months.

"Our family's cabin was over there. It was a pretty good-sized log house, actually. That's where Eldee shot himself. The cabin was torn down a long time ago.

"That bare patch of ground where you can still see foundations is where our community center used to be. It was a long log house with big barrel stoves at each end, and when there was dances we'd bring in a lot of firewood and get those stoves so hot they glowed bright red. Everybody around here used to come to the dances in their horse-and-buggies or spring wagons. Back then, not many had cars. The main families were the Makes Shines, the Blue Horses, the No Waters—they were related to the No Water who shot Crazy Horse in the face after Crazy Horse stole No Water's wife—the Dreaming Bears, the Bear Noses, the Bores a Holes, the Helpers, the Porcupines, the Little Soldiers. A lot of the families still live around here."

Le's stories with horses in them tended to be happier than his stories involving cars; as he talked, and as the miles passed in the vicinity of Oglala and Pine Ridge, remembered car wrecks strewed the roadside. I gripped the steering wheel tightly with both hands. Le offered me a beer, and I told him again that I had quit drinking. I was nervous even breathing the fumes as he and Floyd John went through one after the next and crumpled the cans on the floor underfoot. It was broad daylight, the weather was clear, and I drove expecting at any second the cymbals-crash of the collision that would end our lives. Le pointed out the place where a man had backed up over the man's sister and killed her when they stopped at the White River to get water, and where the ambulance driver fell asleep and went off the road and her passenger hit the dashboard and died, and where the Porcupine boys crashed, and where a nephew hit a bridge abutment and the steering wheel crushed his chest and killed him, and where a car Floyd John was riding in with six other kids spun out at an S-curve at a hundred-plus miles an hour and rolled over many times and the engine block just kept going and ended up fifty yards farther down the road (nobody killed), and where a drunk driver on his way back from White Clay hit two pedestrians and sheared off parts of their arms and legs. Generally his stories did not coincide with the fatality markers which the state has put along the roads. Those markers were for crashes he didn't know about, that happened when he was living away from the reservation, Le said. Occasionally we passed a fatality marker that had been damaged in a subsequent crash.

In the past, the Pine Ridge Reservation has gone through periods of small-scale war. A recent bloody time was in the mid-1970s, when supporters of the American Indian Movement and supporters of the tribal government under tribal chairman Dick Wilson battled each other with gang-style violence that ranged from beatings to firebombings to murder. In a two-year span, 1973–75, there were dozens of unexplained deaths on the reservation. Many AIM supporters lived in the village of Oglala, and a lot of the violence took place around there. Three miles east of Oglala, Le and Floyd John told me to turn off into a pasture pocked with prairie-dog holes. This was the site of the best-known single incident of the 1970s war, the killing of FBI agents Jack Coler and Ronald Williams when they came to question some AIM people staying at the Jumping Bull residence on June 26, 1975. Of the suspects in the killings, only Leonard Peltier was eventually convicted, and he is now serving consecutive life sentences in federal prison. The agents were hit by rifle fire they didn't expect soon after they turned onto the property, and they died from bullets fired at close range as they lay wounded by their cars. Le and Floyd John showed where AIM member Joe Stuntz was killed in the shoot-out with police that followed. They pointed with pride to the gullies and ravines through which everybody else on the Jumping Bull place made their escape through the police cordon. Le and Floyd John laughed at how stupid the police were, but I could see nothing here but murder and sorrow. This nondescript piece of ground—the grass growing in bunches, the gray dirt, the black crickets crawling—seemed unequal to the violence it had borne. We stood there for a while without conversation, then got back in the car.

Driving again, still in the vicinity of Oglala and Pine Ridge, Le providing the commentary: "The people who lived in that house raised a deer. It grew up big and used to run with their dogs and chase cars. One day it heard the call of the wild and disappeared . . . My aunt Rose White Magpie lives back there. There's a black pickup truck in her yard that was in the movie *Thunderheart* . . . Just the other side of the hill is where somebody shot down the FBI helicopter that was lookin' for fugitives after the FBI guys was killed . . . The guy in that house sent

away to the *National Enquirer* for a white woman, and he got one, too."
(Floyd John: "He didn't *send away*. He just mentioned in a story they
did about Pine Ridge that he was lookin' for one, and a woman over in
Europe somewhere read it and came here and met him and married
him.") "That's where Uncle John Bank lived. He always drank Four
Roses whiskey . . . That was Spencer Crow's place. Spencer was our fat
guy. Every town on the rez has its fat guy, and he was Oglala's. He
weighed 470 pounds. He was *strong*. I seen Spencer once pick up a car
engine and bring it to his middle and bump it into the back of a pickup
with his belly. When he died, they needed fourteen pallbearers to carry
his casket, and as they were lowering it with ropes into the grave it almost pulled them in . . . The woman who runs that church is named Sister Kate. She's a nun. She's Wanda's sister . . . That little red house is
where a Frenchman named Daniel lived. He came through the rez on a
vacation years ago and he liked it so much that he stayed. One time him
and me was sittin' around drinking red wine and eatin' kidneys and he
told me that he was an expert at *sabata,* what they call French kick-
boxing. He said he could kick my ass with it. So I said, 'Let's get it on,'
and we went out in the yard and he kicked at me and I hit him on the
side of the head and he fell flat. Then we went back in and started
drinkin' again . . . Down that road is where Alex Scabby Face used to
live . . . That's where the great Lakota singer Matthew Two Bulls lives
. . . In one of them junk cars lives a guy who I ran into years ago in the
Dawes County Jail in Chadron, Nebraska. I was in for something or
other and all these Indian guys in there was moanin' about how the
judge had give 'em thirty days or ninety days, and that guy comes strut-
tin' in so happy—I forget what his crime was—but he was overjoyed,
doin' the quail dance, gettin' down real low and singin' Indian, and he
shouts out, 'Boys, I got two years!' . . . That's where Lyman Red Cloud
lives, old Chief Red Cloud's great-grandson . . . That's where the Young
Man Afraid of His Horses family lives . . . Edison Red Nest lived there
. . . Marvin Dreaming Bear's place . . . Vera Fast Horse's . . . My sister
Aurelia's . . . The sun-dance grounds . . . That's where we used to gather
sweet grass, at a wet place up the creekbed, but the tribe put some new
houses back there and the sewage runoff killed it off . . . Somebody
dumped three 55-gallon barrels of toxic waste in that schoolyard a few
weeks ago . . . That's Tobacco Road, where the Tobaccos lived . . ."

After a stretch of silence, Le added, "But August 1977 was the really sad time on the reservation. They ran out of black crepe in all the stores around here, and all the women on the reservation were cryin'."

"What happened in August 1977?" I asked.

"What *happened*? Elvis died!"

Like many visitors to the reservation, I wanted to see that most famous of Indian places, Wounded Knee. It's about fifteen miles from Pine Ridge. I knew that there isn't much there. The general store that once stood by the Y where two roads meet in the valley of Wounded Knee Creek is gone, as is the Catholic church with the tall bell tower that used to be on a hill above. What remains of the village has moved a half mile up the road, where the tribe has put in a small development of one-family houses. At the Wounded Knee junction, about the only reference points the eye can find are the silhouettes of cemetery gates and stone monuments on the hilltop, the roof of a small church beyond the cemetery, and a couple of pole structures holding pine boughs to shade people selling dream catchers and beadwork at a graveled pullout next to the road. The museum which once adjoined the store was ransacked by rioters in 1972, and its contents dispersed and lost. Students of Lakota history say that among the artifacts were the only known copies of two ancient tanned hides that held the Lakotas' accumulated knowledge of the stars. Now only the museum's stone chimney still stands.

Wounded Knee, the event, has two dates: 1890 and 1973. The history of the Lakota over the last 150 years hangs on those dates like wire on telephone poles. As markers, the years are so prominent that they have become important in the larger history of America as well. The first was the year of the massacre. On December 29, 1890, shots broke out as a cavalry regiment was attempting to disarm Chief Big Foot's band of Minnecojou Indians camped on Wounded Knee Creek, and once the soldiers started shooting they didn't stop until well after all the Indians had fallen or run away. At least 146 Indians died, including 44 women and 18 children. Perhaps 30 soldiers also died. Many of Big Foot's band had participated in the Ghost Dance on the Standing Rock Reservation, and had fled there for Pine Ridge after official attempts to suppress the dance led to the killing of Sitting Bull. The soldiers at

Wounded Knee were also on Pine Ridge because of the Ghost Dance; they had been dispatched to watch and intimidate Ghost Dancing Indians there.

Probably no dance in history ever scared people more than the Ghost Dance scared white people back in 1890. Essentially, the Ghost Dance was an Indian version of the religious revivals so popular on the frontier; but in this case, the Promised Land it evoked would be here on earth, with all the Indians who had ever lived restored to life, and the buffalo herds as well. In this paradise the earth itself would be renewed and would cover all white people and their works to a depth five times the height of a man. What believers must do to hurry the arrival of paradise was dance, leaders of the Ghost Dance said. As the Indians did—as they danced for days, fell in exhaustion, went into trances, awoke, told of the ancestors they had visited on the Morning Star, showed pieces of the Morning Star they had brought back as proof— and as the dance spread quickly on the hungry reservations of the West in 1890, people living near the reservations inclined to panic. The government called out the troops by the thousands. Some of them (the Seventh Cavalry, for example, General Custer's old regiment, ordered to Wounded Knee) were ready to kill, and horror came to pass. The photograph of the frozen body of Chief Big Foot with its fingers contorted and its legs twisted as if trying to get purchase to rise became America's most famous image of homegrown massacre. Killings associated with the Ghost Dance did not stop at Wounded Knee, and two hundred or more died in white–Indian and Indian–Indian violence on the Pine Ridge Reservation in the months that followed.

Wounded Knee's other prominent date, 1973, was the year in which the American Indian Movement occupied the village as a protest demonstration. The occupation, sometimes called Wounded Knee II, lasted for seventy-one days between February and May. AIM members holding the village made demands for political changes and negotiated with the government while various federal agencies, the tribal police, and local volunteer opponents of AIM surrounded them in a porous state of siege. Wounded Knee II was the last in a series of major occupations staged nationwide by Indian protest groups beginning in 1969, when West Coast activists seized the abandoned federal prison on Alcatraz Island in San Francisco Bay. The Alcatraz occupation didn't accomplish much of substance, but it got a lot of press over the eighteen months it lasted, and other occupations followed. Protesters took over an abandoned Coast Guard station in Milwaukee, a Lutheran Church conference in South Dakota, a museum in Los Angeles, the top of Mount Rushmore, the replica ship *Mayflower II* in Massachusetts on Thanksgiving Day, and the headquarters of the Bureau of Indian Affairs in Washington, D.C. The American Indian Movement, founded in Minneapolis in 1968, led most of the big takeovers and emerged as the important voice of Indian miltancy. AIM leaders often talked about Indian self-determination and tribal sovereignty, ideas that had been overlooked in the recent past, when government policy had emphasized moving Indians from reservations into the American mainstream and terminating the official status of many tribes. AIM's real flair was for the defiant gesture in the face of authority. That, combined with its strong sense of Indian history, made it conservative and radical at the same time.

The bloody history of the place was why AIM chose Wounded Knee. The occupiers often said that they were prepared to die there, and that they expected to be wiped out as Big Foot's band had been. Setting aside the occupiers' demands for Senate investigations of all Indian treaties and of the Bureau of Indian Affairs and of all Sioux reservations in South Dakota, the main issue at Wounded Knee II came down to a conflict between progressives and traditionalists on the Pine Ridge Reservation. Loosely subsumed in that were other reservation conflicts—mixed-bloods versus full-bloods, the village of Pine Ridge versus outlying areas, pro–Vietnam War versus anti–, and local politicians versus activists of no fixed abode. Tribal chairman Dick Wilson spoke for the progressives. He wore his hair in a bristly crew cut and called AIM members and their supporters lawbreakers, unpatriotic scum, and Communist agitators. AIM leaders called Wilson a dictator, a thug, and a puppet of the BIA. Traditionalists on the reservation generally sided with AIM. Repeated regularly among the occupiers' demands was Wilson's immediate removal as tribal chairman. AIM said that many Wilson supporters were goons who intimidated people with violence. The Wilson men accepted the name with pride, saying that it was an acronym for Guardians of the Oglala Nation and that they had thought it up themselves. Groups of goons maintained their own roadblocks on the roads leading into Wounded Knee, and in their eagerness for a fight with AIM sometimes drew guns on federal marshals who were trying to restrain them and ended up in jail.

The federal government, for its part, had a legal responsibility to protect life and property on the reservation. Any desire the government might have had to attack the occupiers with full force was balanced by the Nixon administration's fear of another Wounded Knee massacre; the Watergate hearings had just begun, and the administration needed no more bad press. Yet there wasn't much the feds could do about the occupiers' demands, because the crucial one, getting rid of Dick Wilson, could not be granted without involving the government illegally in the sovereign government of the tribe. Whatever the accusations against him, Wilson had been duly elected; the feds feared that if a tribal government could be overthrown by force, the whole structure of government on the reservations would fall apart. Hence, the seventy-one-day standoff, punctuated with many long-range firefights. Bullets probably from the besiegers' rifles killed two occupiers, one of them a man whose grandmother had survived the first Wounded Knee, and a bullet from the occupiers' compound hit a federal marshal and paralyzed him from the waist down.

A fact of Indian political life is its tendency to descend into mind-numbing complications and small print. A good example of this would be the catalogue of proposals, counterproposals, negotiations broken down, negotiations resumed, new negotiating teams, near-settlements, AIM leaders' appearances before Congress, and eventual surrender terms that marked the long occupation. AIM succeeded in the realm of theatrics; its images of long-haired Indians painted for war and carrying high-powered rifles appeared regularly on the TV news, and made a larger point about Indian militancy. But when the occupiers left Wounded Knee not long after the second death there, none of their main demands had been met, and the government's promises led only to a few meetings with low-level officials which most people considered a joke. As at the first Wounded Knee, the events at the second proved to be part of a longer struggle. For years afterward the reservation remained violently divided between AIM and goon. Houses caught fire in the night, shots came through car windows, people usually uncomfortable with guns felt they had to carry them, and the jumpy paranoia that seemed to be everywhere in America in those days reached a high pitch on the reservation. Trying to solve crimes in the midst of this undeclared civil war, the FBI sent its agents. After two of them died at Oglala in June 1975, and FBI men were suddenly all over the place in search of the killers, some residents wondered why the recent deaths of Indians by the dozens hadn't produced a similar response.

Le and Floyd John and I were approaching Wounded Knee from the south. Le said, "During the occupation there were goons right at this junction, the Wounded Knee turnoff. This was where the first roadblock was. From here on you could get shot at, all the way to Wounded Knee. And we're still seven miles away."

Floyd John: "Them goons'd sit around in their trucks drinkin' coffee, drinkin' whiskey. Any civilians that tried to get through, they'd put a gun in their face and turn 'em around."

Le: "At the start, people came from all over to show solidarity with AIM. But if the goons saw a car they didn't recognize—it's easy to tell a rez car—they'd run 'em off the road, terrorize 'em, stay on 'em till they left the rez."

Floyd John: "Wilson made a law that nobody but tribal members could be on the rez if they didn't have official business here. He wouldn't even let that Frank guy that got shot at the occupation be buried here."

Le: "Up ahead is where the pigs had one of their main bunkers—"
(Me: "The pigs?")
Le: "The marshals, the FBI—the *pigs*, man. At the top of that rise was where their lines began. From here their perimeter ran all the way around the Knee, fourteen miles."

Floyd John: "Every so often they put another bunker like the one was here—on high ground so they could shoot down into the village and at the AIM bunkers by the church."

Le: "Them marshals was really gung-ho. You'd see 'em sometimes when they was off duty, down in Gordon or Rushville or up in Rapid. A lot of 'em dressed kind of mod—big wide belts and pants with big stripes on 'em and little caps. They thought they were some cool dudes."

Floyd John: "Sometimes guys'd oink at 'em on the street, but that was about all. Everybody knew when the pigs was off duty they wasn't supposed to mix it up with nobody."

Le: "The marshals and FBI was just the tip of the iceberg. All kinds of military was here—advisers, like in 'Nam. The 82nd Airborne from Ellsworth Air Force Base was ready to take the whole place out in a minute, if they'd got the call."

Floyd John: "There was armored personnel carriers, choppers, reconnaissance planes. After the occupation was over they burned down the church, so nobody could tell from all the holes in it that the pigs'd been usin' 50-caliber machine guns."

Le: "Charley Red Cloud said the only branch of the service that wasn't here was the Navy, and they would've been, too, if the rez had had any water."

Floyd John: "From all the bunkers they was shootin' up flares, every night. One flare after another—and when the flares came down on places where there wasn't no snow, they set the grass afire. The ground was black everywhere."

Le: "They had the guns and they loved to shoot 'em. The pigs must've fired ten million rounds. After they finally left, there was metal cartridge cases layin' all over the place. Some kids went around collectin' 'em, and guys that do traditional crafts made 'em into breastplates and chokers, like they used to in the old days with pipe beads. I heard they sold those cartridge breastplates for a lot of money."

We coasted down the hill to the Wounded Knee junction. Just ahead of us was a Volkswagen bus with oval license plates. It hesitantly turned left, then inched onto the drive that led up to the massacre monument and the site of the Catholic church. The driveway to the monument at America's most famous massacre site is a deeply rutted single-lane dirt track so unpromising as to give any car owner pause. History here has had little time to reflect; it seems to be waiting for further developments, perhaps Wounded Knee III or IV. I parked next to the VW and we got out. Le and Floyd John showed me the long, shallow depression of the mass grave from the first Wounded Knee and the large marker of gray granite with the name of Lawrence "Buddy" Lamont, the Wounded Knee survivor's grandson killed at the second Wounded Knee. They said he was an easygoing guy, a former tribal employee, who was shot in the head by an FBI sniper one morning while on his way to the sweat lodge. His monument had an engraving of an Indian waving as he leaves camp, and a long inscription in Sioux. I picked up the visitors' sign-in list on a clipboard that was chained to a folding chair. Many of the visitors gave European addresses in elegant and unfamiliar handwriting styles.

We looked at the foundations of the church and rectory, and at the places where the bunkers used to be. Vietnam vets among the protesters had deployed and built them, Le said. They were made double-walled, several feet thick, of plywood frames filled with dirt. Now the hill felt as exposed as a countertop; I could not imagine spending seventy-one days surrounded there, bunkers or no. Along the base of the hill runs the narrow valley of Wounded Knee Creek, a winding line of brush, where so many Indians died trying to get away from the soldiers in 1890. Le pointed to a draw a mile or more away to the north. "When I was sneakin' into the Knee at night, I came through that gully," he said. "I snuck in here past the feds eighteen times, carryin' seventy-five- to ninety-pound packs of food, medicine, ammunition, tobacco. I got rides to a drop-off point four or five miles past that butte and walked in through that gully the rest of the way."

(Me:) "Why couldn't the feds just seal the place off?"

Floyd John: "At night they was afraid to get out of their APCs, man. They could see with their nightscopes, but they was afraid to do anything."

Le: "The spirits of the dead at Wounded Knee were up and walking around. Sometimes the feds could see them in the moonlight, hear horses whinnying and babies cryin'. But they'd shoot and it would be just a ghost."

Floyd John: "The marshals set up trip wires and stuff, but that didn't stop nothin'."

Le: "One night I was comin' through the gully with a white guy and a Mexican guy, all of us carryin' packs, and somebody tripped a wire and a flare went off and we hit the ground and crawled on our bellies for a hundred yards faster than you could run. We was laughin' so hard—the flare was bright as daylight, but nobody came after us or shot at us. Some nights I'd get here, drop off the pack, and turn around and sneak back out before morning. Other nights I'd stay—just grab a sleeping bag and crash anywhere. Lots of times there was gunfire. Gun-fire at night is like when you bring a new baby home and it cries in the night—you don't have much choice but to get up and pay attention to it. But after a while you get used to it, and you pay attention to it with-out really waking up."

Le then began to tell a long story about the Indian protest move-ment and his part in it, by way of explaining how he had come to Wounded Knee. He said that he got out of prison in 1968 and went to San Francisco and participated in the occupation of Alcatraz, where he slept in a room in the guards' quarters from November 1969 until June 1971. After Alcatraz, he joined a number of other protests in the Far West—at Pit River Reservation in Northern California, where there was a dispute over fishing rights, and at a store run by the Puyallup tribe in Washington State, fighting for their right to sell cigarettes with-out collecting state sales tax. He said that in 1972 he went to a conven-tion of Indian traditionalists and protesters and their supporters north of San Francisco and became disillusioned and depressed. Everybody was talking about traditional Indian spirituality and getting it all mixed up with mystical beliefs that had nothing to do with it. ("They were talk-ing about stuff like kundalini sweat lodges. *There are no kundalini sweat lodges!*") He said that after the conference he gave up on the protest movement and the whole bunch of them. He wanted to be by himself for a while, and he knew some people in Los Angeles. So, he said, he decided to walk from San Francisco to Los Angeles along the beach.

He said he set out in February 1972 with a backpack, a sleeping bag, four hundred dollars, and 4,600 hits of mescaline. Sometimes he couldn't walk on the beach, because there were only cliffs, and some-times he had to walk around large beachfront installations like Fort Ord, ninety miles south of San Francisco. Along the way he met mi-grant workers, fishermen who shared their fish with him, avocado ranchers, farmers growing roses by the hundreds of acres for use on floats in the Rose Bowl Parade, mission Indians, golf course employees. People usually recognized him for an American Indian—he always wore two eagle feathers in his hair. He said that on the beach near Carmel he met the movie actress Kim Novak painting a watercolor. She was with her Great Dane, and she brought him back to her house and showed him her other animals, including a pygmy goat, llamas, cows, horses, a cockatoo, and little birds in cages. He said that before he left, she gave him an autographed photo.

He said that from Oxnard south to L.A., the beach is all privately owned and closed. He had worn out his shoes by that point and was walking barefoot. It was now July, he had been walking for five months. A man and his daughter gave him a ride all the way to Santa Monica, and when he got there he went under the pier and soaked his feet in the ocean for a long time. Then he walked into a shoe store and told the salesperson his story, and she let him have the most expensive pair of running shoes in the place for five dollars. From Santa Monica he went to his friends' place in Laurel Canyon for a while. Then he hitchhiked to Boulder, Colorado, where he stayed with friends for several months. Then he got a ride to the Rosebud Reservation and stayed at Crow Dog's Paradise, home of the Lakota spiritual leader Leonard Crow Dog. He was living at his aunt's place in Oglala in February 1973 when the occupation began at Wounded Knee.

His mention of the actress Kim Novak made me curious. I wrote her a letter asking if she remembered Le, and sent it to her in Carmel. It came back stamped REFUSED. A friend in New York found me the phone number of Kim Novak's manager, and I called her. The manager said that Kim Novak does not accept mail, but if I were to fax my letter to her (the manager), she would read my fax to Kim Novak. I did, and the manager soon called me back. She said Kim Novak had a vague memory of the incident Le described, but she couldn't be sure, it was so long ago. She said that Kim Novak said that all the details he mentioned—the painting, the house, the animals—were right.

This partial success encouraged me to get in touch with other celebrities Le has mentioned. Apparently he lived in Los Angeles during much of the 1970s after Wounded Knee, and in his stories of that time he sometimes mentions the actor Elliott Gould. A friend of a friend gave me Elliott Gould's phone number, and I left a message on his answering machine. Elliott Gould called me back from New Orleans, where he was touring in a production of *Deathtrap*. He said he certainly did remember Le. He had met him, as I had, on the street. He said that he picked him up hitchhiking in Malibu Canyon and later invited him to his house. He remembered Le afterward coming to his house late one night so high on drugs and alcohol that his body was giving off a ripple effect. He said that he also remembered watching a football game on TV with him, and that Le might have done a curing ceremony for his daughter, Molly, when she had open-heart surgery. He said that the actor David Carradine knew Le much better than he did, and that Le even appears in Carradine's autobiography, *Endless Highway*.

In fact, Carradine devotes an entire chapter of *Endless Highway* to Le. The chapter title is "Lee Warlance"; Carradine explains that he always called him Lee to discourage him from getting too conceited about his Oglala heritage. (Le pronounces his name more like "Leh" or "Lay," in the Lakota style.) Carradine describes Le as an "extremely beautiful man" who came by his house one day and introduced himself because people had told him that he and Carradine looked alike. They got to know each other; "I trusted him. I trusted his instincts and his mystic concepts," Carradine says. According to Carradine, Le said that he was a Vietnam veteran who had a bullet lodged in his head which hospitals were afraid to touch, but which he suddenly felt in his mouth and spit out in the middle of a sweat lodge curing ceremony. (Despite what Le might have said, he is not a Vietnam veteran.) Le apparently also told Carradine stories about Wounded Knee unlike any that he told me; for example, that he helped some reporters and women to escape from the occupation, and that when pursuers shot at them his dog confronted the pursuers and was killed, saving their lives. Of these and other stories, Carradine says, "I was more a listener than an investigator." Carradine also says that through Le he met a number of Indian militants "considerably wilder" than Le. He does not mention that one evening Le brought some of these people and their friends to Carradine's house, that they found no one home, that they hung around for a while, that three of them left in a taxicab, that Le stayed behind, and that the taxicab driver later turned up dead, stabbed many times and stuffed into a drainpipe. Police questioned Carradine about the murder, and Le says that he (Le) was held on suspicion of it for over a month. Le adds that neither he nor Carradine had anything to do with the murder of the taxi driver.

Dennis Banks, with Russell Means the best-known of the leaders of

AIM and a main spokesman for the occupiers at Wounded Knee, more recently headed an American Indian program in Newport, Kentucky. I wanted to ask him questions on several subjects, so I telephoned him there. In the course of our conversation I asked him if he knew Le. He said that he did, and that Le had indeed been at the occupation of Wounded Knee.

CHAPTER

5

Indians are embedded deeply in America. You find them everywhere—in remote places where almost no one else could live, in small towns, and in the biggest cities. 30.9 percent of Indians have incomes below the national poverty line, more than any other race or ethnic group, so the neighborhoods where they live tend to be run-down. But Indian tribes also own high-priced real estate in Las Vegas, Nevada, and Palm Springs, California; five tribes operate gambling casinos that gross $100 million or more a year. The federal government has granted official tribal status to 570 tribes. Over 150 others remain unrecognized but continue to exist all the same. From time to time you read of another officially overlooked tribe turning up in a makeshift community under a highway bridge or in the desert between two Western cities. Of the almost two million people who identify themselves as American Indians on the U.S. census form, about half are enrolled members of a federally recognized tribe.

Most Indians live west of the Mississippi River. More than half the Indians in the United States live within a 300-mile radius of Albuquerque, New Mexico; Los Angeles has the largest concentration of off-reservation Indians in the country. Every Western state has at least one Indian reservation, with the exception of Missouri, Arkansas, and Hawaii. (Of course, native peoples live in those states as well.) Fewer of the Eastern states have reservations. In the nineteenth century, most Eastern states favored removal of all Indian tribes to points west far from their boundaries, they didn't care where. But some Indians refused to go and continued inhabiting unwanted lands where their neighbors often assumed they had died out. Scattered reservations of various sizes, from a quarter-acre on up, remain in many parts of the East.

You could fix a map of the lower forty-eight states to a wall with pins stuck in reservations at each of the four corners. In the Northeast, the Maliseet Reservation is at the very end of Interstate Highway 95, on the border between Maine and Canada. Many of the Maliseet live on the Canadian side. During the hostage crisis in Iran, the chairman of the Maliseet tribe's land-claims committee sent a letter to the Islamic government of Iran asking for financial aid, citing the indifference of the United States to the tribe's complaints. Congress eventually gave the Maliseet a $900,000 claims settlement, which they used for buying riverfront land. Near the other end of I-95, at the tip of Florida in the southeastern United States, the Miccosukee Indians live on a reservation which includes thousands of acres of Everglades swamp. The Florida Miccosukee are descendants of Indians the government couldn't catch and move to Oklahoma after the expensive and bloody Seminole War of the 1830s and '40s. Some Miccosukee villages can be reached only by pirogue or airboat. In the far northwest of the forty-eight states, on the end of the Olympic Peninsula in Washington, is the Makah Reservation. The Makah are seagoing Indians who still build and race large cedar war canoes. Their language is unlike that of any other tribe, but only a few native Makah speakers remain. Recently the International Whaling Commission granted the Makah's request to be allowed to harpoon whales, as the tribe had done in the past for as long as it can remember; in May of '99 the tribe killed its first whale since the 1920s. In the southwest corner of the map, you could put dozens of pins in the many small reservations the United States made of the old Indian missions of the Spanish in Southern California. Some of those reservations are just a ten-mile hike from the Mexican border. Their landscape is mostly hilly desert scribbled with low, spiky greenery. On the horizon stretches the carbon-streaked sky of San Diego and the approaching blue curve of the Pacific Ocean.

Even in the middle of the country, Indians somehow manage to live on the edges. Wherever you are traveling, if your eye pauses on some distant and inhospitable-looking spot, chances are an Indian has already been there, or lives there now. Indians live on islands in the Great Lakes, and at the tip of Louisiana near where the Mississippi empties into the Gulf, and on the Rio Grande border with Mexico. Our wheeled and plumbed and wired society prefers landscapes of a temperate and level kind, but Indian occupation predates the requirements of technology. The Havasupai tribe lives thousands of feet down in a canyon in Arizona that connects to the Grand Canyon. Many of the 650 tribal members still speak Havasupai. The Havasupai's main industry is a tourism business that brings tens of thousands of hikers to the canyon bottom every year. The Timbisha Shoshone have no official reservation, but continue to live in the desert in southeastern California, where summer temperatures reach 134°. In arid parts of Arizona and New Mexico, Hopi and other Indians live in pueblos that are the oldest continually inhabited sites in North America. The Acoma Pueblo, on a butte in west-central New Mexico, is at least a thousand years old, and at the San Juan Pueblo, some of the dwellings have been lived in for seven hundred years. The Hopi Pueblo of Old Oraibi, in Arizona, is even older. Parts of Old Oraibi were built in about A.D. 500. The Spanish explorer Francisco Vásquez de Coronado went there in his search for cities of gold in 1540; the pueblo has had electricity since 1963.

And if the distant place your eye pauses upon happens to be man-made—the top of the Golden Gate Bridge in San Francisco, say, or New York's Empire State Building—Indians have been there, too. For many years, Mohawk Indian high-steel construction crews worked on bridges and skyscrapers from one end of the country to the other. They liked the difficulty and danger of the job, as well as the travel. Sometimes the Mohawks would get bored working on a skyscraper in Manhattan and all pile into their cars and take off for a new job they heard about, three thousand miles away.

Indians are twice as likely as non-Indians to live in a mobile home. The reason for this has partly to do with laws against repossession of tribal land: banks will loan money on reservations only for property which, in the event of default, can be towed away. Ninety thousand or more Indian families are homeless, living on the street or sharing housing with relatives. Forty percent of Indian households are over-crowded or have inadequate dwellings, compared to about 6 percent for the population at large. Indians are about twice as likely as non-Indians to be murdered. Their death rate from alcoholism is four times the national average, and the rate of fetal alcohol syndrome among their children is thirty-three times higher than for whites. Indian babies are three times as likely as white babies to die of sudden infant death syndrome (SIDS). Indians smoke more than non-Indians, and smoking is their leading cause of cancer death. They commit suicide at rates that in certain circumstances approach the epidemic. The American Medical Association says that one in five Indian girls and one in eight boys attempts suicide by the end of high school. In an Indian town in northern Canada, an Indian teenager dead of alcohol poisoning was found to have a blood alcohol content higher than any ever recorded in North America. On and on, the saddening statistics multiply. Any modern study of Indians lists them, unavoidably. They tend to overwhelm the few positive numbers one can point to—the increase in Indian life expectancy over the last twenty years, or the growth in the numbers of Indian college graduates, or the success of the many new tribal colleges, or the large decline in the percentage of Indians living in poverty over the last ten years.

A good example of what Indians have done to survive since white people came is the much-traveled Kickapoo tribe, who to most people are no more than a colorful name. The first reports of the Kickapoo were from French frontiersmen who found them in present Wisconsin in the early 1700s. In the 1760s the Kickapoo moved south to present Illinois and Indiana, home of their relatives the Fox and the Sauk. The Kickapoo fought for the British in the Revolutionary War and in the War of 1812, and with the Fox and Sauk continued fighting the United States in Black Hawk's War. A treaty signed as part of the removal of Indians in the 1830s to lands west of the Mississippi known as Indian Territory—the present states of Kansas, Nebraska, and Oklahoma—gave the Kickapoo land in northeastern Kansas, along with other Eastern tribes. When the United States was deciding what to do about the extension of slavery into the Kansas and Nebraska Territories, no one on either side of the question gave a serious thought to the fate of the Indians recently relocated there. In a unanimity of racism similar to that which would help reknit the country after the Civil War, pro-slavery and anti-slavery politicians agreed on their right to do as they pleased with the Indians of Kansas and Nebraska. The creation of the Kansas Territory greatly reduced the Kickapoo's lands. A large band of Kickapoo who didn't like the outcome simply left their Kansas reservation and relocated a thousand or more miles away, across the border into Mexico.

In 1862, the Kickapoo still in Kansas lost most of their remaining lands in a treaty whose result was the transfer of those lands to the Atchison and Pikes Peak Railroad Company. About a hundred Kickapoo who liked this even less than the high-handedness of ten years before decided to join their relatives in Mexico. There the Kickapoo refugees lived on their own for many years, occasionally raiding across the border. In the 1870s some of the Kickapoo in Mexico were induced to come back to Kansas, to the reduced reservation which remained. The Mexican government eventually gave the Mexican Kickapoo some land, but during a drought in the 1940s a band of them moved north again, to the Texas side of the Rio Grande. In 1981 there were 620 of these Mexican Kickapoo living in reed huts beneath the International Bridge on the U.S. border by Eagle Pass, Texas. An American charitable organization bought them 125 acres along the Rio Grande in Texas in the same year, and in 1983 the U.S. government granted them official tribal status as the Kickapoo Traditional Tribe of Texas. Books about Indians which I read as a child usually divided tribes into geographic categories, such as Woodland Indians, Indians of the Prairies, or Indians of the Southwest; such books never mentioned that a harried tribe might end up falling into two categories, or three.

The most famous removal of Indians, of course, was the removal of the Cherokee from Georgia westward to Indian Territory in 1838 and 1839. There are many accounts of the forced march that came to be known as the Trail of Tears—of the Cherokee's previous peaceableness and prosperity on their lands in Georgia; of the Georgia settlers' hatred of Indians and desire for those lands; of the mercilessness of President Andrew Jackson; of Supreme Court Justice John Marshall's ruling that the removal was illegal; of Jackson's response: "He has made his law. Now let him enforce it"; of the opposition of people as diverse as Ralph Waldo Emerson and Davy Crockett to the removal; of the U.S. soldiers' roundup of the Georgia Cherokee; of the Cherokee's suffering in the stockades and along the trail; of the death of more than four thousand Cherokee, about a third of the population of the tribe, before the removal was through. The Cherokee had their own written language, with an alphabet devised by the Cherokee leader Sequoyah during the 1820s. But their success at following the ways of the whites proved no defense. As would happen again elsewhere, building houses and farms only gave the Indians more to lose when government policy changed.

Some Cherokee escaped the soldiers and stayed in the mountains of their original territory, surviving on little more than bark and grass. Eventually they moved down into North Carolina. Today they have a reservation there and are known as the Eastern Cherokee. The Cherokee who were forced west in the 1830s have no reservation but live spread out through a fourteen-county area in eastern Oklahoma. Their tribal capital is in the Oklahoma town of Tahlequah. Both the Eastern Cherokee and the Cherokee of Oklahoma commemorate the Trail of Tears march with a large outdoor pageant every year. Also, Indians and other people on spiritual quests sometimes walk the historic route of the trail. A Cherokee woman recently walked it from Rattlesnake Springs, Tennessee, all the way to Tahlequah, a distance of 1,100 miles. In 1996, a Pomo Indian minister of an interdenominational church spent four months walking the route carrying a seventy-pound wooden cross.

The Cherokee are among the three or four best-known American Indian tribes. "Cherokee" is especially popular as a brand name, appearing on products from cars and airplanes to hospital scrubs and soda pop. If a person claims to have a little Indian blood, chances are the tribe mentioned will be the Cherokee; Bill Clinton says he is one-eighth Cherokee. In both Oklahoma and North Carolina, the Cherokee are involved in many business ventures, including gambling, tourism, manufacturing, and ranching. In Oklahoma the tribe issues its own VISA card. The Cherokee are sometimes called the largest American tribe. Of those who identify themselves as American Indian on the census form, more say they are Cherokee than say they belong to any other tribe.

The Cherokee are an Iroquoian tribe. That means that their language resembles others—including Tuscarora, Huron, and Erie—which ethnologists have grouped into the Iroquoian language family.

Other Native American language families are the Algonquian, the Muscogean, the Siouan, the Uto-Aztecan, and the Athapascan, each of whose speakers occupied a more or less distinct part of the continent. Of the Iroquoian tribes, only the Cherokee and a few others were not part of the Iroquois Confederacy, perhaps the most powerful Indian force in America at the time white men arrived. The Iroquois Confederacy consisted of five tribes: the Cayuga, Oneida, Mohawk, Seneca, and Onondaga. (A sixth tribe, the Tuscarora, joined later.) The Iroquois lived in present New York State and ruled themselves by a set of laws orally passed down in a tradition of ceremonial recitation which the Mohawk tribe continues today. In domestic matters, government was left to the individual tribe. But in larger questions of war or of relations with other governments or tribes, leaders from each tribe in the confederacy met in council at a longhouse among the Onondaga. These leaders, or sachems, reached decisions through formal debate, and although they had no power of enforcement, their authority compelled obedience. The Iroquois Confederacy could operate effectively on a larger scale than other tribes, and helped the Iroquois to overpower the mostly Algonquian-speaking tribes around them. If Europeans had never come to this continent, perhaps eventually a lot of it would have become an Iroquois dominion, in the way that the Mediterranean and parts of Europe were Romanized in classical times.

As fighters, the Iroquois were fierce. Their large and far-ranging war parties reduced to misery Indian nations as distant as the Illinois on the shores of the Mississippi, the Huron north of Lake Superior, and the Erie south of the lake that has their name. The Iroquois enjoyed torturing captives. Returning from their conquests, they usually made an event of it, with the women and children joining in. To incapacitate enemy warriors immediately after capture, the Iroquois would break the captives' fingers with their teeth. Many accounts of Iroquois torture have come down through records of the early colonial period, especially among the Canadian French. When the torture phase was done, the Iroquois often adopted the survivors. An elaborate system of adoption, with captives parceled out to tribes according to their losses, helped the confederacy to grow.

White people in colonial times and after seem to have feared and admired the Iroquois more than any other tribe. The Iroquois were said to be the bravest, the smartest, the noblest, and the best-looking of all Indians. The American portrait and history painter Benjamin West, upon first seeing the statue of the Apollo Belvedere in the Vatican, cried, "By God, a Mohawk!" I have mentioned above that the example of the Iroquois Confederacy influenced the Founding Fathers of the United States; it also influenced the founders of Communism, Friedrich Engels and Karl Marx. They read about the Iroquois in an 1877 book called *Ancient Society*, by the American anthropologist Lewis Henry Morgan, and made special note of the symmetry between the democracy of Iroquois society and its communal ownership of property. To Marx and Engels, the Iroquois were Communists in a natural state.

With the help of the Iroquois Confederacy, the English had driven the French colonial empire from Canada and the Northeast by 1763. The victory turned out to be bad news for the tribe, however. Once the English no longer had the French to fear, they neglected their Iroquois allies and gave them fewer weapons and presents. Most of the Iroquois remained on the side of the English in the American Revolution, and when the Americans won, Iroquois power dwindled still further. Much of the tribe went to Canada, where its descendants now live on the Six Nations Reserve in Ontario. Other Iroquois stayed; the Cayuga today share a reservation with Seneca in Oklahoma, but the other five tribes of the confederacy still have reservations in upstate New York. When the United States gave all Indians within its borders citizenship in 1924, the Iroquois refused it. They said they were citizens of their own nation and didn't need to belong to another. The tradition of tribal sovereignty, built over centuries, is still strong among the tribes of the Iroquois. They are quick to defend their tribal status, and other Indians look to them for leadership. A few years ago, when the governor of New York State tried to collect sales tax on gasoline and cigarettes sold in Iroquois convenience stores, the tribe stood on their centuries-old treaty rights exempting them from state taxes on reservation lands. The state persisted; the Iroquois protested and set fires along the highways and blocked traffic and threatened to charge tolls on highways crossing their lands. Finally the state of New York backed down.

Two tribes of the Iroquois Confederacy, the Tuscarora and the Oneida, broke with the English during the Revolution. Most Tuscarora

and Oneida warriors either remained neutral or fought on the side of
the Americans. The English told the tribes that for this disloyalty their
lands would be forfeit; after the war, the U.S. Congress rewarded them
by letting them stay where they wanted to be. The Tuscarora ended up
with a reservation about ten miles square along the Niagara River, in
the vicinity of the Falls. In 1790, George Washington told the Tuscarora
and the other Iroquois tribes that their lands were theirs to sell or not,
as they chose. Federal land-allotment policy after 1887 put much of the
land into individual ownership, as happened on reservations nationwide, but for years the boundaries of the Tuscarora Reservation remained the same as they had been in 1784.

Then, in 1959, Robert Moses, head of the New York State Power
Authority, decided he needed a big piece of the Tuscarora Reservation
for a power station reservoir. He duly had the land condemned, and
construction began. The Tuscarora organized protest rallies, blocked
the bulldozers, and filed suit to stop him. The suit went all the way to
the Supreme Court, which ruled for Moses. The Court's majority held
that since much of the reservation land was privately owned, it could be
condemned for public use like other private land. Justice Hugo Black,
for the minority, said that this was ridiculous, that everyone knew the
land was part of an Indian reservation and that "great nations, like great
men, should keep their word." Soon afterward Robert Moses printed at
Power Authority expense a pamphlet he wrote defending his action. He
referred to the Tuscarora with irony as "the noble red men," said they
hadn't been doing anything with the land anyway, and advised them to
"join the United States."

Other tribes of the East: the Pamunkey and Mattapony, descendants of
the Powhatan Confederacy, relatives of Pocahontas, whose state reservations in eastern Virginia are 340 years old and who renew their treaty
with gifts of turkey, fish, and deer brought to the governor of Virginia
every fall; the Passamaquoddy of Maine, who won $40 million in a land
claims settlement with the United States in 1980, and increased it to
$100 million by good investments, and bought a cement company and
sold it a few years later for a profit of $60 million, and became a parable
of smart business dealings in a course taught at Harvard Business

School; the Independent Traditional Seminole Nation of Florida, a tribe without a reservation or federal recognition, which recently won a lawsuit against the county where they live when its inspectors tried to force them to bring their cypress-thatched chickees into compliance with local housing codes; the Shinnecock of Long Island, whose name is also that of an exclusive golf course; the Schaghticoke and the Golden Hill Paugusset and the Paucatuck Pequot and the super-wealthy Mashantucket Pequot of Connecticut; the Ramapough tribe of Mahwah, New Jersey, recently denied federal recognition on the grounds that they were not Indians but descendants of African and Dutch settlers who moved to New Jersey from Manhattan Island in the late 1600s; and the Lumbee of North Carolina, a tribe which has lived for a hundred years in the mountains around Lumberton unrecognized by anyone but themselves; and the Catawba tribe of South Carolina, whose language became extinct in 1996 with the death of its last speaker, a seventy-six-year-old man named Red Thunder Cloud.

A myth about America which we learn early is the story of the first Thanksgiving, when Indians and Pilgrims met to celebrate the harvest in Plymouth Colony in Massachusetts in 1621. The Indians in the story were of the Wampanoag tribe, led by Chief Massasoit, a friend to the whites. He and ninety other Wampanoag attended the Thanksgiving feast and contributed five deer. Squanto, the English-speaking Indian said to have taught the Pilgrims to bury a fish in each hill of corn, was a Wampanoag. About fifty years after the first Thanksgiving, the Wampanoag and other New England tribes rose against the whites in a widespread series of battles called King Philip's War, which killed perhaps a thousand settlers and nearly wiped out many tribes. After that, the Wampanoag seemed to disappear from history for several centuries. In the 1800s, they were among the tribes said to have become extinct. However, they continued to live in the vicinity where the Pilgrims found them in eastern Massachusetts. The Mashpee-Wampanoag have a reservation near Mashpee on Cape Cod, and the Wampanoag tribe of Gay Head has one on the island of Martha's Vineyard. In the late 1970s the Mashpee-Wampanoag filed suit against the town of Mashpee to reclaim land they said was theirs, but a federal jury in Boston decided that the tribe had stopped being a tribe at several key points in their history and so ruled against them. In 1989 a group of Wampanoag on Martha's

Vineyard petitioned Jacqueline Kennedy Onassis for control of an acre and a half of beachfront which she said she needed to keep celebrity seekers at a distance from her property and which the Wampanoag said was the burial site of an ancestor and thus sacred land. (Lawyers for Mrs. Onassis settled the dispute with a land exchange.) Chappaquiddick is the name of a tribe of the Wampanoag.

The tribe with the most enrolled members and the most land is the Navajo. The Navajo Reservation covers 17.5 million acres in Arizona, New Mexico, and Utah, an expanse bigger than New England. It is divided into Western, Central, and Eastern regions, and includes desert, canyonlands, mountains, and badlands. The eroded red-rock spires that have become a visual shorthand for the American West in movies and advertisements are one of its features. Some of the best-preserved pre-Columbian ruins on the continent are in Navajo country, as is the Canyon de Chelly National Monument, with its cliff dwellings dating to A.D. 348 and its ancient cliff-face handprints and pictographs. In 1880, there were about 9,000 Navajo; about 200,000 live on the reservation today, and another 60,000 live elsewhere. Of all North American Indian languages, Navajo has by far the most speakers. Many Navajo children speak it; at a time when tribes are trying to keep their languages alive, Navajo children sometimes must be taught English before they can enter school. In parts of the reservation there are Navajo who speak no English. KTNN, the tribal radio station, broadcasts part of the time in Navajo, and does live coverage in Navajo of Phoenix Suns pro basketball games.

At least 20,000 Navajo on the reservation are homeless. Some Navajo spend their time drinking in "border towns"—places like Gallup, New Mexico, or Winslow, Arizona—just across the reservation's border. The border towns make much of their income selling liquor to the Navajo; travelers who stop in peaceful-looking Gallup on the night of a big rodeo may be surprised at how wild a night in Gallup can be. The big tank, the cell in the Gallup jail where drunks are thrown, holds five hundred. It is said to be the largest jail cell in the country. Navajo by the score have been killed walking back to the reservation along the "hell highway"—a seven-and-a-half-mile stretch of U.S. 666 north of

Gallup. After years of trying, Nancy Bill, an official at the Indian Health Services in the tribal capital of Window Rock, got streetlights installed along that stretch, and the fatality rate went way down. Some Navajo live in hogans, traditional round dwellings of rock, timber, and adobe, and continue to worship the hundred or so deities who help in different aspects of Navajo life. Not long ago a family in a remote part of the reservation said they received a visit from two of these deities, who warned them that the Navajo were risking great danger by giving up their traditions. When the news of the visit got out, thousands of Navajo made pilgrimages to the family's hogan to pray and scatter sacred corn pollen.

People may assume that gambling casinos are now the only business enterprise on the reservations. The Navajo tribe has twice held referendum votes on whether to allow casinos on the reservation, and twice Navajo voters have rejected the idea. Unemployment among the Navajo is around 30 percent. Still, thousands of Navajo work in the coal and uranium mines on the reservation, or in harvesting the reservation's timber, or raising sheep, or in the Navajo's large tourist industry. The Navajo are especially known for their turquoise jewelry and their silver-smithing, and are the only tribe in the Southwest who still weave rugs. The tribe encourages its young people to go to college. Dr. Fred Begay, the only American Indian physicist I know of, is a Navajo. He works at the National Laboratory at Los Alamos, New Mexico, not far from the reservation. Dr. Lori Arviso Alvord is the only Navajo woman ever to become a surgeon. Her practice on the reservation emphasizes *mizhoni*, which means walking in beauty, a measuredness and harmony among all things. She was head resident in surgery at Stanford Medical School in 1990–91, and now is a dean at Dartmouth Medical School.

It's remarkable that the Navajo don't want casinos; hundreds of other tribes do. Since the boom in Indian casinos began about ten years ago, 184 tribes have built casinos, a few tribes have made billions of dollars, and lots of tribes are trying to open casinos of their own. Nowadays, in many people's minds casinos and Indians are one and the same. No other story about Indians in recent decades has received anywhere near as much attention as the casino story, and the image of the casino-rich

Indian has become the latest in a long series of too-simple images pasted over the reality of Indian life. But like most such images, this one is not completely wrong. No tribal enterprise in history has succeeded even remotely as well as tribal casinos. Some tribes with imagination and persistence and reservations convenient to large population centers have become vastly rich with casino dollars, and the rise of tribal gambling has given some tribes economic power greater than Indians have known since the years when they had the continent to themselves.

The success of Indian casinos has largely to do with tribal sovereignty. Basically, a reservation is like a state; federal laws apply to it, but it makes its own local laws, among which are laws regulating gambling. In the 1980s, perhaps revived by the new awareness of tribal sovereignty that was part of the Indian protest movement of the decade before, some tribes realized that they could offer gambling opportunities (larger jackpots, for example) in their little bingo parlors, which the states surrounding them did not allow. The speed with which the new Indian gambling enterprises grew and prospered alarmed the states, mainly because tribal gambling can't be taxed—any more than a state can tax another state's lottery winnings, or the federal government can tax a state's. Frightened at the idea of tribes amassing untaxable gambling riches and building gambling empires within their borders, the states pressed Congress to pass a law regulating Indian gambling. This law, the Indian Gambling Regulatory Act of 1988 (IGRA), gave the states some control over Indian gambling. The IGRA said that a federally recognized tribe could offer gambling on its reservation only after entering into a compact agreement with the state in which its reservation lies. The practical result of this was usually some kind of compromise between the tribe and the state involving a sharing of casino revenues in lieu of tax. After the IGRA passed, the structure it provided helped the Indian gambling boom to take off.

Unlike, say, Christianity or individual ownership of land, gambling was actually part of Native American tradition. Before European contact many tribes played games of chance, often with dice-like stones and marked bones. White travelers who met Indians far from the settlements wrote of their passion for gambling, and recounted with disapproval how some Indians spent long winter nights in riotous gambling, how they sometimes kept playing until they had lost horses, lodges, wives, and everything down to their breechclouts. In the nineteenth century, gambling joined the list of supposed vices which the civilizers of the Indian wanted to eradicate. When Geronimo, the famed war chief of the Chiricahua Apache, lived on a reservation in Oklahoma, he was kicked out of the Dutch Reformed Church for gambling.

The idea to build Indian casinos turned out to be lucky itself. At about the time that the IGRA passed, and in the years since, Americans went gambling crazy. I don't know why. Maybe the reason has to do with the aging of much of the population, and the fact that retirees have more money than younger people, and more free time; certainly, on any given day, people with white hair make up a good segment of the players at most casinos' slot machines. Maybe the reason involves the heralded global victory of capitalism, and the vaulting rise of financial markets using money to make more money without clear connection to anything real. Maybe gambling is just our era's acceptable form of group hysteria. Whatever the cause, the gambling phenomenon is on the order of a continental drift. In the 1990s Americans began to spend more money on gambling than on all other forms of entertainment combined. Gambling meccas like Atlantic City and Las Vegas greatly expanded their hotels and casinos, referred to what they offered as "gaming" to remove any gangsterish tinge, and retooled to accommodate middle-class families. In 1988, the year of the IGRA, Indian casinos took in about $121 million. By 1994, they were making about $4.5 billion. In 1997, Americans bet $638.6 billion—*billion*—on the various forms of legal gambling, and lost about $51 billion of it. The total revenue for Indian casinos in that year was about $7 billion.

Casino money has completely changed the lives of some tribes. Exhibit A is always the Mashantucket Pequot, that small tribe of multimillionaires in Ledyard, Connecticut, just off Interstate 95. Their Foxwoods Casino is sometimes described as the largest casino in the Western Hemisphere, sometimes as the largest in the world. The tribe has become one of the leading employers in the state; it builds museums, funds ballets, builds its own high-speed ferryboats to haul customers from along the seaboard. Recently, the 25 percent of its slot-machine take, which it pays by compact agreement to the state of Connecticut, came to over $14 million in a single month. In other urbanized parts of the country tribal casinos bring in tens or hundreds of millions of dollars every year. Gambling revenues have enabled some tribes to reduce or eliminate unemployment, pay for schooling, hire tribal historians, build clinics and roads and houses, get tribal members off welfare, and in some cases give members per capita payments ranging from thousands to hundreds of thousands of dollars a year.

The fact remains, however, that most Indian reservations are not good sites for gambling casinos. Reservations tend to be far from anywhere, on less-traveled roads, and difficult to promote to gamblers, who, if they travel, usually go to Vegas. Just a few of the tribal casinos—under a dozen—take in half of the gambling dollars. Along with the Pequot, the biggest moneymakers are the Mdewakanton Sioux near Minneapolis, the Oneida of Wisconsin, the Fort McDowell Reservation near Phoenix, and the Sandia Pueblo between Albuquerque and Santa Fe. Hundreds of other Indian tribes don't have casinos, and of those who do, most are making modest profits or just breaking even. A majority of Indians still live close to or below the poverty line. In short, profits from the gambling boom have had little effect on most Indians' lives.

I have been to big-money tribal casinos on both coasts and in Minnesota, and they tend to run together in the mind. They are of a sameness—the vast parking lots, the low, mall-like, usually windowless buildings, the arbitrary Indianish decor, the gleeful older gamblers rattling troves of quarters in their bulging pants pockets, the unromantic expressions in the employees' eyes. Also, going to a major Indian casino is so much like going to a non-Indian one, in Atlantic City or someplace, that you may have to remind yourself exactly why Indian casinos enjoy tax advantages non-Indian casinos don't. The idea of Indian tribal sovereignty, a bit elusive to begin with, can fade out entirely behind the deluge of generic gambling dollars. In the last few years, some state and federal legislators have begun to view tribal casinos in just this skeptical way. Their renewed attacks on tribal sovereignty usually include a lot of rhetoric about the supposed great gambling wealth of Indian tribes nowadays. Regrettably, the resentment against Indian casinos, whose largest benefits go to only a few tribes, may end up threatening the sovereignty of all tribes. Many Indians have worried more about loss of sovereignty since the casino boom began. Some say that entering into compacts with the states is itself a wrong idea, because it accepts state jurisdiction where none existed before. Concern for sovereignty has been a main reason why the Navajo have rejected casino gambling. A Navajo leader said that tribes who accept outside oversight of their gambling operations have allowed a violation of tribal sovereignty; he added, "The sovereignty of the Navajo Nation and the Navajo people is not and should never be for sale."

Tribes do make money at other kinds of enterprises. The Santa Ana tribe, about a hundred households on a small reservation north of Albuquerque, has been able to remain an agricultural tribe by growing many tons of blue corn every year to sell to The Body Shop, a British-based cosmetics company, which makes a blue-tinted natural face cleanser from it. (More recently, the tribe has built a casino, and used its profits to build a multimillion-dollar resort.) The Choctaw tribe of Mississippi, formerly sharecroppers and paupers, have become one of the largest employers in the state; Choctaw factories make circuit boards, wiring-harnesses for automobile dashboards, automotive speakers, and hand-finished greeting cards for the American Greeting Card Company. Almost all Mississippi Choctaws still speak Choctaw. The Bois Forte (Nett Lake) Chippewa Reservation in northern Minnesota grows world-famous wild rice, which the tribe harvests by traditional methods in early fall. Harvesters make their way among the rice stalks in canoes and beat the kernels into the boats with sticks, a method which fills the harvesters' faces with chaff. Waterfowl love the rice, and the Bois Forte Reservation has fine duck hunting.

Wisconsin's Menominee tribe, which has been where it is for five thousand years, occupies a reservation of 235,000 acres in the east-central part of the state. Most Menominee land is managed forest; the tribe had 1.2 billion standing board feet of timber in 1850, has harvested 2 billion board feet since then, and still maintains a healthy forest of 1.5 billion board feet. A tribal corporation limits the annual timber cut and plants replacement trees. The Lac du Flambeau Chippewa, also of Wisconsin, operate Ojibwe Brand Pizza, a chain in seven states; the Eastern Cherokee own the largest mirror company in the United States; the Ak-Chin Community in Maricopa, Arizona, grow top-quality pima cotton; and the Skull Valley Band of Goshute Indians own a rocket-motor test site on tribal land in northwestern Utah. Recently the Goshute have come up with a plan to provide temporary storage on the reservation for spent nuclear fuel.

Many tribes get revenue from energy leases. Although Indian reservations contain just 4 percent of the nation's land, they hold 16 percent of its coal reserves and 4 percent of its petroleum and natural gas. On some reservations, oil has been the major source of non-government income. The Fort Peck Assiniboine Reservation in Montana used to hold a powwow every August to celebrate the discovery of oil there in 1952. On the Wind River Reservation in Wyoming, the Shoshone and Arapahoe tribes made money during the high oil prices of the 1970s; after the prices dropped in the 1980s, the reservation suffered a corresponding rise in suicides.

People who took land from Indians in the nineteenth century thought in terms of farms, railroad rights-of-way, and mines. If they had thought in terms of energy and of what energy resources might be worth someday, Indians might have been left with no land at all. The value of a piece of land, like character, can take time to be revealed. Uranium, for example, turned out to be plentiful in landscapes which no nineteenth-century farmer would have looked at twice—in just the sorts of places where America pushed Indians. Half the nation's uranium reserves now lie under Indian lands. Many of these reserves are in a large mineral belt west of Albuquerque; the reservation of the Laguna Pueblo, near the middle of the deposit, has the largest uranium strip mine in the world. During the Cold War, Navajo miners helped dig the uranium used to make nuclear weapons. When some of them developed lung cancer and sued the government for not warning them of the danger, the government cited the arms race and the need for national security. Tribal revenues from uranium mining, like the uranium business nationwide, have been in decline ever since the near-disaster at the nuclear power plant at Three Mile Island.

One place where you find a lot of Indians is in the Army. Indians have always made good soldiers and have gotten along better in all branches of the service than they often did elsewhere in the non-Indian world. Indians fought in every American war from the Revolution on. Iroquois and other Eastern tribes served in the Continental Army; a while ago the Daughters of the American Revolution gave membership to a full-blooded Indian woman named Neana Neptune Lent, descendant of a Penobscot Indian in that war. Winnebago and Iroquois fought for the North in the Civil War, while Cherokee and Choctaw fought for the South. Stand Watie, a Cherokee politician and soldier, who led a regiment of Cherokee cavalry, was the last Southern general to surrender.

Though most Indians were not U.S. citizens at the time of the First World War, they volunteered at a rate greater than that of any other group. Afterward, partly out of gratitude, Congress passed the law extending citizenship to all Indians. In the Second World War, they again volunteered by the thousands—a thousand from the Oglala alone—and bought lots of war bonds with their scarce dollars and put tribal funds at the disposal of the government. Indians in the service tended to acquire the nickname "Chief," and to win more decorations than their comrades. Notable among Indian heroes of that war was the Pima Ira Hayes, a Marine pfc and winner of two Bronze Stars for gallantry. After a *Life* magazine photographer took the famous picture of Hayes and other Marines hoisting the flag on Iwo Jima, higher-ups brought Hayes back to the United States to make appearances at patriotic rallies and fund-raising events. Hayes quickly tired of the attention and received permission to return to the war.

Biographies of Indian men in their seventies and older almost always include a reference to the Second World War: "He survived the sinking of the U.S.S. *Waters* off Okinawa, one of only thirty-eight found alive from a crew of five hundred"; "He was captured with others of the 36th Texas Division in the South of France, then freed by the 3rd Division, and afterwards wounded by machine gun fire. He had four bullets and one kidney removed, and still has one bullet in his body"; "He served as a fireman and gunner aboard the U.S.S. *Benham* in the years 1944 through 1946 and was awarded five battle stars"; "When a Japanese suicide plane flew into the ship, he was in the water for 52 hours before being rescued." Recently the Ranger Hall of Fame at Fort Benning, Georgia, inducted a Ranger veteran named Norman Janis. Mr. Janis, an Oglala Sioux and a descendant of Red Cloud, was cited for his service with a special unit called Merrill's Marauders in the North Burma campaign. The citation said that once, when his platoon was surrounded, Pfc Janis used his sharpshooting abilities to kill eight Japanese soldiers with eight bullets, all to the head.

In Vietnam, Indian soldiers were more likely to see combat than those of other groups. Many Indians were killed or wounded there; of those missing in action, scientists at first had trouble identifying the remains, because of the similarity of Indian skulls to the skulls of Asian people like the Vietnamese. Indian veterans angry about the war made a large percentage of the membership of AIM and contributed to its militancy. The tradition of Indians in the armed services did not end with that war, however. One of the first U.S. soldiers to die in Operation Desert Storm was a member of the San Carlos Apache tribe named Michael Noline; among the Navy technicians firing Tomahawk missiles at Saddam Hussein was a Crow Indian, Fire Controlman Third Class Wesley Old Coyote. In recent years, many Indian women have joined the military as well.

The military often builds its bases in the neighborhood of Indian reservations. The same remoteness, emptiness, and general unfarmability that resulted in the reservations being where they are proved ideal for the training purposes of the Army and Air Force. Military aircraft on training exercises fly over reservation land all the time. If you drive on Western reservations, sooner or later a B-52 bomber will roar over the roof of your car so close you could almost throw a rock at it, or a Phantom 115 jet fighter will pop out like a genie from around a butte and flit by in spooky silence a second ahead of the sky-filling thunder of its engine. Military overflight has become such a reservation commonplace that some tribes have considered the possibility of restricting their air space. And naturally, every so often a plane flying over an Indian reservation will crash.

On the night of May 10, 1995, an F-117-A Nighthawk Stealth fighter on a training mission crashed into Pia Mesa on the Zuñi Indian Reservation in western New Mexico. Zuñi who saw the plane coming down thought it was a falling star. The plane made a thirty-foot crater and burned, and Zuñi search-and-rescue teams and police and firefighters were the first to reach the crash. Afterward, the Air Force gave all the Zuñi who had been there a detailed health questionnaire. The burning materials in the plane included beryllium, carbon graphite, depleted uranium, radar-absorbent materials, and thermoplastic; Air Force scientists wanted to know what the effects of exposure to such smoke and fumes might be. "I guess they want to know if we are going to mutate into something," Zuñi responder Clay Dillingham said.

The name of this plane, the Nighthawk Stealth fighter, is misleading. It is not a supersonic dogfighting airplane like the Phantom. In fact, its top speed is about that of a commercial jet, well in the subsonic range. The Stealth is designed to fly slowly, undetected by radar, and to drop one or two bombs. It is about the size of a fighter plane and looks like a cross between a boomerang and a grand piano. Its delta-wing shape, futuristic though it may be, suggests to the observer uninformed about aeronautics that the plane might not fly very well. In this case, aeronautics notwithstanding, the doubt would seem to be well founded; of the fifty-nine Stealth built so far, six have crashed, and another caught fire and burned on landing. There has also been a question about the ability of the plane's radar-absorbing skin to resist certain kinds of weather, particularly rain.

As part of most Indian treaties, the United States promised to educate Indian children. Because of this, the Bureau of Indian Affairs is responsible for the public schools on Indian reservations. Recently the BIA has announced that a large number of its reservation school buildings are falling apart. Some buildings are in such bad shape that students have been injured in them, and some have been shut down and replaced with temporary structures until repairs can be made. In 1995 the BIA estimated that the 187 schools it runs nationwide needed between $650 million and $800 million for repairs. The Stealth that crashed on the Zuñi reservation cost $45 million. The fifty-nine Stealths built so far have cost about $2.7 billion. BIA funding in general has been cut in recent years. Its funds for all school repairs and improvements nationwide in 1998 were $32 million, about enough to buy two-thirds of a Nighthawk Stealth airplane.

One of the pleasures of reading about Indians is in the names. In American history, you come across Indians with names like Arm Blown Off (who carried a message between Red Cloud and the soldiers in 1877), or Civility (a Conestoga Indian in Pennsylvania who made a speech to Thomas Penn), or William Shake Spear (an Arapahoe interpreter at the

St. Stephen's Mission in Wyoming in the 1890s) or Spy (a Sioux scout for the Army), or Buttock On Both Ends (a warrior in the Custer battle). In an Army census of about fifteen hundred Indians at the Red Cloud Agency in 1876 and 1877, about seventy Indians gave names which were, by our standards, remarkably obscene. The previous generation or two of pop culture left the impression that most Indians had names like Running Bear or Little White Dove or Running Water. In fact, Indians had and have names of almost every kind, from simple and de-ethnicized to complicated and traditional. Reading about Indians in recent years turns up names like Goofy Killsnight, Toby Shot to Pieces, Rufus White Woman, Gerben D. Earth, Montgomery Ward Two Belly, Heather Whiteman Runs Him, and Whisper Black Elk. Some names are complete sentences, like Randy Falls Down or Michael Stops or Frank Fools Crow or Peter Catches or Bobby Talks Different. An Oglala tribal member sometimes mentioned in news stories about the Pine Ridge Reservation is a woman named Carla Respects Nothing. Then there's Pius Moss, Smile White Sheep, Exactly Sonny Betsuie, Louis Pretty Hip, Melanie Shoot Dog, Octa Keen, Charley Zoo, the brothers Roy and O'Ray Dog, and Frizzell Frizzell, the nation's only American Indian golf course superintendent.

Many Indian last names recall the colonial powers in North America. A few Indians have Dutch last names, more have names that are Spanish, English, or French. In the far Pacific Northwest, where the Russians once built trading posts, some Aleut and Inuit Native Americans still belong to the Russian Orthodox Church and have Russian last names. Bill Prokopiof is the name of an Aleut artist from the Pribilof Islands four hundred miles off the coast of Alaska in the Bering Sea. As the original people on the continent, Indians absorbed groups who came later, and they continue to absorb them. Ethnologists predict that in the next century the number of pure-blood Indians will dwindle to almost none, a prospect which disturbs the many tribes who require that their members be of a certain percentage of tribal blood—usually a quarter or an eighth.

Very likely, future membership in an Indian tribe will depend as much on family tradition and personal affinity as on blood degree, further complicating the already fraught problem of Indian identity. Also, due to the widespread practice of putting Indian babies up for adoption by non-Indian families back in the assimilationist 1950s and 1960s, many adoptees now in search of their parentage are finding that they are Indian. There is even an organization, the Lost Bird Society, to help people find their Indian roots; the tribal enrollment office of the Gila River Pima-Maricopa tribe in Arizona said not long ago that it was getting an average of three requests a day from adoptees in search of their birth parents. A few years past a woman named Yvette Silverman Melanson who had grown up Jewish in New York discovered that she had been born a Navajo. "I thought [Indians] were extinct, like the dinosaur," she told a newspaper.

The idea of belonging to a tribe not by blood but by affinity is less vague than it sounds. Some Indians preferred (and prefer) to live with bands or tribes other than the ones they were born into. An Oglala of the Cut Off band might move in with his mother's relatives among the Bad Faces, a Santee Sioux might journey west from Minnesota and join the Oglala, a Sioux might be adopted into the Cheyenne or a Cheyenne into the Arapahoe. Today there are Oglala descended from Minnecojou Sioux who stayed on Pine Ridge after the massacre at Wounded Knee, or from Cheyenne who came to the reservation and stayed partly due to the friendship of Red Cloud. The power of affinity applies to non-Indians as well. Some people with no Hopi or Zuñi blood at all love the Pueblo Indian culture, and study it and buy its artifacts, and talk about the Pueblo tribes as if no other existed. Germans who like Indians often seem to choose the Sioux or the Apache, while the French favor more northerly tribes like the Blackfeet and Cree. Among Western history buffs it is possible to get into long arguments about which is the coolest tribe, with strong opinions on a number of sides. Every buckskinner— buckskinners are historical re-enacters who dress in buckskin and shoot black powder rifles, for a hobby—has a favorite tribe, and usually a favorite band within that tribe.

Indeed, the Indians of America are so varied that I think you could find an appropriate tribe for almost anyone. The tribes' historical variety is like that of America today, but in seed-crystal form. As we get older, we learn our affinities—for certain foods or kinds of music or seats in an airplane or professions or physical types among the sex we happen to be attracted to. Just through an affinity for a particular part of the country, a person narrows down the number of tribes that would be right for him or her. In the same way that I have gotten used to my liking for hot sauce and my aversion to crowds, I accept that my affections veer toward the Oglala Sioux. Many names of Indian tribes, translated from the original, have a self-praising meaning like "the True People" or "the Human Beings," and Indians will sometimes tell you privately that their tribe is the best of all. Much as I like Indians in general, when it comes to the Oglala, my inclination is to agree. By blood and circumstances, I can never be an Oglala; but by long-standing affinity, the Oglala are my tribe.

CHAPTER

6

I spent the night in a motel in Chadron, Nebraska—the Pine Ridge Reservation has no motels—and in the morning drove the thirty-some miles back to Le's. His door was tied shut with the fish stringer, and on the door was a note addressed to me: "Went to Floyd John's across the river. See U. —Le." I wasn't sure what that meant, so I drove over to Pine Ridge, went to Big Bat's, and had a sandwich. I walked around Pine Ridge for a while, then went to Le's again. This time his door was open and he was sitting unsteadily on several piled-up sofa cushions and looking out through the screen. In his hand was a 24-ounce can of Olde English Malt Liquor. He told me to come in, and then he said, "Listen—I want to tell you something—you know I'm a dog soldier, right? You know what that means? It means I fight for my people, that I'm a warrior. You understand? I'm a dog soldier, today is a good day to die! It's a good day to change the world! I'm standing on my own two feet on the bosom of our mother earth. I go where I want, I do what I want. I take no orders from anybody. The *spirits* tell me what to do. I'm just a man . . ." He began to cry.

He took some dried sage tied in a narrow bundle with red thread, lit it with a paper match, and began to swish its smoke around the room. He was singing Lakota, but so quietly that only occasionally did audible phrases emerge. He said, "I talk to you because you—" He stopped.

"Because I'm your friend," I finished for him.

"I talk to you because you have a curious mind and an innocent heart. And you're not my friend. You're my brother." He set the smoldering sage in an empty can that had once held commodity pears. He sang some more, then took me by both arms and prayed for me, asking that I see with clear eyes that do not judge. He shook hands with me complicatedly, feeling the pulses in my wrists with his thumbs.

We got in my car and drove a few miles north on the highway, then turned off into a pasture. He said that he wanted to collect some more sage and that he knew a good place for it by the sun-dance grounds. We went through several fenced fields, Le getting out to open the gates. Then we came down a small embankment and into an open flat surrounded by cottonwood trees. In the center of it stood a sun-dance arbor—a shelter in the shape of an O, tree-limb posts supporting crossbeams laid over with a roof of bushy pine boughs—and in the center of the O stood the sun-dance pole. From the pole's top fluttered strips of cloth in the four sacred colors, which are red, black, yellow, and white. A sun dance had taken place there a week or so before, and the grasses were still trampled down, and the dusty ground exhaled a good fragrance I couldn't identify. There was not a scrap of litter anywhere. Near the sun-dance arbor remained the willow frame of a sweat lodge, a delicate sketch of a dome just big enough to sit under. By the lodge frame I saw a few remaining pieces of split cottonwood of a deep yellow, a heap of stones, and a sort of whisk made of long-needle pine boughs tied with baling twine. Aside from the twine, the fastenings of blue nylon cord on the sweat-lodge frame, and the cloth at the top of the sun-dance pole, everything in this ceremonial place was made from natural materials found close at hand. Most religious structures look as if they had descended upon the landscape from above; these looked as if they had risen on their own out of the ground.

Le cut sprigs from sage bushes growing at the clearing's edge, singing again in Lakota and telling me Lakota words I should know. The Wild West smell of the sage mingled with the liquidity of the words: *oskí-ski*, which means badlands, and *ih'é-swu-la*, the little stones found sometimes on anthills, and *péji wacáŋga*, sweet grass, and *mitakuye oyasin*, the phrase you say when the heat becomes too intense inside the sweat lodge and you want to get out. It means "all my relatives." Le took a generic-brand cigarette from a pack in his shirt pocket and scattered the tobacco from it to the four directions and said a prayer before we left.

From there we went to Floyd John's. The road to his place had dried to deep ruts, and I walked each tire through them slowly, so as not to jounce Le's neck. Floyd John was on the ground by the propane tank outside his cabin, lying on his back propped up on both elbows. His hair was every which way and his eyes were remote and intent at the same time. He gestured for me to sit on the ground beside him and I did. Then he turned to me and said, "What is love? Love is a piece of shit." He began to talk about love, about the woman and the man, and how one does this and the other does that, and how all of it is shit; meanwhile, he held my right hand in his, emphasizing his points with various shakes and squeezes. I felt something sticky, and when I finally retrieved my hand, I found the palm blotched with drying blood. He and Wanda had had a fight, he explained, and he had broken a glass and cut his hand. Wanda came around the corner of the cabin, gave us an unencouraging look, and went back inside.

The day before, I had loaned Floyd John $20.85 to buy a new regulator for a car he was trying to get running, and he wanted to pay me back. He went in the cabin and came out with an Army fatigue shirt in a jungle camouflage pattern that he had worn in Vietnam. I didn't want to accept it, but I did, thanking him a lot. Then he went in again and this time came out with a belt buckle of embossed and painted leather he had made himself. In the middle of the buckle was the head of a bald eagle in profile superimposed on a black spade, with the word NAM above and the years " '66 '68" below. The edge of the buckle was black leather hand stitching, and stamped on the back was Floyd John's name. I really did not want to take this, and I protested as much as I could, saying that I could never wear it, that I hadn't been in Vietnam. He kept saying he had made it in the V.A. hospital and he wanted me to have it because I was his bro. Finally I took it.

In Pine Ridge I had seen a sign advertising a rodeo west of town that evening, and I wanted to go to it. I had already asked Le if he wanted to go. Now he persuaded Wanda and Floyd John to come along, too. I wasn't crazy about this development, because it looked to me as if the fight they'd been having was far from done. But we all four then piled into my car and drove to Pine Ridge, Wanda and Floyd John continuing to exchange words in the back seat, though I could hear only Floyd John's. In Pine Ridge he told me to pull over at the four-way so we could get out and look at his name on the Vietnam Veterans' Memorial beside the road. Then, by a three-to-one majority, we elected to go to White Clay to buy a case of beer.

We pulled up by the door of the Arrowhead Inn—I am still not ready to describe the town of White Clay—and I gave Le seventeen dollars. He went in and bought a case of Budweiser and three 24-ounce cans of Olde English Malt Liquor. He and Floyd John said they would tell me how to get to the rodeo grounds. On the way there, Floyd John began to tell me about a poem he had written at Khe Sanh, and to lean in my ear and say loud remarks that were hard to respond to. I was in my extra-careful driving mode. Le and Wanda told him to shut up. We missed the turnoff for the rodeo grounds, stopped, and went back. The turnoff was unmarked except by the tracks of many tires, and it led quite a ways off the paved road, over one swell in the prairie and then another, and finally to a gate at a four-strand wire fence where some women were taking admission. It cost us four dollars apiece to get in; again I paid. We drove on to the arena, a corral with nine banks of lights on high poles around it and stock chutes at the far end. There were no grandstands, so we did the same as everyone else and pulled up to the corral fence to watch from our car. Some people had spread blankets on their car hoods to lie on.

There were the usual rodeo preliminaries—the riders guiding carefully-stepping horses among the cars, the bellows from the roping stock, the country music from the scratchy loudspeakers, the small parade featuring the American flag and the flag of the Oglala tribe. The arena lights seemed to get brighter as the sun went down. The first event, the folksy rodeo announcer said, would be Mutton Bustin', a bucking-sheep-riding contest for kids. At an end of the arena the small contestants assembled in a line, many in hats so big and pants so pegged they looked like tacks. One at a time they climbed into the bucking chutes, got aboard, and came out on sheep who flung themselves around more vigorously than I would have believed sheep could move. Some of the kids were quite little and got bucked off quickly. A few began to cry and ran for their dads to the accompaniment of the announcer's uncomforting folksy commentary. Other kids hung on like burrs until the sheep quit bucking, and a swell of applause and honking car horns rose from the spectators. One successful ride prompted the announcer to say that the Oglala ought to consider raising sheep for a living. Perched on my car hood, Floyd John yelled back, "*Sheep?* We ain't no goddamn Navajos!" This got a big laugh, and he yelled it several times more.

I told Le I was going to take a walk and look around. I circled the arena, then headed off across the prairie, stopped on the crest of a rise, and sat down. From here the arena was just a cloud of bright dust rising into the lights, in a vague encirclement of vehicles. The prairie silence stretched on every side to the darkening horizon, and the announcer's voice and the sound of the car horns were faint and faraway. After a while I got up and walked back slowly. Nearer the arena, I noticed that someone seemed to be sitting in the driver's seat of my car. I hurried over to see who it was; I didn't want anyone sitting there. The person turned out to be a cowboy named Jimmy Yellow Boy, an acquaintance of Le's and Floyd John's. He was drinking Budweiser and bully-ragging with them, while Floyd John made threats about kicking his ass. I could not tell for sure how serious he was.

I introduced myself to Jimmy Yellow Boy in a way which I hoped said, "Get out of my car." Jimmy Yellow Boy took no notice, talking instead about the bad bull he had drawn to ride and about bad bulls he had ridden in the past. He said he had been hurt by a bull named Peggy Sue—"I'm all broken up, man. You don't mess with those bulls"—and he showed me his hands. Their multiple breaks and rehealings had given them an odd look, as if they had been drawn by one of those plentiful artists who can't draw hands. Le finally told him to get the hell out so I could sit down, and Jimmy Yellow Boy did, cheerfully telling us to honk our horn for him when he rode.

Each event seemed to take longer than the one before it to get under way. Often a roping steer or a bull would wedge himself crosswise in the chute and bellow and kick and send people leaping back. Many of the hazers and stock handlers had cans of beer in Styrofoam can caddies at convenient spots on the ground along the corral fence and occasionally stepped away from their tasks for long sips, which worked to their disadvantage in dealing with the angry, lively, and sober bucking stock. The announcer called Jimmy Yellow Boy's name, and suddenly we saw the wide blue-and-white stripes of his shirt bouncing from the chute on top of a dark, grunting blur. He had slid to the ground before I remembered to honk the horn. Le and Floyd John were now arguing on a repetitive theme, so I left again and stood behind the bucking chutes. A tall bull rider grinned broadly at a pregnant girl in light-blue cutoffs and asked, "If I ride him, will you name your baby after me?" Then he climbed into the chute, got settled, gave a nod, and went flying off at the second or third buck.

When the rodeo was winding down, Le wanted me to drive around among the parked cars looking for a friend of his, but I ignored him and joined the traffic honking and jockeying at the fence gate in the headlight beams full of exhaust smoke and dust. Le and Floyd John had begun to argue about the Vietnam War, Le calling Floyd John a chump for going and Floyd John calling him worse for not going, keeping up a running argument with Wanda all the while. As we approached Pine Ridge, we came over a rise and saw the lights of the village spread out across the dark prairie. I remarked that they looked like the lights of Los Angeles seen from Mulholland Drive, and said how pretty it was. Wanda said, more clearly than I ever heard her say anything, "It looks pretty, but it's just a slum."

As we drove on toward Oglala, the three-way argument escalated to threats about who would do what to whom. My driving terror reached its peak. In every set of oncoming headlights—or single headlight, or car with no headlights at all—I imagined I was seeing the final frame before the film goes blank. I wondered how I would control the car if the argument suddenly came to blows. Old-time plainsmen used to say you haven't seen a fight until you've seen Sioux fighting Sioux. Then we were bouncing along the drive to Floyd John and Wanda's dark cabin. Because of his bad leg and uncertain balance, Floyd John had a hard time getting out of the back seat, but he finally made it, with a few parting shots at Le and a last complicated handshake for me, along with a promise to introduce me to a rancher named Warren who had known his dad. Le discovered that Floyd John had forgotten his cane in the back seat, and he got out to give it to him. "You're still my bro, Bro," Le said to Floyd John.

Then I drove Le to his house while he told me about two guys he had killed with his bare hands when he was in prison. I backed my car around in his drive to light with my headlights his way into the electricity-less house. He turned at the door and waved and disappeared behind it, like an actor behind a lit curtain. Then I beat it back to Chadron and the motel.

Le had been up for a long time when I got to his house the next day about noon. He had gone to the post office, stacked some firewood, put on a clean shirt, and read some of Stephen Oates's biography of Abraham Lincoln. I noticed it lying on his bed and commented on it. He said he hated Lincoln for hanging thirty-eight Sioux in Mankato, Minnesota, after the Santee Sioux Uprising in that state in 1862. I said that the Minnesotans had wanted to hang three hundred or more, that Lincoln had wanted to pardon most of them, and that thirty-eight was the compromise they made. Le said all the same it was the largest mass execution in U.S. history, and he would always hate Lincoln for it. He said George Washington was another Indian-killer and he hated him, too. I tried to put in a few good words for Lincoln, but failed to dent his opinion.

Florence Cross Dog, Le's older sister, had told Le that she wanted to meet me, so we went to her house at the end of a gravel street of new one-story single-family homes. But Florence had gone to the clinic in Porcupine for her regular kidney dialysis treatment. Le considered for a while and then said, "Well then, let's go see Uncle Edgar." Edgar High White Man, Le's uncle in only the honorific and affectionate sense, lived in a house at the junction of the highway and a gravel road a few miles west of Oglala. Le told me that Edgar High White Man's mother had survived the massacre at Wounded Knee. We pulled into his driveway and got out, and Le called through the back door screen, and Edgar High White Man came out and talked with us as he leaned with one foot propped on the running board of his new red pickup truck. He was short, deeply wrinkled, eighty-six years old, with bowlegs like parentheses. He wore a straw cowboy hat with red, yellow, and black feathers in the hatband; a blue-and-white-checked shirt; blue jeans; blue suspenders; and the gold watch he received on his retirement after thirty years driving the Loneman school bus.

In 1976 Edgar High White Man had testified before Congress as part of the Sioux's attempt to get reparations from the government for Wounded Knee. His mother, Dora, was nine years old at the time of the massacre. She was with her grandmother there, and after her grandmother got shot, Dora ran away over a ridge. A wagon picked her up and carried her to Oglala, where she afterward remained. Edgar High White Man went inside and brought out the transcripts of the hearings, in a thick paperbound volume swollen a bit with water damage that happened when someone he had loaned it to didn't take proper care. He said he testified to the senators about his mother's sufferings for a long time. He and the other descendants of Wounded Knee survivors had hoped the government would agree to reparation payments similar to those given to Japanese interned during the Second World War; but one of the South Dakota senators was working on the Sioux's behalf while the other was working just as hard against them, he said, and nothing came of the hearings in the end.

I asked him if he knew where the name High White Man came from. He said, "Well, that's quite a story. My great-granpa was a respected man and sometimes he would get into a group of younger men talking about expeditions they would like to go on. They'd plan where they wanted to go and they always wanted an older, well-experienced man like him to lead. One older man would lead and another would bring up the tail part, with the younger fellows in between, everybody walking single file just close enough so they could hear each other's steps. Well, on this one expedition they were down south of where Scottsbluff, Nebraska, is now. They never went on the flat like this ground around here, where an enemy could see them. They followed the higher ground just below the ridgeline, and every so often the leader would go up on the ridge and use a bush for cover and look all around. Then he'd go to the next hill and do the same thing.

"Well, my great-granpa was on a hill looking around and he sighted this wagon train coming. So he said to the others, 'This is a tight place. I'll go on ahead and meet the wagon train, and if anything happens to me you can get them when they come through here.' So he went to the wagon train a long way around so they wouldn't know where he had come from, and the fellows that were watching saw the whole wagon train stop. Then they saw the wagon master come over to my great-granpa, and they saw the wagon master shake his hand. The wagon master was a very tall guy with red hair. Well, they saw that, and they decided they had another name for my great-granpa. They said, 'We'll call him Washicun Wankatuya, High-up White Man.' The wagon master gave my great-granpa molasses and bread, and all the others came to the wagon train and got molasses and bread, too, so they didn't have to attack 'em. Our family has had that name ever since.

"It's funny you should ask me that question," Edgar High White Man said. "Just a few weeks ago an auto-glass repairman in Nebraska asked me the same thing."

(I am glad I got a chance to meet Edgar High White Man. He died January 18, 1996.)

On another afternoon, we found Florence Cross Dog at home. Her car was in her driveway, so we pulled in behind it and walked around to the back door, past a black pickup truck with a dead porcupine on the hood. Le said that one of Florence's sons was using the quills for decorative quillwork on a rattle he was making. Le rapped on the screen and someone called to him from inside and we went in. There were a lot of people in the house, and that first time I didn't get them all straight. Several little kids—Florence's grandchildren—came up to us and stared at me and smiled at Le, and held up their puckered lips so he could bend down and be kissed. A girl named Tabitha showed him her new mood ring, and a baby named RaeDawn, wearing only a disposable diaper, yelled something up at us I couldn't understand and then yelled it again and laughed. RaeDawn's mother, Florence's daughter Flora, known as Tweet, was sitting in the living room watching TV. Florence's son John lay asleep on a couch.

Florence came out from her bedroom, where she had been sewing. She is a big-boned woman with short dark hair, high eyebrows, and eyes that take quick measure of what they see. She had on a loose-fitting short-sleeved dress and bandages in the crooks of both arms, from the dialysis. She said that she'd heard so much about me from Le. I said she sure had cute grandkids, pointing down at RaeDawn. Florence said, "That one was born the same day I had my kidney removed, and the papers got the two things confused and wrote that I was in the hospital and had this baby. And I'm five years older than Leonard! I'm sixty years old!"

Immediately she asked me if I would like to buy a star quilt. This is a traditional Sioux style of quilt which has a star at the center with usually eight points radiating to the edges on a plain background, usually white. The star part of the quilt is made of diamond-shaped pieces of cloth all the same size fitted together and sewn on the off side. The pieces can be of all kinds of fabrics and colors, as in any quilt, and their combination and arrangement is a difficult art. I like star quilts, so I told Florence I'd be happy to see hers. She brought out a queen-sized quilt with a star of lavender, light pink, and light blue floral print on a white background. It was not finished yet, and still had blue marks on it from the quilting chalk. She said she wanted $200 for it and needed the money right away. I didn't have $200, but I said I liked the quilt, and I gave her a deposit of $50. I asked her how she had learned to quilt. She led me into her bedroom and showed me her sewing machine.

"It came to me one night in a dream," Florence said. "I never learned quilting from anybody—I just dreamed how to do it. I've been making star quilts for thirty-five years. And I've used this same Singer sewing machine the entire time. You can see how the wood here that the cloth goes over has all the finish worn off, and a layer or two of the plyboard, too. I've made hundreds of plain star patterns, and stars with pictures in the middle—buffalos and eagles and porcupines, and that picture called *The End of the Trail*. The Red Cloud Museum by Pine Ridge only pays $100 a quilt, and the Prairie Edge store up in Rapid only pays $200, and sometimes they turn around and sell them for a lot more, so I don't sell to them no more. Most of my customers are just people who've heard about me, people from all over."

From a bureau drawer she took out a stack of Polaroid photos of star quilts she had made. Reduced to this size, the stars in the middle of each quilt seemed to pulse. Some stars blended colors of the wildest gaudiness into a whole so simple that the eye had to go back over, color by color, to see how the effect had been achieved; others used pastel shades varying in subtle sequence from the center of the star to the tip of the points. Then she showed me a calendar with star quilt photos from the Rosebud Reservation, to compare. On those quilts the colors looked more random, bright but competing with each other in the eye. "Those Rosebudders are good sewers," Florence said, "but they don't understand about the colors, how to put 'em together."

Tabitha and her older sister, Amanda, seeing I was interested in such things, got out their jingle dresses to show me. Le's sister Norma, their great-aunt, had made them. The jingle dress is a ceremonial Sioux garment that goes back at least to the fur trade days. It can be of soft buckskin or cloth, and its main feature is the many little tin cones that hang from it from yoke to hem and that jingle together when the wearer moves. The dress is worn in a traditional women's dance called the jingle dance; Tabitha held her dress to her and did some jingle-dance steps so I could hear how it sounded. Jingle dresses sometimes have 365 cones on them, each representing a prayer for a different day of the year. A woman moving in a jingle dress is a multiplicity of small and soft sounds, like a treeful of dried seedpods rustling in the wind or a river with lots of shards of ice. Under certain circumstances, the effect on the ear can be as beguiling as perfume is on the nose. In former times, the cones were made of tin cut from containers of snuff bought at the trader's. I looked more closely at Amanda's and Tabitha's dresses and saw that on one, every cone was of tin cut from the top of a Redwood chewing tobacco can, and on the other, every cone was from a Copenhagen chewing tobacco can.

Flora took the baby RaeDawn and gave her a bath, and RaeDawn then ran around wrapped in a towel, showing off. John woke up, and he and his brother Rex and Le sat on the couch and began to watch a sitcom called *Major Dad*. Le had seen this episode already and he explained the plot to them. A grandchild of Florence's named E.J. asked if it was okay if he and another little boy went across the street to play on a backhoe at the construction site there. Florence let them. RaeDawn pulled a cushion from an armchair onto the floor and began to do som-

ersaults on it. Le and Rex began to talk about a car, a Volare, that someone was trying to fix up. It had carburetor problems. Florence joined
the conversation, and it briefly switched to Lakota, mixed with occasional English words like "air-filter cover." Through the front window I
could see E.J. and the other little boy climbing all over the backhoe in a
haze of dust blowing down the street.

Another afternoon, Le and I visited his sister Aurelia Two Crow. She is
eight years older than Florence, and shorter and more spry. After her
husband died a few years ago, she moved back to Oglala. She has
medium-length, mostly gray hair and she wears glasses with big round
frames that give her an owlish expression. Her manner is querulous and
lyrical, and her sentences sometimes trail off in a gentle "Uh-huh . . . oh
yes . . ." Her house is far from the road in a grove of tall cottonwood
trees. Her car, an older-vintage Chrysler, was parked among them. We
found her just beginning to wash it. "I was in Rapid, and I wanted to
wash my car it was so dirty," she said. "But they wanted two dollars and
fifty cents for a car wash up there, and I decided I'd rather have a fish
sandwich than a clean car, so I waited to wash it till I got home."
    Aurelia's conversation, spoken as much to the car and herself as to
us, proceeded in phases between filling a heavy black plastic bucket at
the pump, soaping the car from roof to fenders, rinsing with splashes of
clean water, and polishing it dry with a rag.
    "I went up there to visit at the hospital," she said, soaping, "and I
wanted to stay longer, but a storm came up, and I told Floyd John I was
worried about getting back, so we left. The wind started to blow and
tumbleweeds was running back and forth across the road and the sky
got so dark we had the headlights on. Floyd John drove fast on the
wrong side of the road most of the way. He said we was the only people
crazy enough to be out there anyway in that weather, so it didn't matter.
Yes, mm-hmm . . .
    "I got Wisconsin license plates on this 'cause I been living over there
with my daughter. I should be in a nursing home, I'm so old. But instead I'm living in this old place now. I came back here last December
for the holidays and I been here ever since. My kids are all gone, New
Mexico and Wisconsin, and I'm out here by myself. Florence said I

ought to get out and do something, that I'm just vegetating. I said, 'If you think I'm vegetating, I'll run a race against you.' I can still get around good. Oh yesss . . .

"I'm feeling good now that I'm back home out of that damp Wisconsin climate. And I feel a *lot* better now that I don't drink so much anymore. Florence said she quit drinkin' and lost all her friends. Well, I didn't go that far—I have a few beers, but I don't drink so much wine and whiskey like I used to. And I don't try to drink with these guys [gesturing to Le]. I was drinkin' all the time a few years ago and some people told me I was drinkin' too much, that it was terrible. I said, 'Well, all right, Mr. Know-It-All. I worked for fifteen years as a cook at the senior center, makin' Indian food, fresh bread and biscuits and fry bread every day, not boughten bread and crackers like they serve now. And I had my kids and I raised 'em up right, and now they're off and gone, and I don't have no responsibilities no more. So why can't I do what I feel like and drink sometimes if I want to?' Yes, that's so . . ."

She finished polishing the chrome and threw the rags into the empty bucket. Then she stood back and admired her work. "This is a pretty good old car, mm-hmmm . . . Some mornings when it's real cold it don't like to start. But I just take a steel baking sheet from the kitchen and put hot cinders from the stove on it, and then I slide that baking sheet on the ground right under the engine block, and in a half hour or so it starts up just fine. Mm-hmmm . . ."

Aurelia invited us in and gave us mugs of hot tea with honey. She stirred something in a pot on the stove, and Le told me to come look, that she was cooking bull snake. I peered into the pot and saw slices of canned luncheon meat. I said it was a convenient sort of snake, to slice up so nice that way. Aurelia moved boxes of cloth scraps from the couch so we could sit. Late-season flies were buzzing at the windowpanes like wind-up toys running down, and Aurelia swatted vexedly at them with her hand. Then she went and got an aerosol can of hair spray, shook it, and sprayed it at the flies. They dropped in a heap on the sill. She said, "Not a lot of people know that hair spray kills insects almost as good as insect spray—mmm-hmm, it's so."

On the reservation, I noticed that people often told me tips like that. The tips, usually quite specific and informed by experience, reminded me of the woodcraft we were taught sometimes in the Cub Scouts or the Boy Scouts under the heading Indian Lore. That sort of woodcraft seemed to apply to situations that seldom came up—walking backwards in one's own footprints to confuse pursuers, for example, or rubbing two sticks together to make a fire when there were no matches around. But after years of talking to Indians and reading about them, I have found that they do indeed know a lot of more practical precepts that could be described as Lore, such as:

The smoke from anemone flowers burned on hot coals can cure headaches.

When you see cranes flying north, you know the really cold weather is over and spring is on the way. Other birds can tell you the same thing, but cranes are the most reliable.

You find fish in a river wherever there is a whirlpool.

Rainbow-hued sun dogs—bright spots on either side of the sun—mean an enemy is approaching.

If you hear a loud knock on your door and you open it and no one is there, it means that somebody you love has died.

An owl crossing your path can foreshadow tragedy.

After a powwow, there's almost always a party, usually in a motel room or a field. The party is called a forty-nine.

It is impossible to get bloodstains out of wallpaper.

The only way to kill a turtle so its heart stops beating is to boil the turtle for fifteen minutes.

If you kill a rattlesnake to eat, cut off the top six inches of the snake along with the head, because when the snake's muscles contract in death, the poison sometimes works back into the meat.

You cannot claim money that is wired to you by Western Union unless you show a picture ID.

Mussed or frayed eagle feathers may be restored by being dipped in a weak solution of shampoo in water and then hung up to dry.

A good way to break off a cast is by rubbing it on a curbstone.

If you find a dead person in your yard, you must call a sun dancer to come and purify your house.

Ashes will absorb wet blood from a wood floor.

Red willow bark to smoke in a sacred pipe must be gathered in the winter, after the first frost of fall and before the first thunders of the spring.

Deer meat that hasn't been hung up to cure will give you the runs.

If you're out drinking and you get rolled, watch your mailbox, because sometimes your wallet will come back in the mail.

A good fishing line may be made of the white hairs of a horse's tail, braided together.

Warming the hide of a drumhead with a blow dryer before you play it makes the drum sound better.

Hall's Mentholyptus lozenges make singers' voices sound sweeter.

In the old days, big storms always arrived at the death of the moon, but now even the moon lies.

If you're trying to move a house and you can't get it to skid onto the blocks, lubricate the way with liquid dishwashing soap.

Copperhead snakes smell like cucumbers.

A bluish-gray weed called lightning weed, if tied to your golf cart, will keep you from getting hit by lightning on the golf course.

Snakes always come out when it's windy and warm.

That fall a hard winter was on the way. It gave a preview of itself early, as such winters often do. One day we were driving on the reservation in hot sunshine with our sleeves rolled up and the windows down, road dust caking in our sweat. The next morning as I drove to Le's I came over a rise and saw a long, quite low cloud extending before me like the bill of a giant cap. In another minute I was in a white-out blizzard. The snow clouds must have been thin, because the sun lit the whirling whiteness all around until it was almost too bright to look at. I turned the radio off and drove at a slow speed. Soon I had emerged into shafts of sunshine coming down like stilts from among high, fast-moving clouds. To the west I could see more clouds lined up in ranks all the way to the Black Hills.

Le had to go to Rapid City to get a note from his doctor verifying his disability from the car accident, so that he could apply for free firewood and other emergency assistance from the tribe. I went by his house and then we drove to Rapid City and back, almost 160 miles round trip, me watching the weather all the way. The errand took about five hours. Then Le wanted to get his propane fuel tank refilled; besides using the fuel to cook with, he said, he could leave the oven burning and its door open for extra heat on cold days. A friend had disconnected the tank from the inlet out back for him. The tank was the height of a man and a foot or more across, and with his injuries Le couldn't move it by himself. Together we rolled it on its base and wrestled it crosswise into the back of my Blazer.

We drove to PTI Propane, south of Pine Ridge almost to the town of White Clay. PTI Propane is an acre or so of fenced ground with white storage tanks, a trailer house for an office, and a loading dock and scales. I backed up to the loading dock while Le went into the office and paid. Then two women, Patty and Faith, came out with him to fill the tank. We roll-walked the tank to the filler hose, and Patty began to try to open the tank's valve. As she did she told us she was Patty Pourier, wife of Big Bat. He is part-owner of PTI. We talked about him and about his famous ancestor as we each took a turn at trying to get the valve open. Patty is short, apple-cheeked, pretty, and strong. After giving the valve a final hard try, she said it must be rusted shut. She said she could get it fixed for us, but not right away. Le said that he knew where he could find another tank in the meantime and that we'd return soon.

We drove back toward Oglala. Le said he had a tank that someone had stolen from him in a field nearby. He directed me to turn off onto a dirt road which the morning's blizzard had turned to muck. At a place where the road led up a steep embankment, I got out to reconnoiter. Not only was the road muddy and slick and furrowed with small gullies, but its grade slanted toward the downhill side. I walked to the top and concluded my car couldn't make it. As I turned to go back, several dogs at a house beside the hill saw me and set out for me at a run, barking and growling with their teeth bared. I walked quickly but did not run, fearing to enrage them further. I calculated that our paths would converge just about at the car. I was a few feet from it and they were a few yards from me when Le heard the racket, stuck his head from the car door, and growled a word at them in Sioux. His growl was throaty and loud, like that of a dog much bigger than they. The dogs stopped so fast they left skid marks in the mud, and then ran yelping back home. The word Le had said to them sounded familiar. I asked him what it was. He said, "I said to them, 'Wahampi!' It means soup." (And then I remembered—it was the word he had used for the soup we ate in his apartment in New York.) "Dogs on the reservation know the word wahampi because they know they might end up in some soup themselves. Eat a dog once in a while, it teaches the other dogs a healthy respect."

After further complications, and with the help of Floyd John, who we met along the road, we found a propane tank we could borrow. Then we drove back to the propane place. Patty was alone there—it was late in the day by then and Faith had gone home—and she came out to the loading dock when she saw us pull in. We rolled the propane tank up to the filler hose, and she opened the valve and attached the hose. Two guys in a pickup truck had pulled in right after us, and the driver asked if I would mind moving my car away from the dock so he could back his truck up to it. I got in my car and was about to turn the ignition when I heard a pop and a cry and then a loud hissing noise. In the rearview mirror, I saw white fumes billowing. I turned the ignition and pulled the car a few feet ahead. Patty came running at me and yelling, "Turn off your car! Turn off your car!"

I got out and looked back. The filler hose had ruptured at the point where the rubber met the nozzle, and propane gas was spewing out all over. The smell of propane filled the air as the white cloud of gas rose waist-deep around the loading dock and spread slowly across the compound. Le and Floyd John were holding the hissing hose while Patty ran around turning valves, to no effect. Then she told them to let go the hose and get away, and she sprinted for the trailer. Le and Floyd John came over to me, and Le said, "Let's get out of here—the whole place is gonna blow." I remembered when the propane distribution place blew up on the Santee Reservation in Nebraska some years ago. My main thought was that I hated to lose my car. Like an idiot, I went to it and started it again. Patty burst from the trailer waving both arms over

her head and screaming at me not to start my car, was I crazy? I turned
it off and left it regretfully. Then Le and Floyd John and I jog-walked
away down the drive.

A white propane truck came speeding to the bottom of the drive and
stopped. The driver jumped from the cab and ran up to the loading
dock, leaped onto it, and disappeared behind the tanks. In another second the hissing stopped; he had found the cutoff valve. We waited a
while longer, until the gas cloud had dispersed, and then we walked
back up the drive. I got in my car while Le and Floyd John went up on
the loading dock. In the rearview mirror I watched them talking with
Patty. Then I thought I saw them laugh. I looked again; yes, they were
laughing, while Patty shook her head and looked at the ground. Then
she looked up and began to laugh, too.

When they got in the car I asked them what they had been laughing
about. "Oh, we just made some joke about us almost getting blown up,"
Le said. "Patty told us that wasn't nothin' to laugh about. But then she
kind of saw the humor in it, too."

"I don't think it's very funny," I said.

"Well, that's the Indian way," Le said. "We'd rather laugh about still
being alive than moan about how we almost died."

Le and Floyd John speculated as we drove off about how big the ex-
plosion would have been if the place had blown, and what size crater it
would have left. A hundred yards across? Two hundred yards? We got
beer in White Clay and then headed back to Oglala. Le and Floyd John
were laughing about where we would all be now if my car had happened to backfire when I started it just after the hose ruptured. I had
never seen either of them in a better mood. Floyd John's driveway had
returned to its liquid state, and we four-wheeled up it and got out and
stood by his cabin deciding what to do. The wind had begun to blow
hard. Dark-blue, silvery clouds bore down from the northwest, and
prefatory snowflakes whirled. Florence's daughter had asked Le to
bring me to her house for dinner, but I was all in. My nerves were
twanging. I took another look at the clouds and decided to head for
home.

I asked Le and Floyd John to make my apologies to Florence's
daughter, and said to tell her that I'd come another time, that I'd be
back soon. Le imparted some final dog-soldier precepts to me, and

asked for forty dollars to get his reading glasses fixed. I gave him two twenties, and a twenty to Floyd John. After last farewells, I four-wheeled out to the highway. I took deep breaths as the mud clonked around in the wheel wells, and as the tires ran smoothly again on the pavement after the mud was gone.

CHAPTER

7

I came back in November. By then several snowstorms had been and gone, and the grasses lay flat on the prairie waiting for the next. A friend had brought the refilled propane tank to Le's house and hooked it up. Now Le could cook on his stove and use it for heat. He had acquired a too-small green overcoat and an orange-and-white ski cap with the words STATE FARM INSURANCE knit into the design in big letters. His neck brace would come off in a couple more weeks, he said. Floyd John and Wanda were now living in a trailer house across from the Oglala post office. Le said Floyd John had bought it with a VA loan. We drove over there and found Floyd John inside on a couch watching Court TV. He and Le began talking about a car a cousin of theirs had left in the town of Oelrichs, twenty-six miles away, which the cousin had said Floyd John could have if he could get it running before the car crusher came for it tomorrow. The three of us spent the morning and early afternoon in a meandering storyline involving this car.

A mile or two west of Pine Ridge we passed a bearded man in a black cassock and a gray beret who was picking up trash along the highway. Le said he was probably one of the Jesuit fathers from the Red Cloud Indian School nearby. After the car project petered out, I dropped Le and Floyd John off in Oglala and went back to the school to talk to him. The Red Cloud School is a group of brick buildings, some over a hundred years old, south of the highway about three miles from Pine Ridge. The school is down in an expanse of ground between low ridges which give the campus and its drive lined with cottonwoods a sheltered feel. I went into a likely-looking building and found the office of Eva Bordeaux, the school's publicity director. The original Bordeaux in these parts was James Bordeaux, a trader who came to the Plains in the 1830s and married into the Oglala. He remained alive and in business for forty more years, a real achievement back then. At Fort Laramie in 1854 he had the good sense not to accompany the head-strong Lieutenant Grattan when Grattan went to a Sioux camp to arrest those responsible for the theft of a cow from a Mormon immigrant train, and thus avoided the Grattan massacre, which the historians point to as the beginning of the wars between the Sioux and the Army. A marker near the site of Bordeaux's trading post east of Chadron, Nebraska, says that Bordeaux may have sold the Sioux weapons used against Custer's men at the battle of the Little Bighorn.

Eva Bordeaux, a stocky young woman with glasses and a PR director's forthcoming style, said that she was a six-greats granddaughter of James Bordeaux. There are lots of Bordeaux around, she said. I described the man I had seen picking up along the highway and she said that must have been Brother Simon. She led me back through hallways to an office cluttered with papers and livened with hanging plants and goldfish in tanks. There, brother C. M. Simon, S.J., a small man with a spade-shaped gray beard and a long tobacco-stained mustache, greeted me as cheerily as if I had an appointment and was right on time. Eva Bordeaux left us to talk. Brother Simon said he had nothing better to do at the moment; he runs the school's museum of Indian arts and crafts and had to be in his office while an auditor from a firm reviewing the school's books went over his inventory. The auditor, a tall, transparent man, asked occasional questions about one item or another, and Brother Simon answered him in between talking to me. Brother Simon speaks with a stutter which, years ago, kept him out of the Army. Once I caught on to it, I found it more pleasant to listen to than ordinary speech. (I'll omit it here.)

"Yes, I do pick up the trash in the ditches along the road every week or so, just in the vicinity of the school," he said. "One must participate in the community, you know, and occasionally I find some little keepsake, and of course I can recycle the aluminum cans. I am not a teacher at the school. I've been here for thirty-five years, but I've taught nothing, except by my bad example. I've worked in the treasurer's office, and when we had a herd of prize Charolais cattle I handled the paperwork for that, doing yearling weights and genealogies and so on, and for eighteen years I've run the museum and the exhibition of Indian art we have at the school every year. Now, I'm sure in what you'll write you'll say that I'm a monk. Writers always refer to me as a monk when they do stories about me—they get things so balled up. Jesuits are not monks. Jesuits are brothers' or priests. I'm a Jesuit brother, which means that I have no sacramental powers. The responsibility of the brothers is to do the labor of the mission. Priests perform the sacraments and teach— although they'll be happy to tell you that when it comes to labor, teaching teenagers all day is mighty hard work.

"The painted buffalo skull? That's on consignment. It's listed under 'Items on Hock.'

"I was trained in Florissant, Missouri, and came here from a seminary in Mound, Minnesota. My assignment here just happened by circumstance, or maybe because no other house wanted me. Whatever the reason, I came and I stayed. I love the country and I love the people. We have had many fine graduates over the years—Dave Archambault, the former president of Standing Rock College; Shirley Plume, the first woman agent for the BIA; Chuck Trimble, an official in the Nixon administration; Tim Giago, founder and editor of the newspaper *Indian Country Today*; Phyllis DeCory, coordinator of Indian Education for the diocese; Birgil Kills Straight, past president of Oglala Lakota College; so many more. I knew people on both sides of the conflict during and after Wounded Knee. Everybody knows everybody around here, but you have to be neutral. Religion and politics don't mix. Even now, I'd rather not say anything about the Wounded Knee years. It's all still too awful fresh.

"No, no, no—heavens, no. That's not two dozen quillwork armbands, it's only two. See, it's listed here . . .

"There are five brothers and nine priests at the mission, and we cover the entire reservation—eighteen parishes. I believe our church has the most members of any on the reservation. (It depends on who's doing the counting.) The Sioux have traditionally been a Catholic tribe, going back to Father De Smet and the other Jesuit missionaries of the nineteenth century. Of course, there are other churches here as well— Episcopalians, Presbyterians, Seventh-day Adventists, three different Body of Christ fundamentalists, Latter-Day Saints. Then there's the Native American Church, and the traditional Lakota religious ceremonies like the sun dance. Many of our parishioners attend sun dances, too. We don't consider any of the faiths to be competition, and we're glad they're all here.

"The black van door with the windmill painted on it? I don't know what it goes for—I'll have to check.

"It's remarkable, really, when you think about it, how much of their tribal culture the Sioux have retained. Certainly they've retained a lot more than the rest of us. Take me, for example. Two of my grandparents came to Minnesota from Alsace-Lorraine. But would you by any stretch of the imagination consider me an Alsatian? The family has lost its memory of ever coming from there. The old language is lost, the dress is lost, the dance is lost. The Oglala still dance as their ancestors did centuries ago. Can you still do the dances your forefathers did long ago back in Scotland or wherever? For most of us, the only thing we've got left of our Old World ethnic culture is the food. Often in a family a traditional dish or two will survive, but that's about it. I thought it was funny a while ago when Newt Gingrich was trying to get a bill through Congress which would make English the official language of the U.S.A. If we did that, we'd have to hire English teachers from England, because what we speak here isn't English at all, it's American. And, as in any culture that's alive, the American language is changing all the time."

Brother Simon hooked his hands into the cincture of his cassock and leaned back in his chair. The transparent man conferred with him about a clock in the shape of a horse, then faded into columns of numbers again. "I travel sometimes because of the work I do," Brother Simon said. "I go to exhibits of Native American art in cities like Washington and Detroit, but the truth is that I always feel safer here. I think the reservation cops, in general, do a great job. Imagine how hard it is to be a policeman in a place where everyone is a relative—how hard to arrest a cousin or a brother. I do make it a policy never to go out after dark, however. I'm afraid I might run into something on the highway. There are the drunks, of course, especially after the checks come at the first of the month. And perhaps you've noticed that most of the cows around here are black. They don't show up very well at night, even in the headlights. What could be harder to see at night than a black cow?"

When I came out from talking to Brother Simon, the temperature seemed to have dropped about twenty degrees. Full dark had fallen, and wind blew through the tops of the cottonwood trees. I began to see what Brother Simon meant about the dark; on Pine Ridge, dark is darker, somehow. I drove back toward Chadron on the road that led through White Clay. That town was busy. Crowds stood silhouetted in the lighted doors of the package stores, and waiting cars just off the road here and there idled loudly, their brake lights beaming red.

I was going about fifty miles an hour south of White Clay when something hit my car. The impact was so sudden and so loud that I thought at first I must have been shot and could not believe my car was continuing to drive. I thought to pull over, but the road was narrow and cars were speeding by. Neither the car nor I seemed to show any ill effects. I looked all over inside for any evidence of damage I could find, by the dashboard's lonesome greenish light. When I reached the intersection of Highway 20, I pulled over and got out. All along the car, on the driver's side, was a windblown spatter of frozen suds. I took some between my thumb and forefinger and smelled: beer. Scattered among the suds were fragments of brown glass so tiny they had almost returned to sand and a few little pieces of foil label colored red, white, and blue.

Back at the motel, I examined the car again. The bottle, probably thrown from an oncoming car, had hit at the lower driver's-side corner of the windshield frame by the strut that holds the rearview mirror. At that height, if the bottle had hit anywhere but those few square inches, it would have shattered the windshield or the windows on that side. When I went to Le's house the next morning, I pointed out the dent the bottle had made. "Oh, that happens all the time," Le said. "Why do you think there are so many cars on the rez with broken windshields or with left-side headlights gone? You should've chased down the guys that threw it. That's what I'd've done. The last time that happened to a car I was in, we hung a U-turn and chased down the guys that done it and ran 'em off the road. We showed 'em the headlight they'd broke, and they said they was sorry, they hadn't even known the bottle hit us. Then they gave us five bucks to buy ourselves some wine."

A person on the reservation who I especially wanted to meet is Charlotte Black Elk. She is in her early forties, and is the great-granddaughter of the holy man Nicholas Black Elk. Her grandfather, Ben Black Elk, often posed for tourists at Mt. Rushmore in traditional garb and was said to be the most photographed Indian in the world. I had seen Charlotte Black Elk in a documentary on public television talking about the history of the Sioux and about their desire for the return of the Black Hills. I admired her persistent manner, her abrasiveness, and her long dark hair. Because I appeared briefly in that documentary myself, I thought she might remember my name. I called her on the telephone, and although she didn't seem to, she said I could come by and talk to her. The only problem was that she had a bad case of the flu. She told me to call again in a couple of days. "By then I'll be either better or dead," she said.

When I called again she was better, and she told me how to get to her house. She lives on a road that branches from the road between Manderson and Wounded Knee, in the hollow of a creek called Pepper Creek. She said her house looks like a structure built on top of a mine shaft, and it sort of does. It is a gray, two-story house with small four-sided towers and wings and additions that seem to have been built as the need arose. I parked in the narrow drive and knocked on the door. A teenage girl let me in without comment and went back to watching TV; at the time, Charlotte was raising nine children, only one of them her own. I found her in the kitchen kneading apricot-sunflower bread dough on a red-tile countertop under racks of hanging pots and pans. She is a slim, fine-boned woman, and the hand she offered, after rinsing it of flour, was delicate and thin. The part in her long, straight hair is directly in line with the bridge of the round-lens glasses she wears, and she has a smile I didn't remember from TV.

She and her (then) husband, Gerald Clifford, an engineer and accountant who has held many positions with the tribe, are among the leaders in the movement to get Congress to return the Black Hills to the Sioux. Gerald Clifford worked for years as coordinator of the legislative effort of the Black Hills Steering Committee. Charlotte supports the Sioux's claim with a theory based on astronomy and ancient Sioux tradition. Her theory, which she presented during congressional hearings on the Black Hills question, involves the astronomical dating of certain star groups of importance to the yearly rituals of the tribe. Like the Greeks and others, she says, the Sioux had star groups which they named and gave mythic significance to. And like the constellations of the zodiac, certain Sioux constellations were associated with certain times of year. The "Dried Willow" group of stars, for example, once coincided with the sun at the spring equinox. According to tradition, when the path of the sun passed through the "Dried Willow" group, the time had come to break winter camps, begin a series of ceremonies, and follow the buffalo herds.

Due to a fact of the heavens known as precession of the equinoxes, the sun no longer passes through the constellations of the zodiac the same way it did two thousand years ago, when those constellations were named. A slight wobble in the earth's rotation, caused mostly by the gravitational pull of the earth and the moon, causes the path of the sun to cross the plane of the earth's orbit slightly farther to the west all the time, which results in a westerly rotation of the equinoxes totaling a full degree every seventy-two years (and a full 360 degrees every 26,000 years). Precession slowly changes the position of the sun in relation to other bodies in the sky. Today the sun is no longer "in" any of the zodiac constellations at the times of year associated with those signs; its path has moved about thirty degrees westward over the past two thousand years. Similarly, Charlotte argues, precession can be used to date the cultural age of the ceremonial constellations of the Sioux. At the spring equinox, the path of the sun is now thirty to fifty degrees to the west of the "Dried Willow" group of stars. Multiplying those numbers by seventy-two years for each degree of precession, she concludes that the "Dried Willow" star group, as a Sioux cultural artifact, must be between 2,160 and 3,600 years old.

Further, she says, tradition and certain ancient star maps drawn on tanned hide link Sioux constellations to places on the earth, specifically to places in and around the Black Hills. "Seven Little Girls," a constellation identical to the Pleiades, is linked through story to Harney Peak, the "Bear's Lodge" constellation to Devils Tower, the "Race Track" to the red clay valley encircling the Hills, and so on. Using the same calculations of precession as she did for the "Dried Willow" group, she dates the tribe's occupation of the Black Hills between two thousand and three thousand years old. Indeed, it may well be even older, she believes. She scorns ethnologists who, using linguistic similarities between the Sioux language and the languages of Eastern tribes, place the Sioux's more distant origins in the Carolinas. She believes that years immeasurable have made the Sioux and the Black Hills as one. She often refers to the Black Hills as "the heart of our home, and the home of our heart."

When I pulled up a stool and sat at her kitchen counter, she explained her theory to me almost before we talked about anything else. She knows more astronomy and math than I do, and at first I did not follow all of what she said. Later, I found a book with a basic description of the theory, written by her. When I had a better idea of it, I found it less persuasive than she does; historical evidence of the Sioux's migrations over the last 250 years just seems more believable to me. As for the tribe's claim to the Black Hills, the case in their favor is so strong, based simply on facts of history over the last century and a half on which both sides agree, that adding a theory open to debate seems poor strategy. While Charlotte talked, however, I got a sense of what it might be like to live in a place where one believed one's ancestors had lived from the remote obscurities of time. It made me feel like a transient, and a descendant of transients, by comparison.

I asked Charlotte about her great-grandfather, and about his book, *Black Elk Speaks.* "To tell you the truth, I've never had the inclination to sit down and read it," she said. "Being related to someone like Black Elk brings a sense of responsibility that's not very gratifying sometimes, especially when you're a kid. I guess I never really felt I had to read it. As my Granpa Ben told me, 'The book is about this much [thumb and forefinger an inch apart] and you already know this much [arms wide apart].' You probably remember that Black Elk traveled all over Europe with Buffalo Bill's Wild West Show. Well, he spent quite a while in Paris, and when he was there he lived with a Frenchwoman named Charlotte, and that's who I'm named after. I'm named after my great-granpa's chick. Another of my great-grandfathers was Little Big Man.

People think of him as the friend of Crazy Horse who was with him when Crazy Horse was stabbed. But not many people know that Little Big Man wasn't Oglala or Minnecojou—he was a Santee Sioux who fled Minnesota after the Sioux War of 1862 and met up with the Oglala at Rawhide Buttes, near Bear Butte. Little Big Man's brother was one of the Santee captured and hanged after the war. The brother's name was Man Who Stands upon the Earth. I named my son after him. My son is nine now. Usually we don't call him by the whole name. Usually we call him Maka, which means Earth.

"A lot of the Crazy Horse people who stayed on Pine Ridge came to this part of it, in and around Manderson. The Good Thunders, Little Wolfs, He Dogs, Willow Shields, Chips, Little Bulls, Black Tail Deers, Kills Braves, Plenty Wolfs, Protectors—those were the major families. And since a lot of them were ghost dancers in 1889 and '90—Kicking Bear, the ghost-dance leader, settled in Manderson, too—and since the ghost dancers were sentenced to a choice between prison or joining the Wild West Show, there were a lot of Wild West Show veterans around here. The town of Manderson has always been a totally different creature from the town of Pine Ridge. People in Pine Ridge are descended from "friendlies" and treaty-signers who acculturated to white ways back in the 1850s. Some of them were mixed-bloods, who served as interpreters—the Lakota word for mixed-blood, *ieska,* even means interpreter. But a lot of the families around here, around Manderson, became reservation people only very late. Some didn't come in until the 1890s, and some have relatives who never came in, who stayed in Canada. There's a real division between us and the Pine Ridge people to this day. A while ago, when Gerald and I and some others from Manderson walked into a meeting in Pine Ridge, Oliver Red Cloud said, 'Here come the hostiles.' I'm proud of being a hostile.

"When I was younger I used to travel around quite a bit. In general, though, now I stay home. This valley is very quiet. When the snow falls here, it falls straight down, while out on the prairie it's a gale. We've got turkeys and deer around the house, and feral dogs. Actually, I think they're wolf-dog hybrids. They don't bark, and once they kill something, they don't stop eating until they've eaten it all. They ate one of our horses a while ago. With nine kids in the house, I've got enough to keep me occupied here. I don't have all the skills the elders used to have—I

Pine Ridge landscape

Amos Bad Heart Bull drawing of the Manypenny Commission council of 1876
(*courtesy of the University of Nebraska Press*)

Red Cloud about 1872
*(courtesy of the National
Anthropological Archive,
Smithsonian Institution)*

Red Cloud
(courtesy of the Nebraska State Historical Society)

Red Dog
(courtesy of the Nebraska State Historical Society)

American Horse
(Richard Throssel, 1907. Courtesy of the William Hammond Mathers Museum, Indiana University)

Short Bull and Joseph Horn Cloud
(courtesy of the Nebraska State Historical Society)

Little Wound
(courtesy of the James R. Walker Collection, Colorado Historical Society [negative number F-26, 996])

Reverend Eugene Buechel, S.J., c. 1938
(William J. Moore, S.J. Courtesy of Marquette University)

Custer's Last Fight—Anheuser-Busch used this painting
by Otto Becker in its advertisements for years
(courtesy of the Anheuser-Busch Archives)

Bill's Bar (now The Stockman) in Buffalo Gap, South Dakota

Tribal president Dick Wilson at Wounded Knee
(*courtesy of Corbis*)

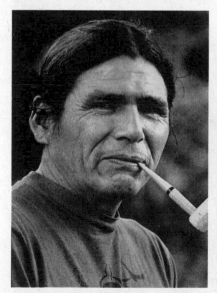

AIM leader Dennis Banks
(*AP Wide World Photos.*
Courtesy of The Chicago Tribune)

AIM leader Russell Means
(*Con Marshall*)

Le War Lance (*above*);

Aurelia Two Crow (*right*)

Florence Cross Dog (*above*)

Le's niece Flora (*right*)

SuAnne Big Crow in third grade

Clockwise from center: her mother, Leatrice "Chick" Big Crow; her sisters, Frances (Pigeon) and Cee Cee; and her niece, Jamie Lea

In the uniform of
the National Indian Team

SuAnne in cheerleader uniform

SuAnne in a 1989 playoff game

Life-size cutout of SuAnne in the trophy room at the Big Crow center

remember watching my grandmother cut a piece of buffalo meat for drying. She'd go to work on it with her knife, a cigarette hanging out of the corner of her mouth, and when she was done that sucker would be a single piece of meat almost as big as this table, thin as tin foil and not a hole in it. I don't know if I could do that. But then I do stuff they never did. When I finish this apricot-sunflower bread I'm going to make cinnamon rolls, and last week we got some piñon nuts and I made piñon–black olive bread, and it was gone in about a second. Going to New York or wherever is interesting once in a while, but basically I try to leave here as seldom as I can. My days of being ready to bum at the drop of a hat are long gone. This is where I want to be."

Le had told me that a medicine man should bless the eagle feather he had given me for my son in the Port Authority Bus Terminal, and that I should bring it with me. I did, and it was hanging by its buckskin thong from a garment hook in my car. One morning I went by Le's house, and then we picked up Floyd John and set out in search of a medicine man named Zachary Bear Shield. Le said that you always must bring a present for the medicine man, so we stopped first at Yellow Bird's store in Pine Ridge and got four packs of king-size generic cigarettes in a brown paper sack. Zachary Bear Shield lived a long way off the pavement in the Wounded Knee district. The dirt drive to his place led over hills and around hollows. At the dicier spots, I first got out and scouted ahead on foot, then proceeded in four-wheel drive. Finally we stopped by two trim house trailers in a pine glen. No cars were parked nearby, the blinds were down. A sleeping dog roused itself and looked at us and yawned; Zachary Bear Shield must get a lot of visitors. Le knocked on the door anyway. No answer. After a few minutes he said, "Well, let's see if we can find Earlie Janis.

"Earlie Janis is a pipe carrier," he continued, getting into the car. "That means he is allowed to hold the sacred pipe at the sun dances and perform other ceremonies. It's not the same as being a medicine man, but almost. Earlie's been around a long time. He's a funny guy. Back in the sixties, when the BIA had this big push to get Indians off the reservations and relocate them in the cities, they came out here to make an instructional film to show to Indians all over the country and they asked

Earlie to be in it. He was supposed to play a young Indian guy headin'
off down the highway with his suitcase in his hand hitchhiking to Rapid
City or somewhere. So he's walking along with his suitcase, and the film
crew is in a car filming him right behind, and this carload of guys he
knows pulls up and tells him to hop in. Earlie says he can't, he's being in
a movie. The guys're all drunk, and they say, 'A movie? Bull*shit*, Earlie!'
and they haul him and his empty suitcase into the car and take off down
the road, with the film crew chasing along behind."

Earlie Janis proved not to be at the end of several long driveways we
tried. Sometimes Le got out and asked directions of people we passed
along the way. One set of directions led to a slab of concrete with wires
and pipes sticking from it, but no walls or roof or other sign of a house
at all. Le said the house had probably just been moved. As we bounced
back toward pavement, I was contemplating a drive to Pine Ridge and a
sandwich at Big Bat's. Then Le said, "Let's go borrow that gun."

He directed me to the town of Porcupine, and to a small blue house
in a row of similar houses with a red school bus parked out front. We
pulled up by the school bus and a skinny white woman in a gray sweat
suit and unlaced fleece-lined boots came out of the house and gave Le
a hug. Le introduced her as Raven. She invited us in. Drying laundry
was hanging everywhere, and there wasn't much of anyplace to sit, so
we stood and conversed around the clothes. We met Raven's nine-year-
old son, Cameron, and her husband, Adam, a quiet, curly-headed blond
man in a blue T-shirt and a blue-and-white-print head rag. We had evidently interrupted Raven in the middle of a speech about what she
would do to her landlady if her landlady did such-and-such to her, and
she picked up again where she had left off. On the floor by my feet was
a copy of *Archaeology* magazine with a cover story on birth control
methods of early man. After the landlady had been taken care of, Raven
started in on the tribal policeman who had come to the house investi-
gating an untrue complaint about Cameron. Le and Floyd John and I
stood nodding politely.

During a pause, Le said that the three of us were going hunting and
wanted to borrow Adam's gun. This was the first I had heard of any
hunting. Adam seemed surprised at the request, but he agreed. From a
back room he brought the gun, a semiautomatic .22 rifle, wrapped in a
crocheted shawl. Then he rummaged around in a gym bag full of or-

ange pill bottles and found the gun clip and a black cloth pouch full of hollow-point bullets, magnum size. He gave the gun to Le, and Le immediately gave it to me, I don't know why. I was uncomfortable standing there in the laundry with it, so I went out to my car and opened the back and laid the gun inside. Then I took the paper bag of cigarettes we had intended for Zachary Bear Shield and gave them to Raven, who was walking Le and Floyd John back to the car. She looked in the bag and then said, "Sir, I thank you," inclining her head and giving me her thin hand. Le told her that we planned to go hunting Sunday morning and would have the gun back to them sometime next week.

Then we drove to Pine Ridge, and to White Clay for the customary purchase. A guy who had promised to cut firewood for Le needed 50-weight motor oil for the chainsaw, so we bought some at the Pine Ridge supermarket, Sioux Nation. Then we headed back to Oglala. I asked Le what the story was with this hunting expedition. He said, "There's lots of mule deer in the hills behind Aunt Rose White Magpie's house. She says she sees them every day. You and me and Floyd John will drive as far back in there as we can get an hour before sunup on Sunday morning and stake out a canyon when they're comin' down to drink, and we'll get us a deer." I dropped him and Floyd John off at Floyd John's trailer and gave them the rifle, happy to have it out of my car. I said I would pick them up about 5:30 Sunday morning, gave Le five dollars he asked for, and left.

On my way I stopped off at Florence's to see if my star quilt was ready yet. I had never been to her house by myself. One of her grandsons saw me through the storm door and called to her, "There's a white guy here!" She came to the door with her face set hard enough to scare away whoever it might be. Then she recognized me and smiled. The transformation from fierce to friendly was so sudden it dazzled me. She said my quilt wasn't done yet, that she'd sent it to the lady who does her batting for her. It should be ready by tomorrow, she said. I paid the balance I owed her and said I'd pick the quilt up on Sunday.

This time I went back to Chadron via a reservation road that's mostly gravel. The sun had gone down, and the sky at the horizon was multicolored, shining pink on the bottoms of dark clouds above. Viewed from high ground, the brightness in the west made the landscape to the horizon a deep silhouette-black, with occasional pieces of silver sky reflected in little stock ponds. But when the road led down into a hollow and out of the glare, then the details—the junipers, the ravines, the fence poles, the grasses—emerged in the twilight. I passed almost no houses, just occasional road signs riddled to steel mesh with bullet holes. I went by what appeared to be a thick paperback lying open in the middle of the road, and I stopped and went back to see. It was a collection of plays by Jean-Paul Sartre, including *The Flies*, *Dirty Hands*, and *The Respectful Prostitute*. It was in pretty good shape. I brought it with me. Ahead, on a small bluff by the side of the road, I saw two boys standing on a ridge, one in a dark hooded jacket. As a car passed coming the other way, one of the boys suddenly and expertly threw something at it, bending at the waist with a quick sidearm motion.

I will now describe the town of White Clay, Nebraska. One morning when I had nothing else planned I walked around the town. White Clay, White Clay! Site of so many fistfights, and of shootings and beatings and stabbings! Next-to-last stop of so many cars whose final stop was a crash! Junkyard, dusty setting for sprawled bodies, vortex consuming the Oglala Sioux! Sad name to be coupled with the pretty name of Nebraska! White Clay, White Clay!

A man who worked for years as a bartender at the Jumping Eagle Bar in White Clay once spread his ten fingers before me and showed me the many scars on his hands from fistfights he'd been in there. He said he often broke up fights with a pump handle, and kept a loaded shotgun hanging behind the bar. So many mournful Oglala stories have White Clay at their end. When I was a kid I liked movies about Wild West towns, those saloon-filled places where a cowboy riding in on Main Street always heard raucous laughter, and a gunshot or two, and glass breaking, and the tinkling of a barroom piano. White Clay is a Wild West town survived into the present that shows how uncongenial such a place would really be. In White Clay, decades of barroom violence have smashed all the saloon windows and mirrors and broken all the stools over people's heads, and now no bars remain. Elsewhere, Indian bars bolt stools and other furniture immovably to the floor and serve drinks only in flimsy plastic cups that can't be used as weapons.

White Clay has gone even further—there are abandoned houses and grain silos where you can drink protected somewhat from the weather, but the town's liquor sales are now all carry-out. Today no commercial establishment in White Clay allows its customers to drink indoors.

White Clay is two rows of stores and houses that line its main street, Nebraska Highway 87, for about a block and a half. Some of the buildings are of wood, with porch roofs extending over the dirt sidewalk and high false fronts like town buildings in Western movies. Others are made of cinder blocks, with thick windows of opaque glass bricks or small, slitlike window openings with bars and steel mesh imprisoning red neon Budweiser signs. About two dozen people live in White Clay. The town has four stores that sell alcoholic beverages—beer and malt liquor only. It also has a Napa auto-parts store (now closed), a Big A auto-parts store (also closed), a car-repair shop that sells auto parts, and a convenience store that sells some auto parts. There's a post office, a secondhand store, two grocery stores, and a pawnshop. Some of the buildings on the main street are boarded shut. The side streets are all unpaved. A wreckage of beer cans and bottles, with other miscellany—a broken shopping cart, a baby's shoe—accumulates in drifts here and there.

Even at 9:30 in the morning, White Clay effervesces and bubbles as if acid were eating it away. On this particular Saturday, there were loud cars cruising slowly, laughter, shouts. A group of tall men drinking 24-ounce beers stood by the side door of the Jumping Eagle Inn, a package store which is not an inn. Two gray-faced women in heavy plaid flannel shirts conferred by the side of the road, then smiled together and set out at a walk. Because White Clay is within walking distance of the reservation, the town usually has a lot of pedestrians. When the crowds get too big or unruly, the Nebraska highway patrol comes and makes everybody who's on foot walk back across the Pine Ridge border. Groups of evictees stagger along the highway out of town; when they see the Nebraska patrolman leave, they come back. Nebraska police made fifty-six alcohol-related arrests in White Clay in 1997. White Clay businesses paid almost $88,000 in Nebraska state liquor taxes in 1997, and another $152,000 in state sales tax, and more than 90 percent of their customers came from the reservation. But Pine Ridge residents jailed in Nebraska can't really get treatment at state-subsidized alcohol treatment centers in Nebraska. Those facilities are intended only for state residents.

Seen from the air, White Clay would look like a small appendage to a multiacre expanse of junk cars. The junkyard, on the prairie behind the Arrowhead Inn, is enclosed by a rambling fence made of corrugated iron alternating with chain-link mesh. The fence is permeable, and the cars provide some of the customers of the Arrowhead Inn with a place to sit as they drink. Women too preoccupied with drinking to be called prostitutes accompany men into the junkyard in exchange for a car radio or a bottle of wine. Large auto junkyards like this one are a common feature of Western towns that sell alcohol on the borders of Indian reservations.

I had brought Le to the Arrowhead Inn a number of times, but had never gone inside it myself. I expected it to be a dive, dark and dank and bestrewn. I was surprised at the near-clinical orderliness I met when I pulled open the heavy steel door. There was an expanse of bare floor ending at a waist-high counter that ran clear across the room, and behind the counter glass-front coolers full of beer in bottles and cans. A man in the back room heard me enter and he came quickly to the counter, ready for business this Saturday morning. Improvising, I asked for a 24-ounce can of Olde English Malt Liquor. He got me one from the cooler and charged me a dollar. He was short, round-cheeked, round-nosed, and bespectacled—like a small Santa Claus, but unsmiling and with security cameras for eyes. He wore jeans, a plaid shirt, suspenders, and a billed wool cap with a ball tassel on top. As I paid, I asked him where all the junk cars out back came from.

"Off the rez, mostly," he said.

"People bring 'em to trade?"

"They bring 'em to sell, trade. Yeah."

"Does the junkyard belong to you?"

"I'm the owner."

"Of this store and the junkyard both?"

"Uh-huh."

I said, "Thanks a lot," and picked up the beer and turned to go. In almost any store in the rural West, the person behind the counter will say, "So long" or "Have a good day," when you leave. But the owner of the Arrowhead Inn and adjoining junkyard said nothing, just watched me as I went out the door.

In the past, I had always thought of the devil as a wild, out-of-control figure—as a half-mad guy lit dramatically from below by leaping flames as his maniacal laughter echoed, a being of chaos caught up in the chaos he spawned. When I came out of the Arrowhead Inn, I had a new thought: If the devil exists, he's probably sober.

On Sunday morning I got up in my motel room at 4:30 and drove to Le's to go hunting. I took the back road from Chadron and saw one other car in thirty-eight miles. I was aware of the dusty smell of the car heater, the staticky uselessness of the radio, and the veering of the headlights back and forth across the darkness as the car swerved through the windings of the road. When I pulled into Le's driveway, I turned off the engine and the lights and stood for a while in the darkness beside the car and looked at the stars. One problem the Pine Ridge Reservation does not have is light pollution. The stars were like bullet holes, the galaxies like patterns of birdshot. I climbed the cinder block by Le's door and knocked. He got up immediately and came out of his dark house, and we went to Floyd John's.

Oglala was dead quiet. Le pounded on the door of Floyd John and Wanda's trailer, the sound distinct and singular in the stillness. A dog began to bark. It took a lot of pounding before a light came on inside, and a while longer before they opened the door. A single pale streak had appeared above the bluffs to the east. I thought we were just there to pick up Floyd John and go, but Le took off his coat and sat down on the couch and began to read a copy of *Reader's Digest*. I had brought some packaged doughnuts and a quart of orange juice, and I set them both on the kitchen counter. Nobody seemed much interested, but Wanda took a doughnut. She wasn't looking at any of us. I did not know her well enough to judge, but I got a feeling she was angry we were there. Le began reading out loud an article about a girl trapped under a derailed train in New Zealand. An infomercial was playing on the TV—about how troubled marriages could be saved through certain unspecified lovemaking techniques which the spokeswoman said were described in more detail on a video you could order by phone.

Outside, the sky was getting lighter. I couldn't understand the delay, but accepted this as the Indian way. Wanda and Floyd John were talking desultorily about a standoff between tribal factions at the Ojibwa

Reservation at Keweenaw Bay, Michigan. They said Oglala policemen might be called in to assist, because of the Oglala's familiarity with such problems. Floyd John began to clean up some messes the cat had made on the lineoleum, and a strong disinfectant smell filled the room. He said something to Le in Lakota, and they went into the hall and talked in Lakota there. After a few minutes Le came back and said that we couldn't go hunting because they didn't have the gun anymore. I asked where the gun was. Le said that it was in Oelrichs, that Floyd John had hocked it with a guy there. They said maybe we could get it back, so we drove the twenty-six miles to Oelrichs and Le and Floyd John knocked on the door of a house behind a gas station at 7:15 in the morning. But they returned empty-handed, and we drove back to Oglala.

And that was it for the hunting expedition. What exactly happened with the gun, and whether Adam and Raven ever saw it again, I never found out for sure. Oddly, I had sort of been looking forward to going hunting. Le had said that if we got a deer we would divide it up and give parts to different relatives. But after that morning we didn't mention hunting again. Back at the trailer, we stood around outside for a while. I had planned to begin the drive home today, so I figured I might as well get going. I said goodbye to Le and Floyd John. I remember seeing Wanda at the door of the trailer, but I don't remember whether I said goodbye to her or not.

Given how the morning had gone so far, I thought there wasn't much point in stopping by Florence's to pick up my star quilt. But I did anyway, and when I knocked at this early hour she answered right away and handed a large black plastic leaf bag with the quilt in it through the door. I put the quilt in the back without looking at it and drove home stopping only for gas—about eight hundred miles in about fourteen hours. My wife was still awake when I arrived. We sat for a while in the living room, and then I remembered the quilt and brought it in from the car. I took it from the plastic bag and unfolded it and laid it on the living-room floor. It was a bit larger than queen size. I could not stop looking at it—at the intricacy of the stitching, at the modulations in the colors, at the parts close up and the whole from farther away. I lay down on it, got up, looked some more. The quilt was like a map of the reservation, with the gravel roads and dirt lanes and one-water-tower towns and little houses in the middle of nowhere stitched together and made shiningly whole. I wished I had a gallery to hang it in.

Bad things seemed to happen on Pine Ridge on holidays in those years. On a Christmas morning, a man named Beto James Rodriguez shot three men with a rifle outside his house in the Eastridge housing in Pine Ridge village. Two were seriously wounded and the other died. They had apparently come to Rodriguez's house at 5:00 a.m., and a fist-fight started. Rodriguez later pleaded guilty to manslaughter and got six and two-thirds years in prison. On a Good Friday, the Holy Rosary Church at the Red Cloud School burned down. For unknown reasons a fire started early in the morning in the small chapel on one side of the church and quickly spread through the building. When firemen came they could do little but watch it burn, and the church was a total loss.

I got home from the reservation a few days before Thanksgiving. The day after Thanksgiving, Le called. He said that early Thanksgiving morning Wanda Kindle had been run over and killed by a car. She had driven to Chadron apparently to do the laundry and was returning by herself to Oglala on the reservation road when her car quit on her. It was about two in the morning. Very likely, no other cars came along. She began to walk. She made it to Highway 18, and as she was walking east toward Oglala, at the junction of the road to Loneman, she got hit by a pickup truck. The truck left the scene, and her body was not discovered until several hours after the accident. The driver, a woman, had been arrested on charges including leaving the scene of an accident and DWI.

I wired some money for her funeral expenses. I had talked to her just five days before. I thought of her leaving the car on that back road from Chadron and walking along in the night. I remembered her eyes that I never saw lit by joy, and the quiet, almost uninflected way she talked, and her dark silence as she moved about her kitchen making coffee on the morning we didn't go hunting. Mostly I remembered the complete conviction, free from any trace of hope, with which she said, "It looks pretty, but it's just a slum," as the lights of Pine Ridge village spread before us on the night when we were returning from the rodeo.

A week or two after her funeral, the newspaper *Indian Country Today* ran an obituary:

OGLALA—Wanda V. Kindle, 45, died Nov. 23, 1995, in Oglala, due to injuries received in an apparent hit-and-run accident.

Survivors include three sons, Shane Herrod and Shaun Herrod, both of Oglala, and Sheldon Herrod, Lawrence, Kan.; one daughter, Sonya Herrod, Ada, Okla.; three brothers, Fred Kindle, Ben Kindle and Ceferino Kindle, all of Oglala; four sisters, Kate Kindle and Catherine Starr, both of Oglala, Minnie Kindle, Columbus, Ohio, and Audrey Wallace, Dallas, Texas; and one grandchild.

Services were at Brother Rene Hall with the Rev. Asa Wilson and the Rev. Simon Looking Elk officiating . . .

Recently, I visited her grave. It's in a corner of Makasan Presbyterian Cemetery, behind the Presbyterian church west of Oglala. Her gravestone is of dark-pink granite carved with two blooming roses above her name. She must have liked roses; a wreath on a marker at the site of the accident always has an arrangement of artificial roses, and someone changes them from time to time. White quartzite stones decorate her grave plot, along with artificial flowers and a pinwheel of bright plastic. Tulips grow by the headstone. Like all the headstones in the cemetery, it faces east, where the view is of a plowed field and the Loneman water tower. To the north is more plowed ground and prairie rolling to distant pink-and-gray buttes wrinkled like old skin. To the west, the horizon is a wavering line. From the south comes the sound of cars on the highway where she died.

CHAPTER

8

Time was, a person could hitch a ride from the reservation up to Rapid City and drink in bars like Fitzgerald's, the Rainbow Ballroom, and the Coney Island Bar. They were "real humdingers," according to old men who remember them, with fights and prostitutes and wild goings-on. The Coney Island and the others are no more; many of the old bars along Main Street washed away in the big flood of 1972. From Rapid City a person could hop a freight and wake up the next day in Billings, Montana. As the train moved slowly, clanging through the center of town, a person could roll off onto the gravel right-of-way and take his pick among dozens of bars lining the tracks for blocks on both sides. A person might begin drinking in Billings one morning in midwinter and still be drinking there in spring. Old-timers remember Billings as a friendly place to drink, well supplied with ranchers who drank themselves and were usually ready to buy.

Streets in Billings are so wide they seem to bend slightly with the curvature of the earth. On the streets along the train tracks were bars called the Buffalo Bar, the Mexican Star, the Yukon, the Oasis, the Wheeler, the Mint, the Western. Of those, only the Western remains; recently, a patron at the Western looked up and down the long bar, whose lines seemed to converge at a vanishing point in the far distance, and asked the only other patron, "Is it always this quiet in here?" The bartender, overhearing, apologized, "Yes, looks like it's going to be pretty quiet tonight." On the adjoining blocks, the other bars are gone. At the Oasis Bar, the neon sign remains, pieces of broken neon tubing hanging down. The sign depicts a camel and a saguaro cactus, an unlikely but thirst-provoking combination. On the building's fake log front, Toni Whitewolf, or someone thinking of her, has penciled her name. At the Mint Bar on April 6, 1947, a ranch hand named John H. Emery was heard to say to a truckdriver named Clyde Kipp, his wife's ex-husband, "You think I'm kidding." Then he pulled a .38 pistol and shot Clyde Kipp dead. Emery was sentenced to life in prison. 2619 Montana Avenue, where the Mint Bar used to stand, is now a lot for guest and employee parking at the Sheraton Billings Hotel.

Why do neon signs look more beautiful in arid places? Take the signs of Los Angeles or Las Vegas, for example—maybe it has to do with the clarity of light in dry desert air. The neon signs of the bars by the railroad tracks in Billings used to be something to see, especially on a summer evening when the sunset was fading in the west and the wind brought the smell of dust and cattle and diesel exhaust. Prominent among these signs was one for a bar called Casey's Golden Pheasant. On top, the sign had a long-tailed bird outlined in neon of yellow-gold, and below that the name of the bar in red and blue. At the bottom of the sign was the word FIREWATER, not in neon but painted, in letters slanted to the right with multicolor flames coming off them. The word suggested that Indians drank in this bar, which was true. A veteran Indian drinker of the 1950s and '60s called Casey's Golden Pheasant "the preeminent Indian bar in this country."

Indians from many tribes drank at Casey's. Its owner, Casey Collett, encouraged them to come; advertising firewater in his sign might have meant that he considered them good for business, too. The reservation of the Crow tribe is closest to Billings, and there were often Crow Indians in the bar. Sioux and Cheyenne drinkers sometimes harassed the Crow for their history of service as scouts for the U.S. Army in the last century, and particularly for guiding Generals Crook and Custer in the Little Bighorn campaign of 1876. The anti-Crow drinkers had a song that ended *"You helped Custer! Yaaaaaaaa!"*—after which the barroom melee usually began. Casey handed out business cards for his bar bearing the motto "All Kinds of Drinks," but the Indian drinkers in Casey's often preferred gallon jugs of wine. Patrons at the bar sometimes chipped in for a gallon of Virginia Dare red to send to the Indians in the back room. That room was called the Snakepit, and according to reputation, awful things went on in there.

2622 Minnesota Avenue, where Casey's Golden Pheasant used to be, is now a vacant lot. It's as you might expect—low heap of concrete rubble, dead pigeon, ground-hugging weeds, water-stained paperback copy of *Fade the Heat*, by Jay Brandon. You can see the shadow outline of the building on the wall of the boarded-up building still standing alongside. I paced off twenty steps from the sidewalk as a guess of where the back room called the Snakepit might have been. If the brawls and gang rapes said to have occurred there left any ghostly traces, they were undetectable by me. It's just a vacant lot like any other. In Billings, an establishment called Casey's Golden Pheasant remains. It's now a restaurant and bar, under different ownership—Casey Collett died years ago—on North Broadway, a few blocks away. It still has Casey's original neon sign. It specializes in Cajun dishes like gumbo and blackened halibut, and has signed photos of celebrities like Lou Gossett Jr., and Tommy Smothers hanging on the walls. I have never seen Indians in there, but then I have been there only a few times. I don't think it is any longer the preeminent Indian bar.

I knew that the old bars in White Clay, Nebraska—Kelley's Cove and Toad's Tavern and the Jumping Eagle, and others—had all closed down. But as I traveled the country and asked sometimes about Indian bars, I found that they seemed to be disappearing elsewhere, too. In Brooklyn, New York, in the neighborhood where the Mohawk high-steel men once lived, the famous Indian bar used to be the Nevins Bar & Grill, at other times called the Wigwam. Joseph Mitchell wrote about it in his great magazine piece "The Mohawks in High Steel." The bar he described was crowded with Indians, and it stocked one Montreal ale and two Montreal beers, for its Mohawk customers from Canada and vicinity. When it was the Wigwam, it had a sign over the door that said, THE GREATEST IRON WORKERS IN THE WORLD PASS THROUGH THESE DOORS. Today there is a take-out pizza place where the Nevins Bar & Grill used to be. It receives money and dispenses pizzas through a security barricade of steel gratings and thick glass or plastic. I hollered through a metal slit to a man back there, and he said that he was the owner and that the Indians now drink at the Doray Tavern, at the corner of Third and Atlantic nearby.

In the Doray Tavern, I found one Indian, a stocky man named Ronnie Tarbell, on a stool at the bar. He wore metal-rim glasses, a blue work shirt, and his thinning brown hair combed straight back. With a Brooklyn accent, he said that he had worked for thirty years as a high-steel foreman and was now retired. Mohawk Indians used to rule this neighborhood, but not anymore, he said. They used to be able to beat up everybody, even the Italians; but where there used to be three hundred Mohawk families on these blocks, now there was maybe one. Bars with mostly Indian customers like the Spar and the Wigwam, he said, were now long gone. Though he spoke of local Mohawks mainly in the past tense, several times he remarked of guys walking by, "He's married to an Indian." The current state of affairs seemed to dishearten him not at all. "I'm not an American and I'm not a Canadian," he said. "I'm a North American from the Kahnawake Reserve, which is older than the U.S. and older than New York State and older than Canada. My people are the natural people, the people of the earth. We've always been here and we'll always be here. After the white man has destroyed everything, and even after the buildings we built for him have fallen down and disappeared, we'll still be here."

Los Angeles, the city with more American Indians than any other, used to have lots of Indian bars. The Columbine, the Ritz, the Shrimp Boat, and the Irish Pub are among the names that people recall. A while ago when I was in L.A. I went looking for those bars without success. I did, however, find the L.A. landmark called Indian Alley. The name appears on no map or street sign, but Indians everywhere know it, and many thousands have been to it. It's one of the most famous unofficial public spaces in the country—a narrow alley in the skid row district of downtown L.A., in the middle of the block bounded by Main Street, Los Angeles Street, Winston Street, and Fifth. The alley also continues partway down the block between Fifth and Sixth. Back walls of commercial buildings enclose it on both sides, and it has the usual skid-row litter of flattened cardboard packing crates, squashed fruit, Styrofoam take-out containers and broken glass. But the tribal names spray-painted on the bricks, the AIM slogans, the sketches of eagle feathers and war ponies, and the scrawled names and hometowns of Indians from reservations all over the country give it an aura of unceded territory, of native ground.

There's an Indian Health Service crisis intervention center at the corner of the alley and Winston Street. Near it I found a tall, copper-red man with pockmarked skin and long gray hair standing with a smaller man in a Hawaiian shirt and black jeans. I asked them if they knew where I could find the Irish Pub—I had read it was in that neighborhood. They said they both had heard of it, but that it closed down long ago. The names of other bars I mentioned rang no bells. A middle-aged woman in a T-shirt that said HOPI came out of the crisis center and joined the discussion, as did two other guys walking by. "There's no bars around here where Indians can drink anymore," the pockmarked man said. "They kick you right out on the street." They all agreed that in L.A. there are no more Indian bars.

Same thing in Minneapolis–St. Paul, in Phoenix, and in Butte, Montana—the bars mentioned in Indian stories from the not-distant past seem mostly to have vanished without a trace. Perhaps new ones have replaced them that I haven't heard of yet. But the Red Front, the Harbor Bar, the Silver King, the Trade Winds, the Busy Bee are forgotten and gone; or perhaps the former bar has been subsumed into a nineties-era hangout for college students, its name changed to Grandma's Saloon & Deli and with a volleyball court added alongside. Bars have an odd relationship to history. Generally they spring up in a moment, provide a setting for all that transpires when people drink, close down without warning, and become a copy shop or similar place containing no clue of what used to be there. Rarely, a momentous event will single out a bar for longer-lasting fame: for example, the No. 10 Saloon in Deadwood, South Dakota, where Jack McCall shot and killed the gambler and gunfighter James "Wild Bill" Hickok as he sat playing poker and holding a pair of aces and a pair of eights, the hand now known as the Dead Man's Hand. Hickok's shooting, in August 1876, was so storied that the bars succeeding the No. 10 on the site have never forgotten it, and posted homemade signs about it that survive in the current occupant to this day. Usually, though, people don't go to bars to remember, and after a particular bar is gone no one much wants to remember it. Not long ago I was walking down the Main Street in Miles City, Montana, where many old Western bars still survive. On the front of the Montana Bar I saw a metal plaque that said this bar, in existence since 1902, had been entered in the National Register of Historic Places. That brought me up short; I had never seen a historic marker on a bar before.

Once in a while I came across a bar I'd heard of that seemed pretty much unchanged. On Highway 39 in southeastern Montana just before the Northern Cheyenne Reservation I stopped at the Jimtown Bar, a drinking hangout of the Northern Cheyenne. It achieved minor fame when it appeared in the 1989 movie *Powwow Highway*. Its door is of splintered plywood painted red and its door handle is a piece of twine, and inside it's your basic Western roadhouse—video poker games, neon beer signs, Beach Boys music on the jukebox. One unusual feature is the bar stools of thick pine log cross-sections bolted to the floor. Outside on a weekend morning eight Indians sat against the wall in the sunshine, waiting for opening time. On the bar's sign on the roof is a large silhouette of that too-common image in Indian country, *The End of the Trail*—the Indian warrior slumped forward on his pony, after the famous sculpture. George Custer passed by the site of the Jimtown Bar in June 1876 as he led the Seventh Cavalry up the Rosebud River valley on the way to the battle of the Little Bighorn. Just across the Rosebud valley and within sight of the Jimtown Bar are the Deer Medicine Rocks, tall sandstone outcroppings carved with Indian pictographs. The pictographs are of buffalo, sheep, the sun, horses, and a convincingly rendered grizzly bear. One of the rocks is marked with a long gray-blue line where lightning struck it. At the base of the lightning mark, and pointing to it with what appears to be a feathered lance, is a carving of a figure in a headdress said to be a medicine man.

The most authentic Western bar I found is the Longhorn Saloon, in Scenic, South Dakota, a little town in badland country about seven miles north of the Pine Ridge Reservation line. The Longhorn used to have a prominent sign in Lakota on its front telling Indians to go away, but changed that policy long ago. It is perhaps best described as a cowboy *and* Indian bar. Its history is long; I know of one murder that has taken place in the Longhorn, though what other acts of violence there may have been I did not ask. The name Scenic is a laconic understatement to describe the landscape that surrounds the town. The immense horizontals stretch all across and around, the long, low buttes and pastel badlands varying endlessly under open sky. The entry to the Longhorn Saloon is beneath a porch roof propped up by unfinished posts and topped with coils of barbed wire. All along the roof and the building's false front are dozens of cow skulls, affixed in decorative profusion. Once you're inside, the skulls make more sense. The saloon's ceiling is low, no more than eight feet high, and the floor is ankle-deep in fresh wood shavings: in the vastness of this near-desert, the saloon suggests the cozy burrow of a predator, complete with an accumulation of bones just outside.

Cattle brands decorate the ceiling. On the walls are pairs of long-horn cattle horns, chaps, spurs, and cartoons of ranching mishaps signed by a cowboy artist named Gumbo Pete. I played the video gambling games and quickly lost fifteen dollars while listening to a weathered blond barmaid tell a story: "He was *old* and he was *bald* and he had *no teeth*, and she was pretty and about twenty-two, so in love with him she sat right here at the end of the bar while he was talking and just *stared!*" The wind-scoured South Dakota sky over the badlands was a bright blue that afternoon, but in the Longhorn Saloon cigarette smoke hung thick. A column of sunlight slanting through it from a window made a luminous gray shaft above an unoccupied table piled with perhaps three dozen empty Budweiser cans.

On the reservation and elsewhere in Indian country you get used to seeing images of the Budweiser brand. If you notice a speck on the roadside up ahead and guess that it is an empty Budweiser case, very often you will be right. Often a trash barrel full to the top will turn out to contain mostly Budweiser cans. The ground at popular outdoor drinking spots—by the cement picnic tables near the powwow grounds, or at a parking area beside a swimming hole on the White River—will often be a mosaic of pieces of broken brown-glass Budweiser bottles, some of the pieces still held together by the paper labels. Bottles thrown at bridge supports and other targets are often Budweiser bottles. The sweetish smell of Budweiser hangs around the places where the bottles are smashed, and in seat covers where Budweiser is spilled, and on people's clothes, and probably sometimes on DWI victims in the morgue. It's a smell you encounter often on the reservation. The distributor of Anheuser-Busch products for northwestern Nebraska sells more Budweiser in White Clay, Nebraska, than in any other town in his territory; package stores in White Clay account for about a third of his total Budweiser sales.

People sometimes say they'd like to buy a whole beer truck full of Budweiser and drink it dry. On the Standing Rock Sioux Reservation in northern South Dakota, a man from the town of Bullhead did. Some years ago the man received an oil settlement of $30,000 and spent $25,000 of it on a Budweiser delivery truck stocked with three hundred cases of beer. He parked the truck beside his house, which it was longer than, and had a nonstop party until all three hundred cases were gone.

Once, as Le and I were driving somewhere, we passed an unusual abundance of Budweiser cases along the road. I asked Le why there were so many of them. Misunderstanding me, he replied, "Used to be you never saw empty beer cases, because everyone on the rez had woodstoves, and they saved the cases and tore 'em up to start their fires. Now, though, people mostly have gas heat. So they just throw the cases away."

"No, I mean why are they all *Budweiser* cases?"

"Well, Budweiser is the biggest maker of beer in the world, so it figures Indians would drink a lot of it. And then Budweiser has all that advertising. Indians buy because of advertising, same as anyone else."

Indeed, Budweiser beer and Sioux Indians have been linked in the company's advertising for more than a hundred years. The brand was created by Anheuser-Busch Breweries in St. Louis in the late 1800s and became the first nationally distributed beer. Adolphus Busch, president of Anheuser-Busch, believed that advertising was vital to selling a beer nationwide. Part of his promotional plans involved "point-of-sale" items—plaster wall mountings, scenes of the Budweiser brewery painted on glass, jackknives bearing Busch's picture, and so on—distributed to bars. In 1888 Busch bought a St. Louis saloon which displayed a large diorama painting of Custer's Last Stand. He hired an artist named Otto Becker to paint a smaller version of the battle scene and make a lithograph of it. Becker produced a 24 by 40–inch painting showing Custer with his sword raised at the center of a maelstrom of Indians and cavalrymen, with Indians on horseback riding from the rear to finish him off and a dust-obscured prairie landscape beyond. (Some of the fallen figures in the painting's foreground Becker took from Gustave Doré's illustration for Dante's *Inferno*, as a scholar recently pointed out.)

Becker finished the painting and had it lithographed in 1896, and the company printed 15,000 copies of the picture bearing the title *Custer's Last Fight*, along with the company's name. Since 1896 Anheuser-Busch has reprinted the picture many times, in over a million copies, and it has hung behind countless bars. Many hours of barroom contemplation have been spent staring at this scene of the final moments of Custer, a circumstance that might have amused him, considering that after an embarrassing episode at the age of twenty-one he never had another drink in his life. In 1939 Otto Becker sold the original of the painting to Anheuser-Busch, and it hangs today in the company's corporate headquarters, where people probably don't think much about the fate of the actual Sioux Indians who drink their beer.

Many fortunes have been made selling alcohol to Indians. John Jacob Astor, America's richest man in the early nineteenth century, amassed his original wealth in the furs-for-whiskey trade as owner of the American Fur Company of New York City. Among the many Indians on the losing end of the trade were the Oglala Sioux, who suffered from the competition between Astor's company and others as traders used free whiskey to lure customers away. Fights brought on by whiskey in the Oglala camps caused deaths and the separation of bands, leaving enmity between them that lasted into reservation times. Throughout the 1800s Congress passed law after law prohibiting the sale of "ardent spirits" in Indian country, to little effect. A man who sold whiskey to Indians on the northern Plains after the Civil War called the laws against the trade "practically a dead letter," in a book he wrote about his career. "I make no excuse for the whiskey trade," he wrote. "It was wrong, all wrong, and none realized it better than we when we were dispensing the stuff."

In the early reservation years, old-timers recalled, alcohol use actually went down. On the Oglala reservation, laws against being caught drinking were enforced with high fines and sentences of a year and a day in tribal jail. But the same act that did away with allotment of tribal lands—the Indian Reorganization Act of 1934, which also provided for tribal constitutions and representative government—allowed for more leniency in anti-drinking laws. By 1940, the alcohol problem on Pine Ridge had become severe. A House Resolution in Congress in 1953 finally removed the old federal laws prohibiting Indians from buying guns, liquor, and ammunition. Control of alcohol on the reservations has since been left up to individual tribes, and today only 91 of America's 293 reservations allow liquor sales. On Pine Ridge, although the suffering from alcohol is ancient, help for it remains hard to find. As far as I know, no one who made money from selling alcohol to Indians has ever contributed anything toward repair of the damage alcohol has done. And although statistics say the alcoholism rate among adults on Pine Ridge is above 65 percent, there is as yet no alcohol treatment center on the reservation.

The late Frank Fools Crow, an Oglala traditionalist, medicine man, and supporter of AIM, still affectionately referred to by some as "Granpa Frank," said in a biography of him published in 1979, "Alcohol is the bitterest curse we have, and it has done more to weaken and destroy us than anything else. We had no strong drink, no such thing as whiskey, before the white men came to our country. We didn't need it then and we don't need or want it now."

About fifteen miles west of the reservation line, by its northwest corner, is the little town of Buffalo Gap, South Dakota. The town is named for a prominent geographic feature about a mile away—a gap in the Black Hills made by the valley of a creek which once provided the buffalo herds with an easy way in and out of the Hills. Charlotte Black Elk says that Sioux cosmology assigned a particular star to Pte Tali Yapa, the Sioux name for Buffalo Gap. She says that in former times, when the star we call Mirfak in the constellation Perseus began to approach the sun, it signaled the beginning of the buffalo's spring migrations through the gap. Wesley Whiteman, a Cheyenne holy man, said that the sun dance sacred to many Plains tribes originated at Buffalo Gap, where the buffalo themselves first performed it and later taught it to the Indians. Two low hills rise on either side of the entrance to the gap; they are hard to miss from Highway 79 as you cross Beaver Creek just east of the Hills. If you turn off onto the gravel road leading up the gap, you proceed along the creek and follow a little north-south sidle around some bluffs. In the next moment you have gone from rolling prairie to mountain canyon as easily as switching geographic channels. In another moment, mountain landscape has enclosed you on all sides. The gap is one of the magical places of the West.

Indians used the gap to enter or leave the Black Hills, and fur trappers and other early white travelers followed them. After the discovery of gold on French Creek in the Black Hills in 1874, thousands of miners and fortune seekers came into the Hills, many of them from the east by way of the gap. A merchant heading for the Hills in 1876 described for a Wisconsin newspaper how his party shot and wounded an Indian who he said sneaked up on their camp in the night; in the morning they found a lariat and some blood nearby, and the place where a pony had been staked, and more blood, about a quarter mile away. The merchant wrote that this happened "at Buffalo Gap where half a dozen battles have already been fought."

In 1885 the Fremont, Elkhorn & Missouri River Railroad built an extension north from Chadron, Nebraska, along the eastern edge of the Hills. The tracks stopped on the prairie near the gap, and there the town of Buffalo Gap was founded. During its time as the railroad terminus and a departure point for the gold mines in the Hills, Buffalo Gap became one of the wildest Western towns ever. It soon had a population of 3,000, many buildings made of green lumber, and hundreds of dwellings of tent canvas. A local history says that it also had "four blacksmith shops, 23 saloons, 17 hotels and eating places, two sporting houses and a whole row of small ones, four general stores, two drug stores, four Chinese laundries . . ." George Boland, the town's first postmaster, responded with irritation to a U.S. postal inspector concerned about Boland's handling of the mail, which he had sorted into the different pigeonholes of a wooden beer-bottle crate. "There's your god damned Post Office, Mr. Inspector," Boland said, throwing the beer crate out the back door of his saloon. "Now you git."

A Frenchman named Galiot François Edmond, Baron de Mandat-Grancey, visited the young town of Buffalo Gap while traveling the West in 1887. He was wry about the real-estate frenzy that had possessed the inhabitants: "The experts predict that Third Avenue is going to become the meeting place of the elite, the fashionable resort—but they ask themselves if Pine Street will be able to contain all the banks which will accumulate there." One night during the baron's stay, some cowboys from a local ranch rode through town and shot out windows in the middle of the night, and when the citizens returned fire, two of the cowboys were killed. The next day the cowboys came back and threatened to burn Buffalo Gap to the ground. The baron noted that what seemed to worry the citizens most about the incident was what it would do to the value of the town's lots.

Like the dreams of many Great Plains towns, Buffalo Gap's did not materialize. The completion of the railroad to Rapid City in 1896 ended the town's importance as a terminus and caused a decline. A big fire one winter destroyed much of the town. The residents built an imposing three-story schoolhouse of red sandstone on a hill, but people continued to move away. By 1910, the population of Buffalo Gap had fallen to 280. The town's reputation for nightlife and "rather wide open dances" (as a county history puts it) endured its change of fortunes, and rowdy evenings still occurred. A shooting just outside the community auditorium in the late 1950s, one longtime resident recalled, "slowed the dances for a while." The last passenger train stopped in Buffalo Gap in 1954; the last high school class graduated in 1963. The Southern Hills Bank, founded in Buffalo Gap in 1910, survived the Depression, only to close in 1994. The schoolhouse continued to hold classes for the elementary grades, but in 1997 it also closed, and the children now go to school in Hot Springs, about twelve miles away. Fewer than two hundred people live in Buffalo Gap today.

I walked around Buffalo Gap's red dirt and gravel streets one summer afternoon a while ago. Though the town has shrunk, the streets remain as optimistically wide as they were in 1895. A Methodist church, gleaming white and with a sign saying EVERYONE WELCOME, anchored one street, tall rows of silver maples held down others. There were some neat one-story houses, a few houses falling down, and a house under construction, evidently abandoned, also falling down. Some of the storefronts had elaborate pressed-tin fronts, boarded-shut doors, and blank display windows. The grain elevators by the railroad tracks were still active, with sparrows eating spills of grain on the ground nearby. Against the side of a building behind the elevator an assortment of galvanized-metal stock tanks of various sizes leaned on their sides, the ten-foot ones inside the twenty-foot ones inside the thirty-footers, like a set of nesting cups.

On a corner stood Buffalo Gap's neat frame post office, a definite improvement on a beer-bottle crate. Across the street was a bar called the Stockman. The doors to the bar, front and side, were locked, and no cars were parked nearby. I walked around the building and looked at it from roof to ground. Its siding was of overlapping fiberboard painted a barn red now so faded you could see in places that it used to be a light bluish-green, with rows of inch-wide unfinished lath running vertically every foot or so for decoration or to help hold the siding on. A rickety false front made the building's single story look taller from that angle, but from the side you could see the roof, half of it wood-shingled and the other half covered with tar paper. Rising from the tar paper was a chimney of cinder blocks extended with a piece of corrugated-iron pipe. If it weren't for the big air-conditioning unit bulging from a window, and the air-conditioner filters lying below it in the heap of silver-maple leaves, the building would have looked just like the ad hoc frontier structures in photos of Buffalo Gap from its boom times over a hundred years ago. People in town believe this building may even be that old.

Twenty-seven years ago this bar was owned by a man named Bill Zuber. Back then it was called Bill's Bar. Zuber bought it from a man named Degnan and remodeled it to make it more homey. He put in a fireplace, enlarged the dance floor, and hired bands on the weekends. Lots of young people came. On Saturday, January 20, 1973, a thirty-year-old man named Darld Schmitz who worked in a gas station in the Black Hills town of Custer drove to Bill's Bar with a friend, Harold Wheeler, and two women they had picked up earlier in the evening in a bar in Hot Springs. Schmitz was an Air Force veteran and father of three. His wife had had their third child in Rapid City just the day before, and Schmitz had visited her there before going drinking with Wheeler. Schmitz and the others had four or five drinks apiece at Bill's Bar and stayed until closing time.

While they were there, a twenty-two-year-old Oglala man named Wesley Bad Heart Bull arrived with some friends. Just outside the bar an argument began, and the bouncer didn't let Bad Heart Bull in. He remained in the street out front rattling an eighteen-inch log chain he carried with him and threatening departing customers. Bad Heart Bull was from Hot Springs and had a record of nineteen arrests for assault and public intoxication. The Bad Heart Bulls were of the same Oglala band as Red Cloud, the *Ite Sica* (Bad Faces), and Wesley's relative Amos Bad Heart Bull was a well-known artist whose ledger book drawings from the late 1800s and early 1900s are an important source for the pre-reservation history of the tribe. Wesley was still standing outside under the single streetlight at 2:00 a.m., when the bar closed and the patrons began to leave.

A man named James Geary, nicknamed "Mad Dog," had words with Bad Heart Bull when he came out. Trina Bad Heart Bull, Wesley's younger sister, later said that Geary picked the fight, jumping from his car and shouting that he could "lick an Indian." All witnesses including Geary agreed that he and Bad Heart Bull began to fight, and most said that Bad Heart Bull then knocked Geary unconscious with the log chain. Darld Schmitz and his companions had left the bar just before the fight started. Schmitz said that they got in their car and saw the fight in the street, and that he and Wheeler and Jane LaChelt, one of the women with them, got out. Mrs. LaChelt ran over to try to get Bad Heart Bull to stop. She said Bad Heart Bull was continuing to beat Geary on the ground, but other witnesses said he had stopped. She knew Bad Heart Bull and was distantly related to him. She said she tried to grab him, but someone pulled her away.

Schmitz said he took out his pocketknife and told Bad Heart Bull to drop the chain. He and other witnesses said that Bad Heart Bull came at him and swung the chain at him. Schmitz said he ducked, tried to push Bad Heart Bull back with his left hand, and stabbed him with the knife in his right hand. Several witnesses said that at about this time they heard gunshots, a coincidence that was never explained. A friend of Bad Heart Bull's tried to hit Schmitz over the head with a bottle, but some people stopped him. Bad Heart Bull fell to the ground, got up, and said, "I've been stabbed." Schmitz said he saw blood on his knife and left immediately.

Bad Heart Bull collapsed again, and friends helped him to a car and drove off toward Hot Springs to take him to the hospital. On the way the car ran out of oil and burned out its engine. The car taking Geary to the hospital passed the stalled car along the road, came back, and loaded Bad Heart Bull in with his victim. The delay occupied some time. Schmitz's knife had just penetrated Bad Heart Bull's aorta, and he bled to death before he reached the hospital.

Bad Heart Bull was stabbed on the morning of January 21. Police arrested Darld Schmitz in Custer the same day. He admitted the stabbing and gave police the knife he had used. After questioning he was released on a $5,000 bond and ordered to appear before the county court in Custer on January 22. Hobart Gates, the Custer County district attorney, did not think he could get a jury to convict Schmitz of any crime more serious than second-degree manslaughter, so he charged him with that. A judge set a date for a preliminary hearing about a month away and released Schmitz on continuation of bond.

At the time of the Bad Heart Bull stabbing, the American Indian Movement had just finished a busy year. In February 1972 it had led a successful protest over the beating and death of an Indian named Raymond Yellow Thunder in Gordon, Nebraska, south of the reservation. AIM had brought hundreds of people from Pine Ridge to Gordon for a rally which shook up the town, got the authorities to make a number of concessions, and won the admiration of a lot of people on the reservation. The big flood in Rapid City in June killed 238 people, nearly half of them American Indian, and AIM helped provide food and housing for the survivors. In October AIM organized the Trail of Broken Treaties, a car caravan that crossed the country from Seattle and San Francisco to Washington, D.C., to remind America of the many treaties made with Indian nations that remained unfulfilled. That protest led in early November to the takeover and occupation of the Bureau of Indian Affairs headquarters in Washington, a much-reported event that lasted seven days.

When AIM learned of the Bad Heart Bull killing, it demanded that the charge against Schmitz be changed to first-degree murder. AIM leaders claimed that witnesses had heard Schmitz say he was "going to kill him an Indian" earlier on the night of the twentieth, that Bad Heart Bull was set upon by white youths who goaded him to fight, and that he was stabbed many times. AIM leader Russell Means called for a conference on the Bad Heart Bull case with county officials to take place in Custer on the morning of February 6, and AIM told its supporters that there would be a mass rally at the courthouse on that day. Custer County had never had a riot before, but people there had seen enough of AIM in the newspapers and on TV to fear one. The county assembled highway patrolmen, federal officers, and FBI agents to keep order, a force of perhaps seventy in all. The governor put the South Dakota National Guard on alert.

An AIM caravan of cars with two hundred people arrived in front of the courthouse early in the afternoon of the sixth. The courthouse was a Victorian-era brick building with high windows and wide front steps leading to wooden doors. The county sheriff met the protesters at the top of the steps and said that only four AIM people would be allowed inside at a time, so AIM leaders Dennis Banks and Russell Means and two others went in. Means, an Oglala on his father's side who had grown up mostly in California, was known for his oratory and his dark, photogenic good looks. He had organized an Indian center in Cleveland, Ohio, and had gained national notice for a protest he led against Chief Wahoo, the caricature-Indian mascot of the Cleveland Indians baseball team. Dennis Banks, a Chippewa from the Leech Lake Reservation in Minnesota, was more a politician and less an actor than Means. He had founded AIM with two other Minnesota Indians, and said that the decision to work for Indian justice had come to him while he was serving time in prison. Craggy-faced as the Indian profile of popular imagination, he sometimes smiled an easygoing smile like a person just having a good time.

When Hobart Gates began to explain to the AIM delegation the reasons for the manslaughter charge, Dennis Banks replied with a long speech about the continuing injustices Indians suffered, pointing out that if the killer had been an Indian and the victim white the charge would certainly have been more severe. Gates tried to answer, but the AIM people kept talking on top of his words. The conference became mostly angry speeches from the AIM side. Russell Means later wrote that the riot started when police on the front steps beat Sarah Bad Heart Bull, Wesley's mother. Other sources say it started when the protesters outside threw rocks through the courthouse windows and broke down the front doors.

Police and protesters began to fight inside and outside the building. The highway patrolmen had recently been issued new riot sticks, but had not been trained in their use, and Indians took the sticks from some of them and clubbed them. The police had helmets, and more Indians than police ended up with head injuries. Outside, two police cars were vandalized and burned. Means says that inside he and his brothers and a Choctaw with a black belt in karate were mowing the policemen down, and that at one point he scratched D.A. Hobart Gates across the face with his long fingernails. AIM supporters did some damage to the gas station where Darld Schmitz worked, and took gasoline to set the courthouse on fire. (Means says the fire was caused by tear-gas canisters police shot in through the window.) A nearby log-cabin building that housed the Chamber of Commerce burned to the ground (also the result of tear gas, says Means), but firemen stopped the courthouse blaze. Amazingly, no one was killed. A former Custer County district attorney who has watched a video of the riot says that for a few frames you can see the finger of a highway patrolman reach for the trigger of his gun, but he has gloves on—snow had begun to fall—and he can't get his finger through the trigger guard.

Police arrested thirty-six Indians, including Dennis Banks and Russell Means. Banks was charged with burglary, arson, rioting while armed with a dangerous weapon, and assault without intent to kill. Means was charged with two counts of arson and one count of rioting. Both were released on bond. On February 9, riots occurred in Rapid City, with damage to several bars and more arrests. A big AIM rally in Sturgis, South Dakota, met a larger force of police and deputized volunteers, and ended peacefully. After the Custer riot, county authorities got reinforcements from the Custer County Civil Defense, the Forest Service, and the Volunteer Fire Department, and no further violence happened there.

Events went rolling on. Darld Schmitz's trial was moved from Custer to Rapid City, but by the time it began, AIM's attention had gone elsewhere: the occupation was in progress at Wounded Knee. AIM's charges against Darld Schmitz did not prove out in court. Schmitz's defense attorney, in his summation, said that Wesley Bad Heart Bull had taken up the sword and had perished by the sword. The jury agreed and acquitted Schmitz. Although the national news had given much play to the Custer riot, Schmitz's acquittal received almost no mention. Wounded Knee had claimed the front pages; no other story on the subject of Indians would get such notice nationwide until a few tribes began to make millions of dollars from casino gambling in the early 1990s. In the midst of the occupation, the actor Marlon Brando, an AIM sympathizer, won an Academy Award for his portrayal of Don Corleone in the movie *The Godfather*. During the televised awards ceremony he sent an Apache actress named Sacheen Little-feather to refuse the award as a protest against the movie industry's treatment of Indians. Among most people who were following the news back then, this is the moment of Native American protest that today remains clearest in their minds.

The Wounded Knee occupation ended in May, and the government arrested over a hundred people in connection with it. Federal prosecutors put some on trial and sent some to jail. Dennis Banks and Russell Means, as leaders, were tried together on charges including grand larceny and conspiracy. A team of lawyers led by William Kunstler and Mark Lane defended them. After a trial of ten months in federal court in St. Paul, Minnesota, the judge dismissed all charges and said he was ashamed of how the government had handled the case. Nine months later, in June 1975, Dennis Banks finally stood trial for the charges resulting from the Custer courthouse riot. As that trial was going on, the two FBI agents were murdered in Oglala. A jury found Banks guilty on the counts of rioting while armed with a dangerous weapon and assault without intent to kill, but acquitted him on the arson and burglary charges. In August he failed to appear for his sentencing hearing and fugitive warrants were issued for him.

After further adventures which the FBI said included aiding the escape of fellow fugitive Leonard Peltier, Dennis Banks eventually turned up in California. Police arrested him in a suburb of San Francisco in January 1976 for the flight charge and the charges from the Custer riot. Banks fought extradition to South Dakota, with California's then governor, Jerry Brown, on his side. In 1978 Brown announced that he would not extradite Banks, and Banks remained in California working at an alternative university he helped found near Davis. When Brown left the governorship in '82 to run for the Senate and law-and-order Republican George Deukmejian succeeded him, Banks fled to the Onondaga Iroquois Reservation in New York State and asked New York governor Mario Cuomo to grant him sanctuary. Cuomo temporized, but the

Onondaga gave Banks permanent sanctuary and said they would protect him. A year later Banks complained that having to stay on the
reservation all the time to avoid arrest was like being in prison. In 1984,
more than eleven years after the Custer courthouse riot, Banks surrendered to police in Rapid City, South Dakota, to face the flight charges
and the sentencing for his riot convictions. His lawyer, William Kunstler, provided the judge with testimonies to Banks's good character
from Jesse Jackson, Harry Belafonte, and César Chávez. The judge sentenced Banks to three years in prison for the riot. Banks served a little
over a year in the South Dakota Penitentiary. After his release, in November 1984, he lived in Rapid City and started his own limousine
service; later he began to work for the cause of Indian sobriety by pro-
moting alcohol-free powwows.

Russell Means stood trial on the Custer courthouse riot charges in
Sioux Falls, South Dakota, in April 1974. His federal trial on the
Wounded Knee charges was then still going on, but the judge allowed
him time off to go to Sioux Falls. At the Sioux Falls trial, another riot
occurred. Means and his co-defendants and their supporters refused to
stand when the judge entered the room, the judge ordered police to
clear the court, and the police and the defendants began to fight.
Means ended up with a number of new felony charges as a result. The
federal judge dismissed all the charges from Wounded Knee in September 1974. Some months later, Means went with a group of friends
to the Longhorn Saloon in Scenic, South Dakota. In the saloon's men's
room, he and an AIM member named Richard Marshall had an encounter with a Lakota from Pine Ridge named Martin Montileaux, and
left Montileaux lying on the floor with a .22 caliber bullet in his head.
Means and companions fled the saloon and drove toward Rapid City at
high speeds with police in pursuit until they were caught on the city's
outskirts. When Montileaux died of his wound, Means and Marshall
were charged with murder. Marlon Brando paid Means's bail.

A few months after that, a BIA policeman on the Standing Rock
Reservation shot Means in the back with a .357 pistol during a traffic
stop. The bullet hit no vital organs and Means was soon out of the hospital. The next month, on the Rosebud Reservation, someone shot at
him from a passing car. The bullet grazed his head but did no serious
harm. In December 1975 a jury found him guilty of rioting to obstruct

justice in the Sioux Falls courtroom brawl. The judge sentenced him to four years in prison but allowed him to remain free on bond. At a party some months later on the Yankton Sioux Reservation, Means and his bodyguard got into an argument with two younger AIM members, who pulled guns and shot them. Means was hit with a .222 rifle bullet in the chest, again not suffering much damage. The bodyguard, shot in the head, also survived.

Means went on trial for the Montileaux murder in July 1976. The other defendant, Richard Marshall, had already been convicted and given a life sentence. Andy Warhol had asked several times that Means come to New York so that Warhol could do his portrait, and Means figured that since he might be in jail for the rest of his life if convicted, he should go to New York now. He flew to New York the weekend before the final arguments in the murder trial. Warhol took many Polaroids of him and entertained him with a night on the town. They and some friends went to dance clubs where Means, a former dance teacher, had a wonderful time. He later called Warhol "a great host." Returning to Rapid City, Means decided that if he was found guilty he would kill the prosecutors and the judge. He and two confederates smuggled pistols into the courtroom in their boots before the verdict was read. Luckily, he was found not guilty. Soon after, he plea-bargained the Custer riot charges to a single misdemeanor and got thirty days in jail and a $100 fine.

In the late 1970s, Means participated in more protest demonstrations and served over a year in prison on the Sioux Falls riot charges. In prison someone stabbed him in the chest with a prison-made knife, but the blade deflected on a rib, and after some stitches he was fine. When he got out he began to work for the return of federal lands in the Black Hills to the Sioux and occupied some Forest Service land there with a settlement he called the Yellow Thunder Camp, named after the man killed in Gordon, Nebraska, in '72. The settlement finally dispersed in the early 1980s after someone was murdered there. In 1983 Means briefly joined the campaign of pornographer Larry Flynt for the Republican presidential nomination, running as Flynt's vice president. In '84 Means traveled to Libya, and in '85 and '86 he went to Nicaragua. His reports of the Sandinistas' brutal treatment of Nicaraguan Indians, and his description of a bombing raid conducted by Sandinista planes on a peaceful Miskito Indian village which he said he saw, lost him support among leftists. The Reverend Sun Myung Moon's Unification Church paid for him to go around the country speaking on the abuses of the Sandinistas. In 1987 Means campaigned in forty-six states for the presidential nomination of the Libertarian Party, but lost a close vote at the party's national convention in San Francisco.

A casting director from Hollywood called him in 1991 and asked if he would try out for the part of Chingachgook in an upcoming movie of *The Last of the Mohicans.* Means went to California and New York to read for the part, scoffing at the script and saying that wasn't how Indians talked. His improvised dialogue impressed the director, who cast him. While filming the movie Means fell in love with acting and decided to make a career of it. In 1995 he did the voice of Chief Powhatan for the Disney animated feature *Pocahontas.* When the movie came out he gave interviews to promote it, calling Disney "revolutionary" for their portrayal of Indians, and adding, "Anybody that nitpicks this movie has buried their childhood, they've buried the child within them."

During the years after Wounded Knee, Means married for the third time, got divorced, then married for the fourth time. He had many children in his four marriages. His oldest son, Hank, went to the South Dakota State Penitentiary in 1982 for his part in a robbery during which one of the victims—a Jesuit priest—died. In 1996, Means's sixteen-year-old daughter Tatewin, his only child by his third wife Peggy Phelps Means, was chosen Miss Teen South Dakota and represented her state in the Miss Teen U.S.A. Pageant.

I thought about this long skein of consequences as I stood in the gravel street where Wesley Bad Heart Bull fell in front of the former Bill's Bar. Then I went into the post office, the one public place in Buffalo Gap that seemed to be open on that afternoon. The only person in the post office was the postmaster, Loretta Schroth, a blond, blue-eyed, frank-faced woman of indeterminate middle age and friendly disposition—another evident improvement over the Buffalo Gap of 1885. We got to talking, and I asked her if she was living here at the time Wesley Bad Heart Bull was killed. "Yes, I was," she said. "Well, not *here*—my hus-

band and I run a ranch just outside of town. When that killing happened my husband was fire chief of Buffalo Gap and he helped orga-
nize the men into neighborhood patrols. AIM was having that uprising
over in Custer, and we didn't want any uprising here. That bar was a
lively place when Bill Zuber had it. The killing didn't hurt business at
all—helped it, maybe. Bill's was still a pretty lively place afterward.
There's been a lot more that happened there—a car ran into the front
of it, there were fights, the law had to be called. Bill Zuber's dead now.
He sold the bar some years ago to Jim and Jo Hayes, who came up from
Colorado. They had it for a while and then sold to Georgia Loberg, who
was an immaculate type of person and a wonderful cook, and she put in
a café and did real well with that. Then she sold it to Sid Hussey, who
sold it to Bill Hartshorn. Bill's not really a bar person—he'd be the first
to tell you that himself. His wife's part-Indian and her relatives had a
band and people weren't too crazy about all the activity that was bringing in. He tried to keep it open just in the afternoons, but he just wasn't
getting the business, so he closed down. I believe he's been trying to
sell it.

"What hurt these little bars more than anything else is these new
laws that say you lose your license if you drink and drive. We're down to
one bar in Buffalo Gap now. People go to Jeannie's—it's a big brown
wood building, one block down and take a left. The fellow who runs it,
he's not a very sociable-type man, and he's got a gun and Mace and so
forth, and the Indians mostly don't go there. Mostly they go to Hot
Springs or Oelrichs. Hard to believe that once there were fifty or more
bars in this town. Well, there's always been a bar in Buffalo Gap, and I
guess there always will be."

The winter after Wanda Kindle died, it snowed and snowed. I stayed at home waiting for a break in the weather and read a book I had bought on a side trip to the Rosebud Reservation—the *Lakota-English Dictionary*, compiled by Rev. Eugene Buechel, S.J. Father Buechel began his work among the Sioux in 1902 and continued it until his death, at the age of eighty, in 1954. He began collecting Lakota words and definitions in 1910, spoke the language fluently himself, and spent much of his free time discussing its intricacies with elders on the Rosebud Reservation. His book of Lakota grammar came out in 1939, but he didn't finish the dictionary in his lifetime. Jesuit colleagues went through his 30,000 note cards and edited them, and the Red Cloud Indian School published the dictionary in 1970. In a picture on page iii, Father Buechel appears as a sagacious-looking man with a high, wrinkled forehead, spectacles, and a well-trimmed gray beard. People on Pine Ridge have told me that the dictionary is overly Christian in tone, and that Father Buechel's informants left out the racy side of the language, an important part of Lakota, because they felt self-conscious talking to a priest.

But Mary Brave Bird, in her book (with Richard Erdoes) *Ohitika Woman*, says that Father Buechel traveled all over the reservation by horse and buggy to say Mass in such remote hamlets as Upper Cut Meat and He Dog, and that the Sioux people liked him for his knowledge of their language, his willingness to eat any food he was served, and the little gifts he brought in his pockets for the children. Mary Brave Bird says that her mother said that she not only learned English from Father Buechel's books but learned her own language better as well.

The dictionary has 853 pages, and I read them all. Father Buechel notes with care a word's shades of meaning, its different uses, and how it changes with prefix and suffix and in idiom. His explanations are always specific, often accompanied with examples. Sioux has lots of words that mean "to bite"; a horse bites with one word, but a mosquito with another. Many Sioux words convey a basic meaning of "to hit or strike," but vary according to the circumstances in which the hitting is done. There are slightly different two-syllable words that mean to make pigs cry by striking, to make dogs cry by striking, and to make boys tough by striking. The act of shooting has a whole palette of words to itself. The word for shooting with an arrow is different from that with a gun, to shoot and miss is a different word from to shoot and hit, to shoot to many pieces is different from to shoot in two.

Sometimes when I travel in the West—on the Great Plains, especially—I find myself in a place too unimportant for people to pay it much attention nowadays; and yet it's a real place, unlike any other and specific to itself, and it always makes me wonder what the lost Indian name for it was. Father Buechel's dictionary contains many words for which the object or action or condition described will probably never come up in ordinary conversation again—that is, the word remains, but what it describes has now been forgotten or lost. Will the Sioux ever again have much use for the word *tacaka*, which means the roof of a buffalo's mouth? Many of the Lakota words in the dictionary are ones I wish we had equivalents of in English. As I read the dictionary, I kept a list of those words and others. Father Buechel devised a complicated orthography for conveying Lakota sounds that don't exist in English; the dictionary's introduction suggests a simpler version of it that uses symbols available on a typewriter. Among my favorite words were:

aca´ hsu, v. To form ice on something in little drops, as on trees, grass, etc.

anpta´ niya, n. Breath of day, the very first glimmerings of morn, vapors raised by the sun.

cui´ yohe, n. Moccasins made of old hides that have served as tents.

glinun´ wan, v. To arrive at home swimming.

hepi´ ya, n. The side or flank of a hill.

hia´ kigle, v. To set the teeth firmly, as a dying person does.

heku´, n. The foot of a hill back from a river.

hena´ gi, n. The shadow of a hill.

ica´ konta, v. To cut a groove in, as one branch resting on another will do when swayed by the wind.

iwa´ glamna, n. An extra or fresh horse.

iyu´ s´o, v. When a man rides through water and gets wet in spite of lifting his legs.

jiji´ lowan, v. To sing in a low, whispering, drawling manner.

kable´ blesic´iya, v. refl. To rest one's mind by walking around after hard work.

mniagla´ pepeya, v. To make a flat stone skip on the water.

nakpi´, v. To crack with the foot, as boys do with the eyes of butchered cattle.

opa´ skan, v. To melt by lying on.

opu´ hli, v. To stuff anything into, as an old coat into a broken window.

pa´ blaska, n. The broad bill of a duck.

Ptegle´ska canli´, n. Bull Durham tobacco.

tiyo´ heyunka, n. Frost settling on the inside wall of houses or tents.

tacan´ hahaka wapa´ha, n. A headdress made from the upper end of the buffalo's spinal column.

waya´ gla, v. To draw out or uncoil, as a dog does when eating the fat from entrails.

wica´ natasloka, n. A dry human skull.

wo´ econla, v. To consider something hard work but it is not.

yugwa´, v. To soften by hand.

yuhmi<u>n</u>´ yan, adv. Off sideways, crookedly, as a ball might go; sliced, as in golf.

yupo´ ta, v. To tear to pieces, as does an eagle a rabbit with the bill and not by scratching.

Just after New Year's, Le called from Oglala and said he was going to Los Angeles soon. He said he needed a full-body CAT scan to qualify him for certain disability payments, and that a friend in Los Angeles had told him she would pay for the test if he had it done there. He was going by car with friends, taking a northern route through Seattle, and said that on their way they would stop and visit me. I had my doubts, as usual. When weeks went by and he didn't arrive, I decided that the trip must have fallen through. Then one Saturday afternoon in late January I got a call from a woman who said that her name was Wendy Cody and that she was with Leonard Walks Out at the corner of Orange Street and Broadway in Missoula. This news startled and worried me. I said my wife was out and I was taking care of the kids, and asked if I could call her back. Wendy said no, she was at a pay phone. I asked her to hold on, and I put the phone down and went into another room and paced around.

I am sorry to say that being generous and hospitable to my friend was not the first thing on my mind. Mainly I was afraid that Le and his friends would come over to my house drunk, and then never leave. But Wendy sounded pretty normal. I picked up the phone again and said they could come by for just a little bit. She said that she'd been driving all night and needed to stop. I gave her directions to my house.

I put on a pot of coffee and did a quick cleaning up of the downstairs. When I looked out the front window, an orange station wagon was pulling into the drive. Le got out of the front seat and stood in the snowy yard with his arms spread wide. I had forgotten what long arms he has. He said, "Give me a hug. I've been lonely out on the highway." His hair was down in his eyes and he no longer wore a neck brace. He was medium drunk—I had seen him drunker. He introduced me to Wendy, the driver, a red-haired white woman in her thirties with blue eyes, one of them bloodshot. Then Le said, "That's Mike Shot in the back seat." Mike did not seem to want to get out and had to be coaxed.

Wendy talked to him for a minute or two, he got out, and we all went inside.

Mike Shot was wearing high laced combat-style boots, a black leather jacket, and big amber-tinted dark glasses. He was in his mid-twenties, and his straight dark-brown hair hung to the middle of his back. He seemed to be about as drunk as Le. Both he and Le had on a lot of cologne. My kids, then four years old and almost eight, came to the front hall to say hello—to stare, really—and Le and Mike hugged them the way sailors who had just survived a shipwreck might hug the beach. The embrace went on and on; Le and Mike didn't say anything, and the kids stood there and let themselves be hugged. Then we sat in the living room, and Le held my daughter, Cora, on his lap on the couch and told her that he was her Indian. I nervously went to the kitchen and brought out cups of coffee. Cora, a talkative child, told Le that she was in first grade and that boys on the playground at school tried to beat her up sometimes. Le said, "You tell them that you have a friend who's an Oglala dog soldier, and that he'll destroy them if they do anything to you!" While he was holding her he spilled hot coffee on her leg, but I had told her to be nice, so she didn't say anything about it until later.

My son, Thomas, wanted to fight with Mike, and stood beside his chair hitting at his knees. Mike parried the attack with one hand. He told me that he had recently gotten out of the Marine Corps. He took off his sunglasses, and I recognized him—I had met him on the reservation the summer before, when I passed him picking chokecherries by the side of the road. He had two big black plastic bags of chokecherries with him then, and he had mentioned the Marine Corps. He had told me that he was about burned out on chokecherries. As I described this incident and what he had said, he slowly remembered it, and smiled a shy, brilliant smile.

Wendy asked me if I wanted to buy a dream catcher Mike had made. A dream catcher is a hoop whose center is strung with a sort of cat's-cradle web of thread or fine string; hung beside a bed, the dream catcher is supposed to intercept bad dreams. I said I'd like to look at it, and Wendy brought it in from the car. Mike had made the hoop part of the catcher from deer antlers bolted together, with the antler points on the outside and a net of tightly strung deer sinew in the center. He had painted the antlers with red and white streaks of lightning and blue deer tracks. I asked Wendy how much they wanted for it and she said $150. I said I didn't have that much money with me, but I could pick it up at a cash machine before they left.

I was acting very flustered and dropped-in-upon, constantly hopping up and fussing with the coffee and so on. I said I didn't know what I could give them for lunch—would peanut butter and jelly be okay? Wendy asked if we had any tuna fish, and I said that was a good idea and went to the kitchen and made a bunch of tuna-fish sandwiches, managing distractedly to use about twenty different utensils in the process. Mike told Wendy to help me, and as she did, she told me that she lived on the reservation and worked with senior citizens, and that she was going to Seattle and L.A. to try to raise money to buy a vehicle to ferry Oglala elders without means to get around. When the sandwiches were done I called Mike and Le, and they sat down at the dining-room table. Le lifted the top piece of bread from his sandwich, stared awhile at the tuna fish, and asked if I had any hot sauce. "Hot sauce? On a tuna-fish sandwich?" I asked.

"Do I look like a white boy to you?" he growled. I brought him a bottle of Louisiana Red and he poured it all over the tuna and began to eat. I gave the kids sandwiches, too, and Mike reached over to Thomas in his high chair and tousled his hair and said to me, "You got beautiful children." That reminded me of the eagle feather Le had given me for Thomas, so I jumped up from the table and went down to my office in the basement and got it. I showed it to everybody and passed it around, and then absentmindedly set it on the table among the lunch fixings. Mike winced slightly and picked the feather up with the tips of his fingers and handed it back to me: I recalled that an eagle feather isn't something you leave lying around next to the mayonnaise. I took the feather and went downstairs again and put it away.

Le sat close by Cora at the table, sketching a picture of her on some paper she brought him and telling her again that he was her Indian and that he was a dog soldier. He asked her if she remembered when she was a little girl and he came to our apartment in Brooklyn and they played on the floor. She said she did. I was eyeing the weather from the dining-room window; the snow had started to fall pretty hard. Suddenly

Mike stood up and said, "It's time to go." Silently grateful, I appeared with everybody's hats and coats. Le took his scarf and wrapped it around Cora's head as a present for her. Just at this point my wife got home, which prolonged the leave-taking. Le hugged me and said a lot more stuff to me, but I disengaged myself and practically pushed him into the car. Mike and Wendy said goodbye and got in, too. Then Wendy hopped out again. She had forgotten her gloves, and she ran back into the house to get them. Such a display of presence of mind gave me confidence in her ability to lead this journey. I had her follow me in their car to the Bi-Lo Supermarket, where I ran in and got $150 from the cash machine for the dream catcher. As I gave the money to Wendy through her window, she asked if I thought that Lolo Pass on Highway 12 would be open in this weather. I said, "Probably," and wished them luck. Then I got back in my car and left them in the supermarket parking lot.

I was not too happy about how I had behaved. Here Le had shown me around the reservation, introduced me to his friends and family, and I could hardly find it in myself to invite him in for a sandwich. I hesitate even to mention this incident, for fear of offending readers who expect likability in the people they read about. But there it is—I was kind of a jerk to Le and his friends when they came to visit me. The memory of my unkindness stayed with me, and had a part in events that came later.

During a clear, cold spell soon after, I went back to the reservation. Around Oglala the wind had blown the prairie free of snow in most places, except for little drifts on the lee side of bushes and tufts of grass. Next to snow fences and in road cuts, big and frozen snowdrifts overlapped on each other, blue as shaving gel in their creases. The badlands looked even more wrinkled on their rock faces than usual, the snow in their eroded fissures bringing the texture into plain relief. The late-February wind just would not quit. Sometimes I couldn't get the car door open against it, other times if I opened it a crack it yanked the door open all the way. Wind sent empty plastic soda bottles skittering across the parking lot at Big Bat's and scattered children as they got off the school buses in the afternoon. Metal clips on the pulley rope kept banging against the flagpole in front of BIA headquarters. Beside the highway tribal policemen sat in their idling cars drinking coffee and chewing sunflower seeds.

On this trip I talked to almost no one. Mainly I read local histories about Pine Ridge in libraries in Custer and Rapid City, and newspaper stories on microfilm at the library at Chadron State College in Chadron, Nebraska, and back issues of the *Sheridan County Star* at the paper's offices in Rushville, Nebraska. One afternoon I went to Oglala and stopped in at Florence's house. She had gone to her dialysis treatment and no one was home but her son, Rex. He told me that Le had gotten back from California a week or so ago and that Florence had kicked him out of her house over by Loneman because she was afraid he would have some accident with the woodstove while drunk and burn the place down. Rex said Le was now staying at Aurelia's.

I was angry at Le because of the way I had acted when he visited me—my behavior had been his fault, somehow—and so put off going over to Aurelia's. The night before I planned to drive back to Missoula, I was sitting in a motel in Custer and I felt a sudden regret that I had not seen him, combined with affection and sentimentality. Instead of heading for home the next day, I went back to the reservation. The morning was sunny and clear, the wind now just a breeze instead of a gale. I drove down the long track across the prairie to Aurelia's house and found her in her yard getting water from the pump. Le came from the house as I drove up. He looked fine and fit, fully recovered from his accident. He wore black stone-washed jeans, a white dress shirt with three buttons on the cuff, low-cut running shoes, and a blue warm-up jacket with the name of a cinematic lighting company on the back in yellow letters. He had gotten the jacket from a movie lighting technician he met in L.A., he said.

I asked how his trip had been. "After we left you it started snowin' a blizzard," he said. "We were driving through that pass with drifts alongside the road three times as high as the car, and it was hairy there for a while. But the weather was good in Seattle, and California had flowers like spring. My friend that was going to pay for my CAT scan wasn't home. Her neighbors told me that she had moved to Eureka, California. So I didn't get the CAT scan done. After Wendy finished some business she had, we drove the southern route through Vegas and Wyoming, back to here."

Le and Aurelia and I talked for a while. Aurelia said she felt bad
about Florence kicking Le out—"My poor boy's got to have a place to
sleep, oh yes, he does"—and I took out my wallet and gave Le the cash
I had left, about sixty dollars. I told Aurelia that I always give Le my extra cash when I'm heading home, and that I had wanted to see him before I left. He walked me back to my car. "How's my little white lady,
my *waschichu* girl, Cora?" he asked.

"She's okay. You know, you spilled hot coffee on her," I said.

He looked away. It occurred to me that what I'd said was no news to
him, and that he already knew I was angry. I told him to take care of
himself, and he replied, "*You* take care of *yourself, too.*" I said goodbye,
and I got in my car and left.

I was in a bad frame of mind. The stories I had recently been reading about Pine Ridge in the local histories and newspapers had left me
with a residue of dread. They all seemed to involve suffering and violence and hopes destroyed, and car wrecks, one after the next. I felt
guilty for my journalistic interest in Le, and for being a chintzy middle-
class white guy. Also, I had gone a while without talking much to anybody, and that always makes me feel lonesome and sorry for myself. It's
better just to overlook these spells, and I generally do. But later, after I
got in the accident, I tried to remember what my mental state had been
just before it, in an effort to make sense of why it happened. The one
lesson I decided to draw from it is: Don't drive when you're feeling
guilty and full of dread.

This trip back, I went from Oglala through the Black Hills, over to
Newcastle, Wyoming, and then northwest to the interstate highway
from there. The day turned balmy. In the prairie past Newcastle, I saw
two bald eagles sporting together high in the blue sky. I took the interstate to Sheridan and spent the night in a motel there. Early the next
morning I woke to the sound of someone scraping ice from a car windshield. I loaded up the car and with the door open drove to a video
store parking lot and scraped the windows there, so as not to wake anyone up myself. The ice was thick and hard, and the scraper made barely
a dent. The windshield wouldn't come clear until the engine had idled
long enough to warm up the car. I looked for a place to have breakfast,
but nothing seemed to be open, so I got back on the interstate thinking
I'd have breakfast in Billings, Montana, a couple of hours away. (An-

other rule: Don't drive hungry.) I tried to find a weather report on the radio but got only mumblings about light snow delivered by a girl disc jockey with a giggle.

Fine snow driven hard by the wind began to come down just beyond Sheridan. The wind was from the west, and the road lay roughly north and south through open country, so mostly the highway was blown clear. I slowed down through road cuts where it had accumulated; I knew the high, narrow Blazer has a tendency to skid. Interstate 90, which I was on, meets Interstate 94 east of Billings. As I came down into the valley of the Yellowstone River just before the intersection, snow was thick in the air and the road had become a hard-polished white. The westbound lanes of I-90 cross I-94 on a bridge, shrink to a single lane, and merge with westbound I-94 from the right. As I went to merge, a white Ford pickup with its headlights on was in the right-hand lane just where I needed to be. Perhaps because the left-hand lane was all snow while parts of the right-hand lane were clear, the pickup didn't pull over to let me in. We were going the same speed. He didn't slow down and I didn't slow down.

We had approached to just a few feet apart when I impatiently stepped on the gas, in order to speed up and go in front of him. At that moment my car went out of control. I was suddenly skidding at 55 miles an hour backwards in the left-hand lane, then into the center divider, back across the right-hand lane, off the right-hand shoulder, and down the embarkment, with plumes of snow blowing past. I crashed sideways through the freeway fence, snapping the barbed wire like string, rolled completely over, and landed on the passenger side in a ditch by an access road.

The seat belt and shoulder strap had held me tight to the seat. I appeared to be all right; later I discovered I had torn a thumbnail. The windshield was broken and the passenger-side window had shattered, and the inside of the car was full of my stuff—briefcase, maps, tapes—all jumbled up with broken glass and snow. Looking at that made me feel as if I were skidding again. I undid my seat belt, and stood on the passenger-side door, opened the driver's-side door above me, pushed it up, climbed out, and hopped to the ground. The white pickup had stopped by the side of the road and its driver, an onion-headed man in a brown corduroy baseball cap, was standing in the snow looking at me with an expression an alien might meet on someone watching him climb from a spaceship. The man asked me if I was okay and I said yeah. He said a woman had already pulled over and had gone for help. He said he would go and call someone, too, and he drove off.

I walked around for a while in the knee-deep snow looking for places in the distance where there might be a phone. I was in the billboard region, near enough to Billings to justify the billboards but too far to have anything more. All around seemed to be nothing but billboards and snow. In a few minutes a highway patrol car pulled up on the shoulder and a patrolman got out and waited for me to walk up the embankment to him. We sat in his car while he wrote down information from my driver's license and called in the accident on his radio. He was black; I had never seen a black cop on the Plains before. He didn't give me a hard time at all or cite me for the accident. When he had finished with the paperwork he walked down with me to look at the car and said, "Maybe you and me could just roll it back up on its wheels." A closer look revealed that would not be possible.

A guy in a small white car pulled up on the access road and sat there for a while looking at my car. Then he got out—a skinny guy with a sparse beard and two cameras hanging from him on straps. He told me he worked for the *Billings Gazette* and was taking pictures of wrecks caused by the weather. I told him I would rather he not take any pictures of my car. He said, "Well, this is the wreck closest to my house, and I'm afraid if I go out on the interstate I'll get in a wreck myself." He unlimbered the cameras and began to snap. I was careful to stay out of the frame.

The tow truck arrived and the jumpsuited driver hopped out, ebullient with all the calls he was getting on this blizzardy morning. He was delighted to learn that his picture might appear in the newspaper and posed for the photographer at the various stages of winching the car upright and hooking it to the tow bar. I climbed into the cab with him and we drove on the access road toward town. I asked how much the tow would cost and he said $80, cash or check. I had no checks and had given Le most of my cash, so the driver took me on a long detour to a cash machine in the middle of Billings. Then we went to a Sinclair station by the interstate which he said was the only place where I could get work done at this hour on a Sunday morning. The guys at the Sinclair station, young fellows with long hair straggling out from ski caps, looked at the car and at me and said, "You must've been wearing your seat belt!" One of the guys told me that I was in luck, that he was a student at an auto-body-repair school. The next time I looked, he was lying on his back on the driver's seat and kicking hard at the crumpled-in roof with both feet. I went across the street to a place called the Lucky Stiff Casino and had breakfast.

When I got back, the roof had been raised enough that it didn't brush the top of my head when I sat up straight. It was still pretty low-slung, though. The guys had taped a piece of heavy cardboard with a few lug-soled bootprints on it over the broken window, and had also duct-taped the bigger cracks in the windshield, and along the lower edge where it had come loose from the frame. They had replaced the various fluids that had drained out when the car was on its side, and had pushed the smashed-in wheel wells out so that the tires wouldn't rub against them. A blond guy in a red jumpsuit, the most talkative of the crew, said that the car was probably drivable but that the state wouldn't let you drive a wreck on the highway unless you first got permission and a sticker from the highway patrol. I did not want to bother with any red tape; for some reason, I just wanted to get back on the highway and keep going. I paid the guys and thanked them, and to their skeptical farewells I backed out of the service bay and headed for the interstate.

By now the snow was coming down so hard I could see only a short distance ahead, and when semis passed me, I could see almost nothing but the snow they swirled. The road was a dim blowing world in which headlights suddenly appeared in the rearview mirror and red taillights suddenly flew by and disappeared. The tape holding the windshield to the frame quickly came apart, and the windshield hung loose like a drapery, bouncing with every jolt and letting snow in to pile up on the dash. The car made a strange noise at speeds above thirty miles an hour and refused to go much faster than thirty-five. I anticipated the start of a skid in every shimmy and gust of crosswind. Ragged breaks in the snow berm showed where other vehicles had skidded off the road. After about forty-five miles and ninety minutes of this, I pulled off at Columbus, Montana, and went to a Super 8 Motel right by the exit. The motel had a lot of trucks in its parking lot and a long line at the check-in desk. When I finally got to the head of the line, the lady there said she had just a few rooms left. She said there had been a wreck with fatalities on the interstate some miles to the west and the truckers had heard about it on their radios and had decided to quit for the day.

Once I got in my little motel room, the unshakable sensation of skidding really took hold. I was skidding as I paced the narrow piece of carpeting between the bed and the bureau, skidding like mad as I lay on my back in the water in the shallow bathtub. I called people on the phone and told them what had happened, pacing around. I watched the Weather Channel for a while, and finally it occurred to me that these interchangeable weather people massaging satellite photos of the United States with their manicured fingernails might as well be talking about storms on Mars. On the subject of the blizzard happening at that very moment in central Montana, they had nothing to say. I ate dinner at a café and came back to the room and tried to sleep. At about three in the morning I woke up and stood at the window watching the snow fall and the traffic go by on the highway. There were no cars, only occasional trucks, but they seemed to be getting through okay. The snow was falling less hard than before. I packed my suitcase, warmed up the car, and set out again.

This time the going was a little easier, with the traffic not as heavy and the wind not as strong. I turned my emergency flashers on—I hadn't known how to turn them on before—and kept a steady thirty-two miles an hour through the dark windings along the Yellowstone. I got to Livingston, about eighty miles farther, as dawn was breaking. A woman followed me off the highway and flashed her lights, and I pulled over in irritation to find out what she wanted. She said that she had been praying to her angels to get me to stop, because my left rear wheel was wobbling as if it was about to come off. She recommended I go to a Tire-Rama nearby. At the Tire-Rama they told me my left rear axle was bent. They didn't have the part, but called the Tire-Rama in Bozeman, which had it there. I bought new studded snow tires in Livingston with a credit card and then wobbled twenty-six miles over the pass to Bozeman. At the Bozeman Tire-Rama they said they could have the axle fixed by late afternoon.

I walked over to the Bozeman public library and happened on a copy of the play *Eleutheria* by Samuel Beckett at the new-arrivals shelf right by the door, and I spent the day reading it. It is a wild play, in which a shoe gets thrown through a windowpane every few scenes and there are characters named Monsieur Krap and Dr. Piouk. Late in the play a "Chinese torturer" named Tchoutchi climbs onto the stage from the audience and begins to torture the characters to get them to tell him what the play is about. I went back to Tire-Rama at about four and they were still working on the axle, so I looked at magazines in the waiting room. A teenage boy and a teenage girl were sitting there. The girl kept saying, "I can't believe I dyed my hair!" accenting a different word in the sentence with each repetition. Her hair looked like any other teenage girl's to me. I was idling through the newspaper, when suddenly I saw my car. On page 1 of the B section of the *Billings Gazette* was a large full-color photo: my car's intricate underside against the white of a snowscape, the winch cable connecting the capsized vehicle to the tow truck, the happy tow-truck driver in the foreground. I took the page with the photo and hurried back into the Tire-Rama work bays past the CUSTOMERS KEEP OUT signs and showed it to the man working on the axle. When he finally understood what I was talking about, he was unimpressed to be working on a famous car featured on page 1 of the *Gazette*'s B section.

The blizzard hit Pine Ridge, too. Le called my house to make sure I'd gotten back all right; my wife told him I had been in a wreck but was okay, and she didn't know when I would be home. He said he would pray for me. He called again soon after I had finally arrived. "I hear you rolled that car of yours off the highway," he said.

"Yeah, I wrecked the body pretty bad and took out some fence, but I had my seat belt on."

"The eagle feather I gave your son was protecting you and your whole family," he said. "That's why you survived, and nothin' happened to your wife or babies while you were gone. Plus I was prayin' for you, and so was Aurelia and Florence and Norma. She's a sister you haven't met yet, the one that prayed for me in the hospital. I've been in eleven car wrecks myself, and I'm still alive. Some of 'em people died in, some of 'em nobody got hurt at all. The thing about a car wreck, even if you don't get hurt you feel strange in your body for a long time after—you'll be sittin' in a chair and you'll think the chair is about to crash into the wall. A wreck shakes up your nerves in a way that's totally uncalled for. I learned that when I was driving stunt cars in the movies. When I was drivin' those stunt cars I was cool on the outside. Like, before a shoot, I was, 'Hey, let's get it on!'—real unconcerned. But inside I had that strange sensation like I'd been in a wreck, all the time."

We talked a lot more about wrecks and disasters. My being in a wreck had somehow restored a balance between us; the bad feelings of the last month went away, and we could act like friends again.

Then it was summer, and across the reservation locusts sizzled in the cottonwood trees. At the outskirts of Pine Ridge village, in the grove with graffiti spray-painted on their trunks by the picnic area, I napped in my (now-repaired) car. On the windshield, ants investigated the remains of smashed insects, while across the field someone tested the loudspeaker system at the powwow grounds. Dust had fallen so thickly that it coated the weeds and grasses, and it rose in puffs wherever you stepped. An invasion of grasshoppers had arrived on a hot wind. Behind the stores of the village, when the wind gusted, it blew dust and grasshoppers above the buildings in clouds. The hoppers had eaten the green off the sweet clover and left it bare as broomstraw, and had eaten the yellow petals of the sunflowers clear down to the brown center. A man collecting empty cans in a big plastic sack walked across a vacant lot with the cans crinkling in the sack and the grasshoppers rising around his legs in such numbers that they collided with each other in the air. Inside the houses the sound of windblown hoppers against the walls and window screens sometimes became a thudding fusillade.

The powwow grounds and the picnic area where I was napping are on the west side of town. The field that includes them is a hundred acres or more of tribal land bordered on its western edge by the brushy course of White Clay Creek, and past the creek is Pine Ridge High

School. Students from distant parts of the reservation board during the school year in brick dormitory buildings on campus; the main classroom building is a newish structure of glazed brick decorated with geometric patterns in the sacred colors of red, yellow, black, and white. The sound of bouncing basketballs echoes from the school's gymnasium, whose doors are often open when the weather is warm. The amphitheater-style football stadium sits below the school buildings in a hollow of White Clay Creek. During the time of the ghost dance, the dancers often gathered in a big hollow farther up the creek because they liked the way the drumming and singing sounded there.

I have already mentioned the center of town—the intersection of Highways 18 and 407 which people still call "the four-way," and Big Bat's Texaco and the tribal office building and Billy Mills Hall. To the south is the Nebraska state line and the town of White Clay. On a hill just north of the intersection is the old IHS hospital and the tribal senior citizens' home. On the town's east side is the new IHS hospital, with a doorknob-shaped light-blue water tower behind it. A row of new streetlights in Pine Ridge village runs from the hospital along Highways 18 and 407 all the way to the town of White Clay, a connection which appears more than coincidental. Developments of one-story homes on gravel streets follow the creek or stretch across the prairie. People sometimes refer to different developments by name, and to addresses like Crazy Horse Street or Eagle Court, but since the town has no street signs, I usually cannot say for sure which developments or streets they mean.

People in Pine Ridge also talk about places in town that disappeared long ago. They talk about the old golf course—not much in the Pine Ridge landscape of today immediately calls a golf course to mind—or about the Pejuta Tipi, the drugstore that was once downtown. They sometimes mention the bowling alley, the moccasin factory, Gerber's Hotel, the motel. All these establishments have closed down for good, with no successors taking their place. A remembered name that comes up often is the fishhook factory. In 1960, the Wright & McGill Company of Denver, manufacturers of fishing tackle, opened a factory to make snelled hooks in Pine Ridge. A snelled hook is one with a short section of monofilament tied to it; a loop at the monofilament's other end makes the hook easier to attach to a fishing line. No machine satisfactorily ties monofilament in knots that small, so the tying must be done by hand. In the early 1960s Wright & McGill was employing over five hundred people at factories in Pine Ridge and other towns on the reservation. Most of the employees were Oglala women who earned from about $45 to about $140 a week, a real addition to the Pine Ridge economy. In 1968, citing foreign competition and a rise in the minimum wage, the company shut down all of its Pine Ridge operations. Today the packages of most Wright & McGill fishhooks bear the words *Made in the U.S.A.* and a picture of the American flag. On the snelled-hook package, however, it says *Hand tied in Mexico.* Today the snelled hooks are made in the Mexican city of Agua Prieta, just across the Arizona border, where the knots may be more cheaply tied than in Pine Ridge, year after year the poorest place per capita (says the Census Bureau) in the United States.

Many towns in rural America, and especially on the Great Plains, have lost businesses over the last thirty years. Vacant storefronts and boarded-up buildings along a town's main street are a common sight. When the businesses go, usually the people go, too; kids grow up and move to big cities, parents age and enter nursing homes, the few residents who remain drive long distances to do their shopping in super-stores, and the town begins to die. Oddly, the village of Pine Ridge fits only part of this pattern. Although it has lost many businesses over the last thirty years, during the same period its population has more than doubled. The U.S. census counted 1,256 residents of Pine Ridge village in 1960 and 2,596 in 1990. The tribe estimates that 28 percent of the people on the reservation are homeless, so it is likely that even more live in the village than the census was able to find. The tribe says that about 20,500 people live on the reservation as a whole.

Meanwhile, the population of almost every town neighboring the reservation has declined. Rushville, Nebraska, had 1,228 people in 1960 and 1,127 in 1990; Gordon, Nebraska, went from 2,223 to 1,803; Hot Springs, South Dakota, from 4,943 to 4,325; Custer, from 2,105 to 1,741. Only Chadron, Nebraska, home of a state college, gained in population. The phenomenon of the dying Western town has been reported often before. But on Indian reservations, despite a lower life expectancy, population figures have been on the rise. If the trend continues, perhaps in a hundred years most of the descendants of the pioneers who settled in the West will have left the still-rural parts of it, and the descendants of the Indians will have increased their numbers to more than they were when the first pioneers arrived.

I walked all over Pine Ridge village that hot, windy summer—along the banks of White Clay Creek, up the hill to the old hospital, across the playing fields behind the high school, across the rolling prairie behind the powwow grounds, to the town limits of White Clay, to the houses under construction by the new hospital. Much of the way I followed footpaths worn into the ground. Many tourists and other wanderers show up in Pine Ridge in the summers, so I felt less conspicuous than I had in the winter and fall. Sometimes, though, local people noticed me; they would wave from their cars and ask, "Didn't I see you walking out by Merrival's this morning?"

In some of the developments, I passed houses with lawns and lawn sprinklers and asphalt driveways and basketball hoops. Some houses had large plastic butterflies, for decoration and luck, on the wall beside the front door. Chain-link fence topped with barbed wire surrounded a development just south of town where entering drivers opened the front gate by inserting a plastic card in a key box. In other parts of town, the houses were a sprawl of neglectedness and decay. I saw partly burned houses, a house in which all the windows had been smashed out and an American flag hung as a curtain in the doorless front door, yards full of car parts and skinny dogs. Gang graffiti—"bL%d$," "Lakeside Posse," "BAB GUZHISH will rock your crotch," "NOMADZ are shit-takin' wannabes"—covered some of the walls. Plastic and paper and aluminum trash strewed the streets, sun-faded and wind-torn plastic bags flapped from the branches of the trees. At a corner I stopped to look at the singed, melted trash conspicuous in an empty lot where a recent fire had burned the vegetation away. From a front stoop, a young woman in a wheelchair watched me through her dark hair. Someplace close by, an unmuffled car engine started with a burst like a brick of firecrackers going off.

The run-down parts of town are usually the ones that news stories and TV documentaries concentrate on. These neighborhoods are used to illustrate poverty, an inescapable fact of the reservation. According to the 1990 U.S. census, Shannon County—the county in South Dakota that includes Pine Ridge village and much of the reservation—has the largest percentage of people living in poverty of any county in the nation: 63.1 percent of Shannon County residents have annual incomes that fall below the national poverty line. Of the ten poorest counties in the United States in 1990, four were on Indian reservations in South Dakota. Shannon County has appeared at or near the bottom in earlier censuses as well. Few reports about Pine Ridge fail to mention that it's the country's poorest place, and the fact usually provides reporters with their opening paragraph: "This is as poor as America gets," the stories sometimes begin.

The stories never mention, just as a point of reference, what the richest county in America might be. After reading this lead for the dozenth time, I began to wonder. It turns out that the richest part of the United States is suburban Washington, D.C. According to the same census, the richest place in America is Falls Church, Virginia (technically a city, but it would be considered part of a county elsewhere). The second-richest place is Alexandria, Virginia, and the third-richest is Arlington County, Virginia. Two other counties among the richest top ten are in the suburban Washington, D.C., area.

Only about three people in ten on Pine Ridge have jobs, and those are mostly with the Bureau of Indian Affairs, the Indian Health Service, or the Oglala tribe. The BIA and the IHS are federal agencies, and much of the money the tribe receives comes from treaty and other payments made by the federal government. The wealth of the suburban D.C. counties is due to their closeness to the capital, with income from government-related businesses such as lobbying, law, and consulting firms. Like the poorest place in the country, the richest places get their money mainly from the federal government.

Perhaps because I often had to follow footpaths to find my way, in Pine Ridge I kept my eyes on the ground. The paths' dust was marked with many tracks—of dogs, of bicycles, of the brand-name-pattern soles of expensive running shoes. Occasionally I saw the parallel prints left by wheelchair wheels. For several days, shag-carpet shreds were everywhere. The carpet had been olive, and olive pieces of it blew across the parking lots and along the road; later I found olive shag-carpet shreds stuck to a piece of electrical tape on the wheel of my car. On the dust-and-gravel lot around Yellow Bird's gas and convenience store, flattened yellow plastic Pennzoil bottles dotted the ground. At the picnic area by the powwow grounds, a litter of bitterroot rinds covered the usual flooring of Budweiser shards. Grasshoppers had chewed irregular holes serrated with tiny grasshopper bite marks into the glossy pages of the March issue of *Glamour* magazine lying by the gate to the Pine Ridge cemetery. Some of what I came upon I put in my pocket and kept: the cover from a gangsta-rap CD (*Uncle Sam's Curse*); a rectangular pink rubber eraser which had been carefully colored in pencil to look like an American flag; a piece of ruled notebook paper on which the sentence "I will not run wild when Mrs. Iron Cloud is away" had been written out in pencil thirty times.

Nineteenth-century travelers sometimes commented on the bones and animal hair and broken tipi poles and other detritus that accumulated in encampments where Indians stayed for any length of time. As in these villages, Pine Ridge has plenty of stuff on the ground. Sometimes I would stop and examine a piece of it as if I were a nineteenth-century traveler and this a strange artifact I'd found. Usually, the artifact closest to hand would be a discarded food package of some kind. I would sit on the ground—unlike in other towns, a person sitting on the ground in Pine Ridge does not draw stares—and read the words on the bottle or can. I had not realized before how many warning labels our packaging now bears. On a plastic A&W root-beer bottle it says, *Caution: Contents Under Pressure. Open With Care.* An aluminum nut-can lid warns, *Caution: Sharp Edges.* A plastic press-on coffee-cup lid announces, *Caution May Be Hot Sip With Care.* On a Berry B. Wild Squeezit drink bottle: *Twist off top with hands only. Do not put in mouth.* On a 20-ounce plastic Dr Pepper soda bottle: *Warning: Contents under pressure. Cap may blow off causing eye or other serious injury. Point away from people, especially while opening.*

As I sat, traffic in Pine Ridge came and went around me. Two boys of elementary-school age zipped by on a gas-powered motor scooter, whooping and bouncing across the prairie at twenty or thirty miles an hour; neither had a helmet on. A pickup truck full of people roared down the highway ahead of a thick trail of exhaust, the half-dozen teenagers perched on the sides of the truck bed flying briefly into the air at every bump. A couple of lanky young men in cowboy hats pulled their truck to the side of the road and hopped out to ask a friend for money, taking no time to remove their seat belts, since they had never had them on. Most passersby in the village seemed to live in a way that ignored the cautionary tone of the messages on the roadside trash.

Every summer Pine Ridge opens out in early August like a road map unfolding, as people begin to arrive for the big tribal powwow. First you see one motor home with an unfamiliar license plate, then you see three, then ten. They have lawn chairs strapped to the back or the roof, and they're emblazoned with brand names like Tioga or Itasca or HitchHiker or Wanderer. Suddenly the village seems enlarged—a spread-out encampment rather than a small town. Here and there cars are pulled off the pavement alongside the road, and people in shorts and carrying cameras or binoculars are stepping through the sagebrush in the fields. A pale bunch of teenagers sits on the curb outside Big Bat's licking ice-cream cones, making a row of white knees. At the cement picnic tables west of town a family of seven—two white-haired oldsters, blond dad, blond mom, and three blond children—carefully lay out seven places for a picnic lunch. Then they sit, hold hands, and all bow their heads in prayer; their extra-long motor home has Utah plates.

At Yellow Bird's store, cars wait in line for the gas pumps. At the traffic light downtown there's sometimes a mini–traffic jam. It's loud; with plenty of partly muffled reservation cars in it, a Pine Ridge traffic jam really throbs. The loudspeakers at the powwow grounds are now on all the time, even though no events have begun and workmen are only setting up there. A guy is talking on the public address system as the spirit moves him, commenting on the goings-on: "Get that sod laid down good and tight, boys. We wouldn't want any of our fancy dancers to trip and mess up their two-thousand-dollar fancy-dance costumes . . . And look who's driving up the road now! It's Charlie-Boy Pourier with the water-sprinkler truck. Good to see you, Charlie—let's see if you can get that pesky Pine Ridge dust to lay down . . ."

Some early arrivals pitch tents and lay out campsites among the trees just west of the powwow grounds. There are two-man and four-man high-tech nylon tents in luminous shades, and old-fashioned canvas wall tents, and several white canvas tipis with pennants of colored cloth hanging from the ends of the tipi poles. People indicate their campsite boundaries with low fences made of wooden stakes connected by twine or strips of yellow plastic tape bearing the words POLICE LINE DO NOT CROSS. Next to many tents are stacks of freshly split firewood logs. The tent neighborhood grows, and soon acquires at least two sketchy streets with many vehicles parked along them. One morning the big tractor-trailer trucks begin to arrive—first the stock trucks with the steers and bucking horses and bulls for the powwow rodeo, and then the long caravan of carnival attractions and rides. The stock trucks park by the rodeo corrals, where the bawling of the animals echoes all around. The carnival trucks assemble in a bunch at another part of the field, sort of like circled wagons. Skinny, muscle-y, bristly-haired carny guys in sleeveless T-shirts get out of the trucks and stretch and smoke and holler remarks at each other. The carny vehicles include three electric generators the size of small boxcars, each with a thick umbilical of cable coming from it. The carny guys begin plugging cables to other cables to yet more cables, until in about an hour the whole carnival encampment is linked to the generators by a web of wires trailing through the dusty grass.

I generally got my breakfast early at Big Bat's, before the morning crowds showed up. The village had a pleasant feeling of expectancy in the cool, just-after-sunup time. One morning as I was staring out the window at the still-empty street and waiting for my Bat's Special Breakfast (two eggs, sausage patty, hash browns, and toast), I noticed Patty Pourier, Bat's wife, sitting two tables away. When my order number was called, I paused by her table, caught her eye, and asked her, "Do you recognize me?" She stared at me for a moment; then the memory of that day when the propane distributorship almost blew up clicked in her eyes. "I thought you looked familiar—we almost died together!" she said. "It's nice to see you here on earth, at Big Bat's, rather than on a cloud someplace in heaven!"

Sometimes when I stopped at Big Bat's I was hugged by a young man whom I'll call Germaine. He seemed to spend a lot of time at Big Bat's sitting at a table or standing just outside waiting for people to hug. As near as I could tell, he hugged only out-of-towners. His hug was unstudied and unhesitant, like a child's. He went right to the person he intended to hug as if magnetized, and during the embrace he rubbed his forehead on the other person's. The first time he hugged me he took me by surprise and his head knocked my hat to the floor. When I tried to disengage myself after a moment, he made a wordless noise of protest. The next time he hugged me he said, happily, "Remember me?" and of course I did. Usually we had conversations. He would say, "Where're you from? Are you married? I'm single. Do you have any children? I like you." Then he would hug me again.

I noticed that the other people Germaine hugged responded in different ways. A number of Pine Ridge's visitors during powwow season come from foreign countries, and occasionally these visitors reacted to Germaine's hugs with a stiffness suggesting that hugging was not a big part of their culture back home. Indeed, many of the people he hugged seemed surprised and even a bit frightened, as I had been myself the first time. I could imagine that in their years of dreaming in Berlin or Paris about the Oglala Sioux of the American West they had not expected to be nearly tackled in Pine Ridge by one of them the minute they stepped out of their rented camper van. But I noticed, too, that almost all the people soon understood the gesture's gentle spirit, and went along.

The sound of foreign languages on the streets of Pine Ridge—a not uncommon sound during powwow time—raises this place to a category of its own among mid-American towns. It reminds you that Pine Ridge village is also the capital of a nation, one that receives emissaries from far away. The fascination many German people, for example, have with the Oglala had seemed merely odd to me until I saw German and other foreigners at the powwow. They were excited, all eyes and ears and electronic gadgetry, and they made what surrounded them seem exciting, too. I reflected that the moment in history when white people and Native Americans first discovered each other was so momentous and fateful and even thrilling for each culture that some of us feel compelled to reenact it again and again. Nor was the powwow's mood of curiosity about the Other limited to just the visitors' side. One evening

during powwow week I went for a walk along a dirt road in an out-of-
the-way part of the village, and as I came down into a little hollow I met
five or six Oglala boys sitting on bicycles. By accident or on purpose
they were in a line across the road, blocking it so that I had to stop.
Around the road on both sides midsummer foliage screened out all
other sights and sounds; we could have been on any creek-bottom road
on the Plains. The boys looked at me with unblinking dark eyes. Then
the biggest boy, straddling his bicycle and bumping it back and forth
between his knees, said to me, "Where did you come from—Europe?"

Most of the time during the week of the powwow I hung out by myself.
Le and Floyd John did not seem to be around. Floyd John had left the
reservation for Santa Fe or Colorado, depending on which relative I
asked. As for Le, all anyone could tell me was that they hadn't seen him.
I stopped by Florence's house a couple of times, but no one was there.
As I was driving east of Pine Ridge one afternoon, a car came up behind me and blinked its lights and passed, and then arms from the open
windows waved me to pull over. I did, and it was Florence and her son
Rex and daughter Flora. Florence was on her way to the Porcupine
clinic, so sick she looked green. She said she thought Le might be in
White Clay, or he might have gone down to Scottsbluff. She said everybody went to the first night of the powwow and I'd surely run into him
there. Flora said it was strange that none of us had even seen him walking along the road. I gave them some gas money and went back to Pine
Ridge and took a walk on the mown jogging track in the field behind
the old IHS hospital. Suddenly from far away I heard a voice shout,
"*Hoka hey!*" A figure was waving at me from the road. I went over toward it and soon recognized Le.

His hair was messed up and he had bags under his eyes. He shook
my hand. He was carrying his cowboy boots under one arm and wearing
a new pair of tassel loafers which he said the Porcupine boys had given
him, for reasons he explained to me but I didn't follow. Then he said,
"I've been in jail the last five days. The judge just let me go half an hour
ago. They picked me up Thursday night driving back from White Clay
with my niece Verna Yellow Horse. (She's my niece, but she's only
eleven months younger than I am.) We was drinking in White Clay, and

then we came back in her car, and I was driving, and they pulled me over for not having my headlights on. I thought I'd hit the dimmer, but I guess I'd turned the lights all the way off. They pulled me out of the car and tried to give me a Breathalyzer test, and I told the tribal cop who was arresting me that he was a guppy-faced immigrant punk and I'd kick his ass for him and put him in the hospital. So they locked me up for drunk and disorderly. They locked Verna up, too. I had to wait to see a judge for a hearing, and the jailer told me I'd be in until after powwow. I said to him, 'No way.' So this morning a judge showed up, and when I went before him he said, 'The famous Mr. Walks Out!' See, he recognized me from your book. He asked me what I was doin' in there, and then he gave me a new trial date and let me go. As I left I said to the jailer, 'I told you so.' They're gonna need the room in the jail during powwow days, anyway."

Le came with me back to the jogging path and we walked a lap together, splashing up grasshoppers at every step. Le said, "They made this path for the people who worked up at the hospital. The doctors and nurses used to walk on it and jog on it for exercise. They was always tryin' to get Indian people to exercise more, for their health and especially so they wouldn't develop diabetes. They didn't persuade too many people, though, so really the only people you ever saw out here were doctors and nurses. Then the hospital moved to the other side of town, and not even doctors came here anymore. We still call this the Path the Doctors Walk On."

At my car I offered to give him a ride to Oglala, where he'd been heading when he called to me. A mile or two from Pine Ridge we passed two women walking along the road. "Hey—that's Verna!" Le said. "They must've just let her out, too." We stopped, and Verna, a heavyset woman with long, tangled hair, got in. Her friend Kay, who was shorter and fatter and had glasses, followed her. They both seemed to be pretty drunk. Verna told me her name several times, and said she had been lucky to be in a cell with Kay, because they were old friends. She told me her age to the month, corroborating Le's story of the difference in their ages. She said, "I'm so stiff from sleeping on that hard cement floor!" She and Le talked in English and in Sioux, apparently comparing notes about their arrest and their appearance before the judge. Verna and Kay got out in Oglala by the post office. Le waited until they had crossed the road, and then he asked me for some money. I gave him a five, which he pocketed without comment. I asked him what he was going to do, and he said, "First I'm going to check my mail, and then I'm going to hitchhike to Oelrichs and buy a gallon of wine." I said I didn't want to go to Oelrichs. I asked if he would be at the powwow tomorrow night and he said yes. We said we'd see each other there. He must've been happy to get out of jail; he smiled broadly and waved as I drove away.

By Wednesday afternoon Pine Ridge was jumping. The rodeo was going on—the "Old Man Events," for cowboys forty-five and older—and the powwow would begin that evening. Wherever you looked, near or in the distance, you saw people, and yet somehow at no single place did they constitute a crowd. Many had dressed up specially for the day's events, even more had not. For a while I just went around checking out what people wore. A group of Oglala veterans who would march in the powwow's grand entry parade stood talking by an olive-drab van with white lettering on its sides listing the names of battles in Vietnam. They had on berets, service patches, medals, and feathers; one guy was in crisp jungle-camouflage fatigues, his trousers bloused below the knee into jungle boots of olive nylon and shined black leather. On his head he wore a black baseball cap with a single eagle feather on a leather thong hanging down behind. As I looked at him he nodded back at me and asked if I was a veteran. One of his companions had a clipboard with a list of names; they needed more guys to march in the parade. I said no, I wasn't, and I half-slunk away.

I saw a young woman in dark-purple jeans, silky black blouse, sunglasses, and silver earrings in the shape of baying coyotes, her straight black hair hanging well below her waist and held by a single tie between her shoulder blades; a young man all in denim from his jeans to his sleeveless vest to his oversize Superfly-style denim cap, on which was pinned a large button that read, "I Like A Good Beer Buzz In The Morning"; limping Indian rodeo riders with their identifying numbers still attached to their backs and orthopedic bandages peeking out from their shirts at the wrist or wrapped around the outside of their blue jeans at the knee; a slim young man in a black T-shirt with white lettering that said, "My Heroes Have Always Killed Cowboys"; a one-armed man in a turquoise T-shirt that said "I'm No Wimp"; old Indian men in light-colored Western dress shirts with dark string ties and their hair slicked back; old Indian women in flouncy, many-colored Spanish-style skirts with their hair held in combs and piled up high; little girls in buckskin dresses decorated with elk's teeth; a big, long-haired man wearing a blue-and-white head rag, narrow reptilian sunglasses, a loud Hawaiian shirt unbuttoned over his stomach, and a heavy chrome-silver watch chain looped from his belt to his right front jeans pocket; and a curly-haired man with a drink-ravaged face, a beaded belt that said "Bull Plume," a yellow straw cowboy hat, pegged jeans, and pointy-toed cowboy boots cut off below the ankles so they resembled slippers with high heels. Of course, most people had on the usual shorts-T-shirt-and-sneakers combination of the summer fairgoer, which made the exotic getups look even better.

All the activity—the rodeo, the vehicles and horses, the thousands of strolling feet—stirred up a great dust that rose above the village and hung high in the air. Late in the day as the sun declined, it illuminated the dust and gave the sky a reddish tinge. Pinkish-red light glowed on the western sides of the Pine Ridge water towers. The carnival rides began, and neon tubes in soft shades lit up on the whirling armatures of the Tilt-A-Whirl ride and the Mad Hatter's Tea Party. The carnival's three electric generators roared. Speakers on the façades of the rides played loud rock-and-roll music, and as I stood at a point with speakers on one side and the generators on the other, I decided there wasn't much difference between the two sounds. At sunset storm clouds appeared in the west, and the sky in that direction turned an ominous yellow, and the wind rose. A man named René Shoulders—he had introduced himself to me earlier in the day, not far from the veterans' van, where he, too, had asked if I was a veteran—saw me looking fearfully at the sky. He told me I shouldn't worry. A tornado had been sighted nearby, he said, but the medicine men had prayed and caused the tornado to veer away.

I went into the powwow grounds, passing through a gate in the chain-link fence that surrounded it. Admission was free; among the acts of former tribal chairman Dick Wilson that really irked people back in the seventies was his decision to charge admission to the tribal sun dance. At the center of the powwow grounds, and at the center of the powwow, is an open space about forty steps across where the dancing competitions and other ceremonies and contests are held. A circular structure, poles supporting a roof, encloses this space. The structure includes a raised booth for announcers and officials, with stairs leading to it. Spectators gather under the structure as if at a theater-in-the-round. Some stand or sit on the ground, but most sit on folding lawn chairs they have brought. The best way to observe a powwow is from your own lawn chair, and you may feel a bit unmoored and not-quite-present if you haven't got one. Outside the ring of spectators is a kind of circular promenade lined with booths selling Indian tacos and crafts and lemonade. Many powwow goers occupy this zone, walking round and round.

I did not know for sure what was going on. No program notes had been provided; as at most powwows, events seemed to proceed by spontaneity, with tacit understanding among the main people involved. A tribal official was talking at great length on the loudspeaker, allowing himself many weighty pauses. The spectators remained attentive to the still-empty powwow circle, as if expecting that at any minute something would materialize there. After a while the waiting made me nervous, and I wandered away. When I came back fifteen minutes later, I had just missed the Grand Entry parade. People were refurling flags and folding star quilts and banners. A dozen little girls in jingle dresses ran by, and I saw a young woman with lustrous, yard-long hair who had on a sash proclaiming her this year's powwow queen. Dozens of drum groups, from Pine Ridge and other reservations, had arrived. A group of men in matching ribbon shirts carried a flat drum the size of a truck wheel to a place near the announcer's booth, and a minute later they had set it up and had begun to drum and sing.

The men sat on metal folding chairs in a circle around the drum, hitting it hard with leather-wrapped drumsticks and singing a traditional song in loud, high-pitched unison, above which a single higher voice occasionally rose. Full dark had fallen by now, and the overhead lights had come on, but many corners of the powwow grounds were half-lit or in shadow. Shadows made it hard to see all the singers' faces. In a circle around them, intent white people watched and listened, some holding microphones to catch the sound. The observers' faces were wide-eyed, but the singers, as they leaned into the light and back out of it, had their

eyes screwed shut and their mouths wide open in song. Some of the
singers held a hand to one ear to plug it, the way musicians in recording
studios do. They sang at full voice, from deep inside themselves, all of
them hitting each note and word with vehemence and at exactly the
same time. The singing, a survival from hundreds of years ago, filled the
arena and echoed to the prairie sky.

I walked around in the promenade zone looking among the spectators for Le and for Florence's family, but they weren't there. For a while
I kept pace with a man named Rick Weiland, a candidate for Congress
from that district, who strolled along introducing himself to people in
the crowd. He kept meeting powwow fans who would be small help to
him at election time; I heard him say, hiding his vexation, "New
Zealand! Wow! There are people here from everywhere!" I saw two
other journalist-types like me with notebooks and gave them a wide
berth. Suddenly out of the shadows a pair of arms reached to embrace
me—it was my friend Germaine. "Remember me?" he asked, rubbing
his forehead to mine. After he released me he continued around the
circle, hugging every stranger he came upon. Those he hugged hugged
him back with powwow enthusiasm, happy that someone had wel-
comed them. Everyone I saw walking away after a hug from Germaine
had a smile.

Elaborately feathered dancers entered the powwow circle for the
men's Traditional Dance competition. The crowd of spectators standing
behind the rows of lawn chairs grew, and those in back couldn't really
see. The view from there reminded me of a crowded exhibition of famous paintings I went to once in a museum in New York City: occasionally a gap in the throng would occur, and through it come a dazzling
glimpse of color and form; then the ranks would close and all you could
see was the backs of people's heads again. At a less crowded spot I
worked my way to the front. The dancers were all going counterclock-
wise, each dancing as if alone, stepping to the drum music, some
crouching down low. All of them had numbers pinned on like those
worn by rodeo riders or distance racers; the powwow judges would
award cash and other prizes to the best dancers in each category and
subcategory. A dancer came right by me. He was a big man, and in his
costume—turkey-feather bustle three feet across, feathered anklets,
feathered gauntlets, beaded headband, tall roach made of a porcupine

tail atop his head—he seemed magnified in every dimension, almost a spirit-being. Then I saw the wristwatch he had on beneath the gauntlet, and the sweat on his temple, and the concentration in his eyes.

Now I wanted to be someplace quiet and empty. I maneuvered through the crowd, went by the taco and lemonade stands, out the gate in the chain-link fence, through the field full of parked cars. The carnival had shut down and the rock-and-roll no longer played, and only one generator still purringly ran. I walked to downtown Pine Ridge, past the tribal building, up the hill to the old hospital, and then onto the open field of the Path the Doctors Walk On. I went half a lap around and sat down. The grass was damp; dew had begun to fall. I could hear the amplified voice of the announcer at the powwow. Then his voice stopped, and the only sound was the singing and drumming. It came through the darkness high and strong and wild as if blown on the wind. It could have been ten voices singing or it could have been a thousand. At moments it sounded like other night noises, coyotes or mosquitoes, or like a sound the land itself might make. I imagined what hearing this would have done to me if I were a young man from Bern, Switzerland (say), traveling the prairie wilderness for the first time in 1843. I knew it would have scared and thrilled me to within an inch of my life.

CHAPTER

11

One morning I wandered into the main tribal building in downtown Pine Ridge and found the door of the circular council room wide open. The Oglala Tribal Council—seventeen members elected from the reservation's nine districts, plus an executive committee of five—meets here. The council room was empty, so I went in. Its roundness and its chairs set in a circle on ascending tiers around an open space at the center gave the room an intimate feel; its lack of windows, low ceiling, and brick walls added the battened-down quality of a war room. A man came in and sat on a chair in the front row and began to look through some papers. He was tall, probably in his fifties, with a butch haircut, a widow's peak, a prominent nose, and dark-rimmed glasses. I expected he would kick me out; but he said hello amiably, as if I were someone with important business there myself. I thought I recognized him from newspaper photographs. I asked, "By any chance, are you Oliver Red Cloud?"

"Oliver's my father. I'm Lyman Red Cloud," he said.

The photographs I remembered had accompanied a news story about a TV movie on the life of Crazy Horse that had aired not long before. The news story said that the Red Cloud family was suing Turner Network Television for the movie's portrayal of their ancestor Chief Red Cloud. I had seen the movie and could understand why the Red

Cloud family was annoyed. I mentioned the lawsuit to Lyman Red Cloud, and he said, "That's right! We're suing TNT and Ted Turner for $100 million for lying about my great-great-grandfather. They made Chief Red Cloud into an evil savage who was trying to kill Crazy Horse practically from the day he was born. If you believed that movie, the Lakota were constantly fighting with each other and trying to kill each other back then. The Turner people told us they'd do right by Red Cloud, but they disgraced his history. That TNT is a bunch of rippers."

"I thought the nude love scene between Crazy Horse and Black Buffalo Woman was especially bad," I said.

"They put in all that nudity just to draw an audience," Lyman Red Cloud said. "The Oglala people didn't walk around naked like that. And they wouldn't be makin' love outdoors where people could see. The Oglala were chaste and careful about their courtship. Crazy Horse would have *never* done that."

I said, "Another thing that was dumb was when the young Crazy Horse went on a vision quest, and his horse stood nearby, and the horse turned at one point and lifted its back foot, and you could see a shiny steel horseshoe."

"You weren't the only one that grabbed that detail, brother," Lyman Red Cloud said. "We were watching the movie on a VCR and we stopped the action right then. There it was—on the right hind foot—a horseshoe! Sioux people didn't have iron shoes on their horses back then. A man like Crazy Horse, he was a spiritual man, he didn't need shoes on his horse. A man like that, his spirituality protected the whole horse."

The council room began to fill up for a meeting, so I left. I was delighted to have met a Red Cloud. The original Red Cloud, in a sense the founder of the Pine Ridge Reservation, was perhaps the most important Indian leader of the nineteenth century. Other Indians would be more famous than he, and would live longer in myth and popular imagination; none would have more influence on the government's Indian policy. Red Cloud was born on the banks of Blue Creek, near where it meets the North Platte River in present western Nebraska, in 1821 or 1822. A meteor that crossed the sky in September 1822 was recorded in a Sioux pictorial calendar of the time, as well as by U.S. soldiers at a fort in Minnesota. According to some sources, Red Cloud's name referred to the meteor's light in the sky at his birth; others say that the name was in the family and had been his father's and his grandfather's. Red Cloud lived to be eighty-seven, feeble and blind and forgotten, and he died at his government-built frame house west of Pine Ridge village. Father Buechel, the Jesuit and lexicographer, recalled that just twelve Indian policemen came to Red Cloud's funeral on a cold winter day in 1909.

As an admirer of Crazy Horse, I at first had contempt for Red Cloud. Red Cloud did not participate in the Battle of the Rosebud or the Little Bighorn, where Crazy Horse won fame; Red Cloud had been at peace with the whites for almost eight years by then. After Crazy Horse surrendered and came in to the agency in 1877, Red Cloud bore tales against him to the authorities, and very likely conspired in his death, out of jealousy. Certainly, the death of the popular warrior removed a threat to Red Cloud's power at the agency. Red Cloud's behavior at that time is the worst that can be said about him, and is hard to forget. But it is also true that Red Cloud's biography tells the bigger story of the Oglala in the second half of the nineteenth century. As the tribe's leading chief for much of that time, he continued to work for his people, and had some successes, under circumstances where failure seemed to be built in. The destruction of the Indian way of life in those years was such that no Indian leader really survived it; Red Cloud almost did. Crazy Horse, who died in his thirties, is a good hero for someone young. As you age and see more of life's complications, you may find sympathy, if not admiration, for Red Cloud.

He was a big man, over six feet tall and two hundred pounds. A correspondent for *Harper's Weekly* who saw him in 1870 described him: "of herculean stature, six and a half feet in height, and large in proportion." An Army wife at Fort Laramie when he came there in the 1860s said he had "a pleasant smile." He grew up in the camp of a chief called Smoke, his mother's brother. His own father, sometimes called Lone Man, died of drink when Red Cloud was a boy. In 1841, taking Smoke's part in a quarrel, Red Cloud shot and killed Smoke's rival, a powerful chief called Bull Bear. The killing added to Red Cloud's reputation but divided the Oglala for decades. Red Cloud told interviewers in later years that he had been in eighty battles. Unfortunately for his national fame, most were with other Indian tribes and occurred before many white men had arrived. The autobiographical narrative which he related to a friend in old age is full of the killings of Pawnee and Shoshone and Omaha, the wiping out of fifty families of Arapahoe, the scalping alive of Crow.

The country at large first heard of Red Cloud after the Civil War. Gold seekers headed for Montana had put a wagon road through the Powder River country, the Sioux's favorite refuge and hunting ground in present eastern Wyoming. Red Cloud, by then the Oglala's most powerful war chief, led a campaign of large and small attacks over several years that ended up closing the trail and destroying the forts the Army had built to protect it. The war, first called the Powder River War, came to be known as Red Cloud's War; he was the only Indian ever to win a war with the United States. In 1868 he signed the Treaty of Fort Laramie, a peace agreement of such generosity to the Indians that the government would soon regret it.

In 1870, Eastern advocates of peace with the Indians brought Red Cloud to Washington and New York City. The trip made Red Cloud a star. He spoke at New York's Cooper Union to an overflow crowd that applauded and cheered after his every translated sentence; the New York *Tribune* called the speech "a triumph." Crowds lined Fifth Avenue to watch him and the other Sioux of the delegation walk by. A newspaper correspondent afterward wrote: "His name has been heralded with electric speed, within a month, to the remotest parts of the civilized world." The trip was, of course, a great encouragement for the policy of peace with the Indians as well. One reason for the enthusiasm of Red Cloud's reception may have been the fascination with the West that appeared in the years after the Civil War. For a country that had been painfully divided, the myth of the West—of the cowboys, of dime-novel gunfighters and heroes, of wide-open spaces, of undefeated Indians like Red Cloud—reimagined America as a place without boundaries, still new and whole.

Red Cloud would make many more trips to the East to meet with the government on his people's behalf. His later middle age was spent in a series of political and policy disputes with Indian agents and officials from Indian Affairs. Not long after the Fort Laramie treaty of 1868, the government had second thoughts about the boundaries it had set for Sioux lands. Specifically, it wanted the Black Hills. There had

long been rumors of gold in the Hills; then, in 1874, a treaty-violating
Black Hills expedition led by General George Custer reported "gold in
the roots of the grass," and a gold rush began. Red Cloud did not like
Custer going into the Hills and said so. When a government commission came to his agency in 1875 and tried to get the Sioux to sell the
Hills, Red Cloud called the commission offer of $6 million "just a little
spit in my mouth." He said that the Black Hills were "the head chief of
the land," and suggested $600 million as a more realistic price. The
commission concluded that the Indians valued the Hills beyond any
price that could be paid. After Custer's death at the Little Bighorn, the
United States finally got an opportunity to take the Hills at a bargain.
Threatening to cut off the rations of agency Indians, it forced a token
number of Sioux to agree to the sale. Red Cloud signed the treaty with
reluctance, and later said he hadn't understood what he had signed.
Among Lakota today who work for the return of Black Hills land, Red
Cloud's agreeing to the sale of the Hills is his most egregious sin.

The main struggle of Red Cloud's leadership period was over the lo-
cation of the Oglala's permanent home. In five years during the 1870s,
the Red Cloud Agency had four different locations. ("Agency" meant
the place where the Indian agent lived and tribal business was done; in
a larger sense it meant roughly what "reservation" does today.) The first
site was on the northern bank of the North Platte River, just down-
stream from Fort Laramie, where, for strategic reasons having to do
with the Oregon Trail and the railroad, the Army did not want the Sioux
at all. The next was on the White River in western Nebraska; the Ne-
braskans had said repeatedly that they did not want the Sioux within
their borders. From Nebraska the Sioux were made to move to an
agency on the Missouri River in central South Dakota in 1877. They
never quite got there, stopping short of the Missouri at a site on the
lower White River for about a year, then turning around and moving
back to the valley of White Clay Creek just north of the Nebraska
line, where Pine Ridge village is today. Each of these new locations involved the uprooting of thousands of people, the construction of new
agency buildings, much planning and debate. As I mentioned in Chapter 3, most of the turmoil was the result of the railroad interests' imper-
atives pushing the Indians around, a fact Red Cloud never seemed
to grasp.

Red Cloud spent the last thirty years of his life at the house he shared with his large family about a mile west of Pine Ridge village. The foundations of his house still remain, in a thicket of chokecherry bushes. His later years saw his powers as an Oglala leader and advocate decline. He refused offers to join the Wild West Show and exhibit himself, as Sitting Bull and others did, preferring to keep his dealings with the whites on a dignified level. At various times he worked for better rations, better Indian agents, Catholic missionaries to replace the Episcopalians the government had sent. In an attempt to humiliate him, General George Crook had deposed Red Cloud as chief in 1876; apparently the demotion didn't take, because an Indian agent who hated him and wished for his death tried to depose him again in 1880. Red Cloud's later trips to Washington never equaled the success of the trip in 1870. During the Ghost Dance troubles he was kidnapped by ghost dancers fleeing Pine Ridge after the massacre at Wounded Knee. The Indians who took him fired their guns around him to speed him up, and when he returned home after many days, he found his house and barn had been plundered. In 1898 he unsuccessfully opposed the building of fences on reservation land. In 1894, on a trip to visit hot springs on the Shoshone reservation, Red Cloud was arrested and jailed in Casper, Wyoming—the center of the Platte River country he used to roam—for killing a deer out of season. He used two horses to pay the $66 fine.

When the Oglala had finally settled on upper White Clay Creek, the site that would remain their permanent home, Indian agency officials debated about what to name the agency. Red Cloud had long advocated this site and had mentioned it to the President in person and in a letter. But government officials chose not to name it after him—perhaps to curtail Red Cloud's power, perhaps to avoid associations with the controversies about various sites which had gone before. Someone suggested the agency be called Oglala, but the Indian Commissioner objected that "not one in a hundred can spell Ogalala [sic] correctly." Pine Ridge was the name officialdom decided on. Its generic blandness and vaguely bucolic quality anticipated similar names—the Oak Parks and River Groves and Lake Forests and Chestnut Hills and so on— which would appeal to other planners of real estate across the land. Beneath the reservation's name of Pine Ridge, ineradicable as a watermark, the name of Red Cloud survives.

•   •   •

Most places in Pine Ridge village, if they're named for anyone, are named for people I had never heard of. Sometimes I asked around to find out who these people are or were. Behind the main tribal building, on the other side of a parking lot, is the Moses Two Bulls Tribal Court Building. One afternoon I went in there and asked a lady behind a desk who Moses Two Bulls was. She said he was a respected judge who served on the tribal bench for a long time and died about twenty years ago. She said his daughter, Joan, worked in the tribal enrollment office in the BIA building. I went to the enrollment office and stood in a long line of people with complicated questions, most of which seemed to involve getting their children enrolled. When I finally reached the head of the line, an Indian couple showed up, and the woman at the door naturally took them first. Only after the couple had left and I was waiting there alone did she turn her attention to me.

Joan Two Bulls, who had short hair, glasses, and a pained expression, seemed reluctant to admit even that she was she. I explained that I was writing a book and wanted to know about her father, who I assumed had been a great man in the tribe. She said that she did not think it was right to share information about him with an outsider. She said she would talk to her sisters and see whether they thought she should talk to me or not. If I came back in a month or two, she might be able to talk to me, she said. (I did, but she hadn't changed her mind.) All I was able eventually to learn about Moses Two Bulls was that he had belonged to the Seventh-day Adventist Church, often handed down strict sentences, and wore a hearing aid which he was suspected of turning off when arguments in his courtroom went on too long.

A short walk from the building named for him is the tribal senior citizens' home, known locally as the Cohen Home. Directions to that part of town often refer to it: "Take your second right past the Cohen Home." Its official name is the Felix S. Cohen Retirement Center. Places named after Jews are rare on the Great Plains; finding one on an Indian reservation might seem unlikelier still. One afternoon I entered the gate into the Cohen Home's fenced-in parking lot and grounds, passing five different signs that said intoxicated visitors would be taken to jail and another that warned visitors not to ask residents for money.

The young man at the security desk by the door did not know who Cohen was, though he did know his first name was Felix. He called for the director, and after I told her what I wanted, she let me in. She was Yvonne "Sister" Wilson, a short, vivid woman with dark, curly hair. She had on a turquoise turtleneck top and blue slacks. (Her late husband, Dick Wilson, was the tribal chairman and *casus belli* during the years of the Wounded Knee takeover.) She led me on a tour of the center— through the large living room with its tall windows flecked with BB-shot holes and its many armchairs and ashtrays aligned facing the TV, down the hall lined with paintings of old cowboys sitting around the campfire, into the dining room, where a few residents were playing bingo as a caller read out letters and numbers through a loudly amplified microphone. Yvonne Wilson said the center is for residents still able to care for themselves, and that when they no longer can, they go to a nursing home. Guests sleep two to a room and pay a total cost of about $200 a month, most of which comes from Social Security.

The home was built in 1965, she said. She didn't know who had suggested naming it after Felix S. Cohen, but thought the idea might have been the contractor's. She said that Cohen was a lawyer who did some work for the tribe and might have written the tribal constitution and by-laws back in the 1930s.

Felix S. Cohen, I later learned, was the leading expert on federal Indian law of this century. Indeed, probably no one in the history of the country has known more about the subject than Felix Solomon Cohen. He was born in New York City in 1907. His father, Morris Raphael Cohen, came to America from Russia when he was twelve and eventually became a professor of philosophy at the College of the City of New York (CCNY) in Manhattan He was a widely renowned philosopher, and the main library at CCNY is named for him. Felix's mother, Mary Ryshpan Cohen, a schoolteacher, tutored Felix at home until he was eight. Felix went to Townsend Harris High School and entered CCNY early, graduating magna cum laude at eighteen. He paid some of his way through college by collecting and trading stamps. After CCNY he went to Harvard, where he received an M.A. in philosophy in 1927 and a Ph.D. in 1928. He got his law degree from Columbia Law School in 1931. By then he was twenty-four.

In that year he married Lucy M. Kramer, a graduate student at Columbia with an M.A. in mathematics whom he had met at a Halloween party when both were eighteen. They would have two daughters. As a young man Felix Cohen wrote many philosophical articles on such subjects as "What Is a Question?" and "The Ethical Basis of Legal Criticism," but he believed that philosophy should engage itself with problems of the real world. To him, the law was where the two met, and he regarded law as the central, all-inclusive institution of civilization. He also believed strongly in ethnic culture—he liked to sing folk songs of different nations—and he envisioned the country's future as a place of many ethnic groups working together and appreciating each other and getting along. His ideology and his learning made him an obvious choice to serve in the New Deal government that took over in Washington in the thirties. John Collier, the new head of Indian Affairs, wanted bright young people sympathetic to tribal concerns. The administration hired Felix Cohen as an assistant solicitor to draft Indian legislation, and he moved to Washington in 1933.

Federal Indian policy has historically been a crooked path swerving between two extremes: one, the attempt to abolish all Indian tribes, end all treaty obligations, and assimilate Indians into the American mainstream (a policy sometimes called termination); and the other, the attempt to increase tribal sovereignty, encourage traditional Indian culture, and reduce federal and state involvement in the governing of the tribes. Felix Cohen arrived in Washington at the beginning of a big swerve in the second direction. For the previous half century, termination had ruled, with a policy of land allotment designed to make Indians property-owning citizens like everybody else. The legislation Felix Cohen worked on ended allotment, increased tribal landholdings, and strengthened the sovereignty of Indian tribes. It had at its center a deep belief in the curing power of democracy. The Wheeler-Howard Act of 1934, called the Indian Reorganization Act (IRA), gave the tribes many of the powers previously held by the federal government. It also said that tribes could vote on whether they wanted to govern themselves as constitution-style democracies. Disappointing the drafters of the IRA, about a quarter of the tribes voted not to accept the act at all. The Oglala accepted it and adopted a tribal constitution. Felix Cohen did not write it for them, although he may have consulted with them on it, and his department may have given them a model constitution to work from. A generation later, when factional fighting broke out on the reservation in the 1970s over opposition to the elected tribal government, some Oglala traditionalists blamed the changes brought by the IRA. They said that majority-rule democracy was wrong for the tribe, which had previously ruled itself more loosely, with various headmen in charge of different groups and no dissenting group absolutely compelled to go along.

Part of Cohen's work for the government involved a review of all existing federal Indian laws for the Interior Department. From this came the achievement for which Cohen is most remembered, his *Handbook of Federal Indian Law* (1941), which went on to be the standard text on the subject. Cohen left the government for private practice in 1948, but continued his interest in Indian affairs. He believed that "our democracy entrusts the task of maintaining its most precious liberties to those who are despised and oppressed by their fellow men," and Indians were foremost among the oppressed in his mind. He wrote passionate essays about their contributions to the world, represented individual tribes in lawsuits, and traveled widely with his family on the reservations. The Blackfeet tribe of Montana adopted him and gave him the name "Double Runner." He worked for legislation that included Indians among those entitled to Social Security benefits, and he won several lawsuits against states that had not allowed Indians to vote.

In 1953, at the age of forty-six, Felix Cohen died of lung cancer. He had been a vigorous man—he climbed forty of the forty-six Adirondack peaks over 4,000 feet high—and aside from an occasional Parliament cigarette in the evenings, he did not smoke. The notices of his death were filled with eulogy. He was remembered for his scholarship, his selflessness, his integrity, and the "almost saintly qualities" he attained in his later years. John Collier praised him as "an enemy of the drive toward cultural homogeneity, the enforced cultural flatland." Cohen's rabbi said of him, "His words flowed softly like the waters of Siloam out of the sanctuary of his being." Supreme Court Justice Felix Frankfurter, with whom he had studied, said that Felix Cohen carried out his earthly pilgrimage "with high adventure and the gallantry of the wise and the good."

Admirers recalled the poetic sense of harmony that Cohen brought to the work and hobbies he loved—to writing, teaching, tending his vegetable garden, collecting stamps, rooting for the CCNY basketball team. His college was one of the great loves of his life, and he kept up with fellow alumni and stayed in touch with the school. After his death the CCNY alumni magazine printed a memorial to him, along with a poem he had written just before graduation:

> *O City College, castle of the mind,*
> *I could not see your towers in the sun;*
> *I climbed your stairways confident and blind;*
> *The way was pleasant and the way is done.*
> *Within your walls my days of springtime lie . . .*
> *Gray towers melt away into the sky.*

Several places in and near Pine Ridge village are named for athletes. There's the Paul "Dizzy" Trout Field House at the Red Cloud School, named for the Detroit Tigers pitcher who led the American League in wins in 1943. Dizzy Trout was an active member of an Illinois athletic club that raises money for the school; he died at about the time the field house was built, and his friends asked that it be named after him. Billy Mills Hall, the auditorium at the corner of 18 and 407 in downtown Pine Ridge, honors the Oglala runner who won the gold medal in the ten-thousand-meter race in the 1964 Olympics. No other American has ever won a gold in that event. Billy Mills was born and raised in Pine Ridge village, and he trained for the Olympics while in the Marine Corps. He is now a spokesman for a charitable organization and makes motivational speeches and videos. He lives in California.

The Leroy "Sunshine" Janis Memorial Park—the official name of the picnic area by the powwow grounds—is dedicated to a well-known Pine Ridge resident who died of cystic fibrosis in 1984. Sunshine Janis was born in 1927 and grew up in a remote part of the reservation called the Gunnery Range, used back then by the Air Force for target practice. His siblings remember the recurrent sound of gunfire and the shells that would buzz over the house sometimes. Sunshine was a good amateur boxer and fought many bouts when he was in high school. After his junior year he dropped out and joined the Army Airborne. He liked the military and might have made a career of it, but ruined his knee on a jump when another soldier got tangled in his parachute. He came back to Pine Ridge and worked various jobs and was a tribal po-

liceman for a while. In his spare time he organized and coached a boxing club for Pine Ridge kids, and for many years drove the boys to
matches in the big Buick Specials and Ford station wagons he favored.
He stood over six feet tall and weighed 220 pounds. He loved to play
practical jokes and sing funny songs and clown, imitating popular
singers and movie stars. People remember especially how he used to
wear an old black hat, put his false teeth in upside down, and recite the
Pledge of Allegiance in the voice of the actor Gabby Hayes.

Next to the Leroy "Sunshine" Janis Memorial Park is the Delmar
"Fudd" Brewer Memorial Field, where local softball leagues play.
There are a lot of Brewers in Pine Ridge. Someone told me that Delmar's brother Dennis is head of the BIA's highway maintenance shop in
town, and I found him there, in his small office with safety posters on
the walls beside a hanger-sized garage full of dump trucks and road
graders. A crackling shortwave radio on a shelf relayed a conversation
between road crews in an outlying district who were trying to contain a
grass fire. Dennis Brewer is a stocky man with glasses, close-set eyes,
big arms, and a shock of hair across his forehead. He was happy to tell
me about his brother, and asked me to sit down. "There was nine of us
kids," he said. "Six boys and three girls: Dave, Deane, Duane, Dennis,
Delmar, and Rich; and Colleen, Judy, and Doris. We just lost Dave here
about a month ago. He was head of records out at Pine Ridge Hospital.
The other one that died was Delmar. He was born February 23, 1951,
and he died March 14, 1991. I was born in 1948, and he was the
brother closest to me. When we were kids we lived in Rapid City, but
then my dad—he was a construction worker—moved us down here to
Pine Ridge.

"Us boys grew up playing baseball. We lived and died it, we couldn't
wait for spring. A lot of times it was just me and Fudd—everybody
called him that, because of Elmer Fudd, ever since he was a kid. We
played this game we made up, with a flat wooden stick for a bat and one
of those yellow plastic ReaLemon juice bottles for a ball. They're
shaped like a lemon, you know, and you can make 'em do all kinds of
things when you throw 'em. Fudd had a good screwball. I couldn't hit
that sucker, but I had a backup ball, and Fudd couldn't hit that. So it
would be me against him, with our two dogs, Sparky and Duke, in the
outfield. They were Lab-shepherd crosses, and they could really play

ball. Them dogs could catch anything—pop-ups, long flies, line drives—and if the dogs caught it, you were out. We played hour after hour, all summer long. After we'd perfected this game, we got other kids to play it, and I'll tell you, it was a great game, more competitive than baseball.

"Fudd was an all-around good athlete, though. He was about five-nine and 155 pounds, and he had an excellent arm. As soon as he was old enough, he played regular ball: Little League, Pony League, then American Legion ball. He played a lot of positions, but he was best as a pitcher. He always went into a game knowing he was gonna win, and usually he did. Every year he won fifteen or twenty games, and he once struck out twenty-two guys in a game. If he hadn't been sick, he could've played pro ball. His best pitch was his fastball, and he didn't walk many guys. I played, too—I was a catcher. Plus, him and me always played in a fast-pitch softball league, travelin' to games all around here. Some Saturdays or Sundays we'd play a baseball double header in Pine Ridge in the afternoon and then in the evening drive to Rushville or someplace and play a fast-pitch softball game. It was just in the blood, it was fun. In 1987 our team won the state championship in fast-pitch softball.

"We gave Fudd the trophy. He'd had to quit by then. He finally got too sick—he had childhood diabetes and it began to affect his eyesight. It was hard for him to hang it up. He still came with us to the games, supporting and coaching. He lived here in Pine Ridge and worked in the property and supply office at Pine Ridge Hospital. He was real professional about his job; he started there right after high school and stayed right straight through almost until he died. The people at the hospital was the only ones in town that called him Delmar. After his health declined he watched a lot of sports on TV. He had to have a leg amputated, and an arm. He joked about it sometimes. He was just a happy guy who joked a lot and made other people feel good. He was married twice, had a couple of kids. People around town loved Fudd. After he died, G. Wayne Tapio, a tribal councilman, came up with the idea of naming the field after him and the park after Sunshine, and on Labor Day a couple years ago they had the dedication ceremony."

•   •   •

One afternoon Le and I were driving on Highway 18 in Pine Ridge when I noticed a single-story factory-style building across a weedy field. It had some lettering and a mural of a landscape on the front. A sign by the highway said it was the SuAnne Big Crow Health and Recreation Center, and below that were the words "Happytown, USA." I asked Le if he knew who SuAnne Big Crow was. He said, "She was a basketball star for Pine Ridge High School who helped 'em win the state championship and died in a car wreck a few years back. It was when I was living in New York, though, so that's about all I know."

A day or two later, I drove up to the building and parked in the dirt parking lot out front. Up close, I could see that the mural painted on the building's wall of corrugated steel depicted Sioux country from the Black Hills to the prairie and Pine Ridge. The tops of the letters of "SuAnne" in the center's name were lost in the white clouds over the Hills. A chunk of cinder block propped open the green steel front door. I went in. First to greet me was the smell of hamburgers frying. In the many times I would return, that frying smell would always be there. I would bring it away with me in my clothes and even in the pages of my notebooks, and when I happened to meet it in other places, I would always think of the SuAnne Big Crow Center. I had never much liked hamburgers or their smell before, but now it is a happy and inspiring aroma in my mind.

The entry hall had fluorescent lights above and a banner that said WELCOME TO HAPPYTOWN, USA. The images in the hall were a temporarily confusing combination of Oglala pride and 1950s-revival style. The words for "Boys" and "Girls" on the restroom doors on my left were in Sioux. On a table in a corner was a highly polished pair of brown-and-white saddle shoes. Above them hung the flag of the Oglala nation, and next to the flag was a large framed portrait of a young Elvis Presley—a more Indian-looking Elvis, it seemed to me, with a darker complexion and blacker, straighter hair. Framed photographs of a teenage girl smiling in a basketball warm-up jacket, making a shot in a basketball game, looking serious in a formal dress next to a boy in a tuxedo, gave the place the additional aura of a shrine.

The hall led, on the left, to a café in a big room with a lunch counter and tables and booths. The back end of a 1955 Packard affixed to one wall held potato and macaroni salads in its open trunk. A few late lunch customers were eating burgers at the booths or helping themselves to salad. A loud jukebox played fifties and sixties songs. Old-time Pepsi-Cola memorabilia decorated the walls, along with black-and-white photo portraits of John F. Kennedy and Martin Luther King, and several more portraits of Elvis. Kids of junior high age and younger were hanging out—eating ice-cream cones, playing video games.

At the end of the hallway on the right was a smaller room with glass trophy cases along the walls. The trophies all were from the athletic career of SuAnne Big Crow, the teenage girl in the photos, the person for whom the center was named. I looked at the trophies, I watched a short video playing on a VCR in the room, I read some framed news stories about SuAnne Big Crow, and a sense of discovery came over me. Here was a hero—not a folk hero, a sports hero, a tribal hero, or an American hero, but a combination of all these. I had thought that Oglala heroes existed mostly in the past. But a true Oglala hero appeared in the late 1980s, while the rest of the world was looking the other way, in suffering Pine Ridge, right under everyone's noses: SuAnne Big Crow.

If you ask people nowadays to name a hero, probably they'll say Michael Jordan, or maybe Mother Teresa, or maybe AIDS researcher Dr. Mathilde Krim. In the public sphere, the pickings have become pretty slim. Or else they'll mention someone unknown to the public at large—perhaps a parent, or a dedicated teacher they had in high school. The first kind of hero is admired by millions and exists for us mainly through the newspapers or (most often) on TV; the second kind has dozens or at most hundreds of admirers, and is seldom or never in the news or on TV. Historically, though, the distinction between the two kinds of heroes has been much less clear; that is, in the past a hero to the public at large might also have been someone you knew or knew of from your community—someone you would see on the street now and again, an acquaintance, a friend-of-a-friend. Also, for most of history, the first news of a hero came not through any written or broadcast word but by word of mouth.

For the Oglala, heroes have always been of the first and second kinds simultaneously. Crazy Horse, for example, was just a guy you saw around from time to time, herding his horses, sitting before his lodge, smoking with his friends. And yet he was also . . . *Crazy Horse*: the near-magic warrior, the victor of many battles, the man never wounded once in a fight, the famous destroyer of Custer and the Seventh Cavalry. Our usual experience of heroes today is so divided between the one or the other kind, and so diminished in general, it may be hard to imagine how someone who is both kinds of hero at once can elevate your soul. Imagine that when you were a little kid you thought, as kids often do, that your father was the strongest man in the world; but when you got older, you discovered that in your case your father actually *was* the world's strongest man, and you watched him win the gold medal in weightlifting in the Olympics. Or imagine that an older kid you looked up to when you were in elementary school, instead of fading in luster in the usual way as time went on, not only fulfilled every expectation you had for him but surpassed these with glorious public feats you never dreamed of.

Imagine that the hopeful, innocent, unbounded fantasy you had about someone you really admired when you were a child did not meet the usual puncturing and deflation but simply continued to grow; that you kept it with the same innocence and hope, finding more justification for it every day; that the person you admired, someone as familiar to you as yourself and yet at the same time set apart, took the hope invested in her onward into the larger world without a hitch, increasing her fame and achievements and admirers geographically along the way; and imagine that against odds upon odds she *won*, won at everything important she tried, won so blithely as to hardly show her strength; and that she carried the hope invested in her unstoppably aloft, defying the death and fear in the world. And imagine that as she did this she somehow carried you with her, lifted you, too, above the fear and the death, and gave you and all the people around you someone to be—a self, a freedom, a name. Warfield Moose, Sr., SuAnne's teacher of Lakota studies at Pine Ridge High School, said of her, "She showed us a way to live on the earth." Such was SuAnne's stature and generosity, she was able to do that not only for her Oglala people but for those who knew her and knew of her in the state of South Dakota, and beyond.

Reader, books are long, and I know that even the faithful reader tires. But I hope a few of you are still with me here. As much as I have wanted to tell anything, I want to tell you about SuAnne.

CHAPTER

12

SuAnne Marie Big Crow was born on March 15, 1974, at Pine Ridge Hospital—the brick building, now no longer a hospital, just uphill from the four-way intersection in town. Her mother, Leatrice Big Crow, known as Chick, was twenty-five years old. Chick had two other daughters: Cecelia, called Cee Cee, who was three, and Frances, called Pigeon, who was five. Chick had been born a Big Crow, and grew up in her grandmother Big Crow's house in Wolf Creek, a little community about seven miles east of Pine Ridge. Chick had a round, pretty face, dark eyes, a determined chin, and wiry reddish-brown hair. Her figure was big-shouldered and trim; she had been a good athlete as a girl. Now she worked as an administrative assistant for the tribal planning office, and she was raising her daughters alone with the help of her sisters and other kin. People knew that Everett "Gabby" Brewer was the father of the two older girls, but Chick would never say who SuAnne's father was. If asked, Chick always said she didn't want to talk about it. When SuAnne got old enough to wonder, people sometimes told her that her father was Elvis. And sometimes, when SuAnne wore her hair a certain way with a curl in front, you would have to admit that a resemblance was there.

SuAnne's birth came at a dark time on the reservation. The ongoing battle between supporters and opponents of Dick Wilson's tribal government showed no signs of letup, with violence so pervasive and unpredictable that many people were afraid to leave their homes. Just the month before, a nine-year-old boy named Harold Weasel Bear had been shot and seriously wounded as he sat in his father's pickup in White Clay; his father was a Wilson man. Russell Means had campaigned against Wilson for the tribal chairmanship that winter and got more votes than Wilson in the primary. In the runoff election, however, Wilson won, by about two hundred votes out of the more than three thousand votes cast. Means had promised to "destroy" the present system of tribal government if he won, and many people were glad he wouldn't get a chance. He accused Wilson of stealing the election, and the federal Civil Rights Commission later agreed, saying that almost a third of the votes cast seemed to be improper and that the election was "permeated with fraud."

The beatings and stompings and shootings and bombings on the reservation would continue until the killing of the FBI agents the following year, after which a general exhaustion plus the presence of hundreds of FBI investigators brought the violence level down. In those days, if you were on the Pine Ridge Reservation you picked a side, and Chick Big Crow was for Dick Wilson all the way. She still calls Dick Wilson one of the greatest leaders the tribe ever had. Distinctions between those with anti– and pro–Dick Wilson loyalties, between AIM and goon, mean less today than they did then. Before SuAnne's sixteenth birthday, she would have a lot to do with causing those divisions to heal.

As a Big Crow, SuAnne belonged to one of the largest clans—the Lakota word for the extended family group is the *tiospaye*—on Pine Ridge. In the Pine Ridge telephone directory, Big Crow is the fourth-most-common name, behind Brewer, Pourier, and Ecoffey. (This method of figuring is not definitive, of course, since most people on the reservation don't have phones.) Chick Big Crow's mother, Alvina Big Crow, was one of nine children, and Chick had many Big Crow first cousins, as well as many with other last names. Her mother's sister Grace married a Mills; Olympic champion Billy Mills is a first cousin of Chick's. Chick's uncle Jimmy Big Crow married a woman named Marcella who bore him twenty-four children, including nine sets of twins. TV shows sometimes featured Jimmy and Marcella Big Crow and their family, and for a while they were listed in the *Guinness Book of World Records*. Basketball teams at Pine Ridge High School have occasionally been all or mostly Big Crow brothers or sisters and their first cousins.

The name Big Crow comes up rather often in the history of the Sioux. Big Crows are mentioned as headmen, though not as leaders of the first rank like Spotted Tail or Red Cloud. They seem to have been solidly upper-middle-class, if such a description can apply to nineteenth-century Sioux. When Francis Parkman arrived fresh out of Harvard to visit the Oglala in 1846, he stayed in the well-appointed tipi of a man called the Big Crow (Kongra Tonga), who was known for his friendliness to the whites. Parkman described in his book *The Oregon Trail* how the Big Crow sat in his tipi at night telling stories in a darkness suddenly made light by the flaring of a piece of buffalo fat on the fire, and how the Big Crow returned from a buffalo hunt with his arms and moccasins all bloody, and how he particularly vexed his lodger by getting up every midnight to sing a long prayer the spirits had told him to sing. In 1859, this Big Crow or another was killed by Crow Indians on a raiding expedition; the event appears in a Sioux winter count which marks 1859 with a pictograph that translates as "Big Crow was killed." In 1871, a Big Crow is listed among the chiefs who accompanied Red Cloud to a council at Fort Laramie. In 1877, when Crazy Horse fled the Red Cloud Agency to seek refuge at the Spotted Tail Agency, a Brule Sioux named Big Crow confronted him and lectured him, saying that Crazy Horse never listened but that now he must listen and must go with Big Crow to the commanding officer.

Leatrice "Chick" Big Crow does not know for sure whether any of these Big Crows is an ancestor of hers, but she thinks not. She says that her branch of the family descends from Big Crows of the Sans Arc Lakota, a tribe much smaller than the Oglala, who lived on the plains to the north and west. A medicine man has told her that among the Sans Arc long ago lived a chief named Big Crow who was greater than any chief we know of. This chief was also so wise that he never put himself forward and never identified himself to the whites so they could single him out as chief; he knew the jealousy and division this would cause.

For years the chief led the Sans Arc in war and peace, carefully avoiding all notoriety as the tribe prospered and grew strong. After he died, the tribe began to quarrel among themselves and dwindled away. The memory of this chief vanished except among a few, according to the medicine man. After SuAnne died, the medicine man told Chick that she had been the spirit of this great leader come back to reunite the people.

SuAnne grew up with her sisters in her mother's three-bedroom house in Pine Ridge. She was an active child; she sat up on her own while still an infant, and walked at nine months old. From when she was a baby, she wanted to do everything the bigger girls could do. When she was two, she told her mother that she wanted to go to school. She walked with Pigeon and Cee Cee to the school-bus stop in the mornings and often had to be restrained from getting on. Pigeon's memory of SuAnne is of her looking up at her from under the bill of her baseball cap. She was always looking up at her sisters and following them. When they went places around town, she went with them, telling Pigeon, "I'll walk in your footsteps." She played easily with kids much older than she. Chick came home from work one afternoon and found that SuAnne, then only four, had escaped from the babysitter and gotten on a big kid's ten-speed bicycle. Chick saw SuAnne coming down the hill, standing on the crossbar between the pedals and reaching up with her arms at full length to hold the handlebars.

Even today, people talk about what a strict mother Chick Big Crow was. Her daughters always had to be in the house or the yard by the time the streetlights came on. The only after-school activities she let them take part in were the structured and chaperoned kind; unsupervised wanderings and (later) cruising around in cars were out. In an interview when she was a teenager, SuAnne said that she and her sisters had to come up with their own fun, because their mother wouldn't let them socialize outside of school. Pigeon remembers Monopoly games they played that went on for days, and Scrabble marathons, and many games of Clue. In summer they could take picnics to White Clay Creek and spend the day there in the shallows, lying back and seeing different shapes in the clouds. One summer when Pigeon was in summer school the girls had their own school in their basement when she came home in the afternoons, with a full schedule of math and geography and English and so on. They played badminton in their yard and did Tae Kwon Do, and they made up a version of kickball played under the sprinkler on their lawn's wet grass where they could slide for miles. On evenings when their mother bowled at a league in Rushville they held road races with shopping carts on a track they made in the basement; they later said that the shopping carts taught them how to drive. At night, though they were sent to bed early, the three girls would read by flashlight under the covers or by the light from the hall—they liked the Nancy Drew mystery books and the Little House on the Prairie series, and the stories of the Babysitters' Club, and books by Beverly Cleary and Lois Duncan and Judy Blume. They had a little radio they kept under the bed, and when a local station signed off at ten o'clock with the national anthem, they would unharmoniously sing along.

Chick Big Crow was (and is) strongly anti-drug and -alcohol. On the reservation, Chick has belonged for many years to the small but adamant minority who take that stance. When SuAnne was nine years old, she was staying with her godmother on New Year's Eve when the woman's teenaged son came home drunk and shot himself in the chest. The woman was too distraught to do anything, so SuAnne called the ambulance and the police and cared for her until the grown-ups arrived. Perhaps because of this incident, SuAnne became as opposed to drugs and alcohol as her mother was. She gave talks on the subject to school and youth groups, made a video urging her message in a stern and wooden tone, and as a high-schooler traveled to distant cities for conventions of like-minded teens. I once asked Rol Bradford, a Pine Ridge teacher and coach who is also a friend of her family, whether SuAnne's public advocacy on this issue wasn't risky given the prominence of alcohol in the life of the reservation. "You have to understand," Rol Bradford said, "SuAnne didn't *respond* to peer pressure, SuAnne *was* peer pressure. She was the backbone of any group she was in, and she was way wiser than her years. By coming out against drinking, I know she flat-out saved a lot of kids' lives. In fact, she even had an effect on me. It dawned on me that if a sixteen-year-old girl could have the guts to say these things, then maybe us adults should pay attention, too. I haven't had a drink since the day she died."

• • •

As strongly as Chick forbade certain activities, she encouraged the girls in sports. At one time or another, they did them all—cross-country running and track, volleyball, cheerleading, basketball, softball. Some of the teams were at school and others were sponsored by organizations in town. Chick's sister, Yvonne "Tiny" De Cory, had a cheerleading drill team called the Tiny Tots, a group of girls eight years old and under who performed at local sporting events and gatherings. SuAnne became a featured star for the Tiny Tots when she was three; many in Pine Ridge remember first seeing her or hearing about her then. She began to play on her big sisters' league softball team at about the same time, when the bat was still taller than she was. Coaches would send SuAnne in to pinch-hit, hoping for a walk, and telling her not to swing. Often she swung anyway; once, in a tie game, she swung at the third strike, the catcher dropped it, and several errors later she had rounded the bases for the winning run.

Pine Ridge had a winter basketball league for girls aged seven to eleven, and SuAnne later recalled that she played her first organized game in that league when she was in kindergarten. She had gone with her sisters to a tournament in Rushville when a sudden snowstorm kept some of the players away. The coach, finding himself short-handed, put SuAnne in the game. "It was funny," SuAnne told a basketball magazine, "because all I really knew how to do was play defense, so that's all I did. I not only took the ball away from our opponents, but also from my own teammates!" A coach who watched her play then said, "If you ever saw the movie *Star Wars*—well, you remember the Ewoks? Well, SuAnne was so much smaller than the other kids, she looked like one of those little Ewoks out there runnin' around."

In the West, girls' basketball is a bigger deal than it is elsewhere. High school girls' basketball games in states like South Dakota and Montana draw full-house crowds, and newspapers and college recruiters give nearly the same attention to star players who are girls as they do to stars who are boys. There were many good players on the girls' teams at Pine Ridge High School and at the Red Cloud School when SuAnne was little. SuAnne idolized a star for the Pine Ridge Lady Thorpes named Lolly Steele, who set many records at the school. On a national level, SuAnne's hero was Earvin "Magic" Johnson, of the Los Angeles Lakers pro team. Women's professional basketball did not exist in those years, but men's pro games were reaching a level of popularity to challenge baseball and football. SuAnne had big posters of Magic Johnson on her bedroom walls.

She spent endless hours practicing basketball. When she was in the fifth grade she heard somewhere that to improve your dribbling you should bounce a basketball a thousand times a day with each hand. She followed this daily exercise faithfully on the cement floor of the patio; her mother and sisters got tired of the sound. For variety, she would shoot layups against the gutter and the drainpipe, until they came loose from the house and had to be repaired. She knew that no girl in an official game had ever dunked a basketball—that is, had leaped as high as the rim and stuffed the ball through the hoop from above—and she wanted to be the first in history to do it. To get the feel, she persuaded a younger boy cousin to kneel on all fours under the basket. With a running start, and a leap using the boy's back as a springboard, she could dunk the ball.

Charles Zimiga, who would coach SuAnne in basketball during her high school years, remembered the first time he saw her. He was on the cross-country track on the old golf course coaching the high school boys' cross-country team—a team that later won the state championship—when SuAnne came running by. She was in seventh grade at the time. She practiced cross-country every fall, and ran in amateur meets, and sometimes placed high enough to be invited to tournaments in Boston and California. "The fluidness of her running amazed me, and the strength she had," Zimiga said. "I stood watching her go by and she stopped right in front of me—I'm a high school coach, remember, and she's just a young little girl—and she said, 'What're you lookin' at?' I said, 'A runner.' She would've been a top cross-country runner, but in high school it never did work out, because the season conflicted with basketball. I had heard about her before, but that day on the golf course was the first time I really noticed her."

SuAnne went to elementary school in Wolf Creek, because of her family's connections there. Zimiga and others wanted her to come to Pine Ridge High School so she could play on the basketball team, and finally they persuaded Chick to let her transfer when she was in junior high. By the time SuAnne was in eighth grade, she had grown to five feet, five inches tall ("but she played six foot," Zimiga said); she was long-limbed, well-muscled, and quick. She had high cheekbones, a prominent, arched upper lip that lined up with the basket when she aimed the ball, and short hair that she wore in no particular style. She could have played every game for the varsity when she was in eighth grade, but Coach Zimiga, who took over girls' varsity basketball that year, wanted to keep peace among older players who had waited for their chance to be on the team. He kept SuAnne on the junior varsity during most of the regular season. The varsity team had a good year, and when it advanced to the district playoffs, Zimiga brought SuAnne up from the JVs for the play-off games. Several times she got into foul trouble; the referees rule strictly in tournament games, and SuAnne was used to a more headlong style of play. She and her cousin Doni De Cory, a 5'10" junior, combined for many long-break baskets, with Doni throwing downcourt passes to SuAnne on the scoring end. In the district play-off against the team from Red Cloud, SuAnne scored thirty-one points. In the regional play-off game, Pine Ridge beat a good Todd County team, but in the state tournament they lost all three games and finished eighth.

Some people who live in the cities and towns near reservations treat their Indian neighbors decently; some don't. In cities like Denver and Minneapolis and Rapid City, police have been known to harass Indian teenagers and rough up Indian drunks and needlessly stop and search Indian cars. Local banks whose deposits include millions in tribal funds sometimes charge Indians higher loan interest rates than they charge whites. Gift shops near reservations sell junky caricature Indian pictures and dolls, and until not long ago, beer coolers had signs on them that said, INDIAN POWER. In a big discount store in a reservation border town, a white clerk observes a lot of Indians waiting at the checkout and remarks, "Oh, they're Indians—they're used to standing in line." Some people in South Dakota hate Indians, unapologetically, and will tell you why; in their voices you can hear a particular American meanness that is centuries old.

When teams from Pine Ridge play non-Indian teams, the question of race is always there. When Pine Ridge is the visiting team, usually their hosts are courteous, and the players and fans have a good time. But Pine Ridge coaches know that occasionally at away games their kids will be insulted, their fans will not feel welcome, the host gym will be dense with hostility, and the referees will call fouls on Indian players every chance they get. Sometimes in a game between Indian and non-Indian teams, the difference in race becomes an important and distracting part of the event.

One place where Pine Ridge teams used to get harassed regularly was in the high school gymnasium in Lead, South Dakota. Lead is a town of about 3,200 northwest of the reservation, in the Black Hills. It is laid out among the mines that are its main industry, and low, wooded mountains hedge it round. The brick high school building is set into a hillside. The school's only gym in those days was small, with tiers of gray-painted concrete on which the spectator benches descended from just below the steel-beamed roof to the very edge of the basketball court—an arrangement that greatly magnified the interior noise.

In the fall of 1988, the Pine Ridge Lady Thorpes went to Lead to play a basketball game. SuAnne was a full member of the team by then. She was a freshman, fourteen years old. Getting ready in the locker room, the Pine Ridge girls could hear the din from some of the fans. They were yelling fake-Indian war cries, a "woo-woo-woo" sound. The usual plan for the pre-game warm-up was for the visiting team to run onto the court in a line, take a lap or two around the floor, shoot some baskets, and then go to their bench at courtside. After that, the home team would come out and do the same, and then the game would begin. Usually the Thorpes lined up for their entry more or less according to height, which meant that senior Doni De Cory, one of the tallest, went first. As the team waited in the hallway leading from the locker room, the heckling got louder. A typical kind of hollered remark was "Squaw!" or "Where's the cheese?" (the joke being that if Indians were lining up, it must be to get commodity cheese); today no one remembers exactly what was said. Doni De Cory looked out the door and told her teammates, "I can't handle this." SuAnne quickly offered to go first in her place. She was so eager that Doni became suspicious. "Don't embarrass us," Doni told her. SuAnne said, "I won't. I won't embarrass you." Doni gave her the ball, and SuAnne stood first in line.

She came running onto the court dribbling the basketball, with her teammates running behind. On the court, the noise was deafeningly loud. SuAnne went right down the middle; but instead of running a full lap, she suddenly stopped when she got to center court. Her teammates were taken by surprise, and some bumped into one another. Coach Zimiga at the rear of the line did not know why they had stopped. SuAnne turned to Doni De Cory and tossed her the ball. Then she stepped into the jump-ball circle at center court, in front of the Lead fans. She unbuttoned her warm-up jacket, took it off, draped it over her shoulders, and began to do the Lakota shawl dance. SuAnne knew all the traditional dances—she had competed in many powwows as a little girl—and the dance she chose is a young woman's dance, graceful and modest and show-offy all at the same time. "I couldn't believe it—she was powwowin', like, 'get down!' " Doni De Cory recalled. "And then she started to sing." SuAnne began to sing in Lakota, swaying back and forth in the jump-ball circle, doing the shawl dance, using her warm-up jacket for a shawl. The crowd went completely silent. "All that stuff the Lead fans were yelling—it was like she *reversed* it somehow," a teammate said. In the sudden quiet, all you could hear was her Lakota song. SuAnne stood up, dropped her jacket, took the ball from Doni De Cory, and ran a lap around the court dribbling expertly and fast. The fans began to cheer and applaud. She sprinted to the basket, went up in the air, and laid the ball through the hoop, with the fans cheering loudly now. Of course, Pine Ridge went on to win the game.

This story, which was published first in a newspaper article at the time of SuAnne's death, is not quite accurate. The game took place not in 1988 but in 1987, when SuAnne was in eighth grade, and Pine Ridge did not win it, but lost in the last three seconds, 66–64. Today no one in Lead seems to remember SuAnne's center-court dance. But because the story sums up so well the way people in Pine Ridge felt about SuAnne, and because it recounts one of the coolest and bravest deeds I ever heard of, I would like to consider it from a larger perspective that includes the town of Lead, all the Black Hills, and 125 years of history:

Lead, the town, does not get its name from the metal. The lead the name refers to is a mining term for a gold-bearing deposit, or vein, running through surrounding rock. The word, pronounced with a long *e*, is related to the word "lode." During the Black Hills gold rush of the 1870s, prospectors found a rich lead in what would become the town of Lead. In April 1876, Fred and Moses Manuel staked a claim to a mine they called the Homestake. Their lead led eventually to gold and more gold—a small mountain of gold—whose value may be guessed by the size of the hole its extraction has left in the middle of present-day Lead.

In 1877, a mining engineer from San Francisco named George Hearst came to the Hills, investigated the Manuels' mine, and advised his big-city partners to buy it. The price was $70,000. At the time of Hearst's negotiations, the illegal act of Congress which would take this land from the Sioux had only recently passed. The partners followed Hearst's advice, and the Homestake Mine paid off its purchase price four times over in dividends alone within three years. When George Hearst's only son, William Randolph, was kicked out of Harvard for giving his instructors chamber pots with their names inscribed on the inside, George Hearst suggested that he come West and take over his (George's) share in the Homestake Mine. William Randolph Hearst chose to run the San Francisco *Examiner* instead. His father gave him a blank check to keep it going for two years; gold from Lead helped start the Hearst newspaper empire. Since the Homestake Mine was discovered, it has produced at least $10 billion in gold. It is one of the richest gold mines in the world.

Almost from the moment of the Custer expedition's entry into the Black Hills in 1874, there was no way the Sioux were going to be allowed to keep this land. By 1875, the Dakota Territorial Legislature had already divided the Black Hills land into counties; Custer County, in the southern Hills, was named in that general's honor while he was still alive, and while the land still clearly belonged to the Sioux. Many people in government and elsewhere knew at the time that taking this land was wrong. At first, the Army even made halfhearted attempts to keep the prospectors out. A high-ranking treaty negotiator told President Grant that the Custer expedition was "a violation of the national honor." One of the commissioners who worked on the "agreement" that gave paper legitimacy to the theft said that Custer should not have gone into the Hills in the first place; he and the other commissioners reminded the government that it was making the Sioux homeless and that it owed them protection and care. The taking of the Black Hills proceeded inexorably all the same.

Sioux leaders of Crazy Horse's generation began working to receive fair compensation for the Hills in the early 1900s. The Black Hills claim which the Sioux filed with the U.S. Court of Claims in the 1920s got nowhere. In 1946, the government established the Indian Claims Commission specifically to provide payment for wrongly taken Indian lands, and in 1950 the Sioux filed a claim for the Black Hills with the ICC. After almost twenty-five years of historical research and esoteric legal back-and-forth, the ICC finally ruled that the Sioux were entitled to a payment of $17.5 million plus interest for the taking of the Hills. Further legal maneuvering ensued. In 1980 the Supreme Court affirmed the ruling and awarded the Sioux a total of $106 million. Justice Harry Blackmun, for the majority, wrote: "A more ripe and rank case of dishonorable dealings will never, in all probability, be found in our history"—which was to say officially, and finally, that the Black Hills had been stolen.

By the time of the Supreme Court ruling, however, the Sioux had come to see their identity as linked to the Hills themselves, and the eight tribes involved decided unanimously not to accept the money. They said, "The Black Hills are not for sale." The Sioux now wanted the land back—some or all of it—and trespass damages as well. They especially wanted the Black Hills lands still owned by the federal government. These amount to about 1.3 million acres, a small proportion of what was stolen. At the moment, the chances of the Sioux getting these or any lands in the Black Hills appear remote. The untouched compensation money remains in a federal escrow account, where it, plus other compensation moneys, plus accumulated interest, is now over half a billion dollars.

Inescapably, this history is present when an Oglala team goes to Lead to play a basketball game. It may even explain why fans in Lead were so mean: being in the wrong to begin with can make you even ornerier sometimes. In all the accounts of this land grab and its aftermath, and among the many greedy and driven men who had a part, I cannot find evidence of a single act as elegant, as generous, or as transcendent as SuAnne's dance in the gym at Lead.

For the Oglala, what SuAnne did that day almost immediately took on the stature of myth. People from Pine Ridge still describe it in terms of awe and disbelief. Amazement swept through the younger kids when they heard. "I was, like, 'What did she just do?'" recalled her cousin Angie Big Crow, an eighth-grader at the time. All over the reservation, people told and retold the story of SuAnne at Lead. Any time the subject of SuAnne came up when I was talking to people on Pine Ridge, I would always ask if they had heard about what she did at Lead, and always the answer was a smile and a nod—"Yeah, I heard about that." To the unnumbered big and small slights of local racism which the Oglala have known all their lives, SuAnne's exploit made an emphatic reply.

Back in the days when Lakota war parties still fought battles against other tribes and the Army, no deed of war was more honored than the act of counting coup. To count coup means to touch an armed enemy in full possession of his powers with a special stick called a coup stick, or with the hand. The touch is not a blow, and only serves to indicate how close to the enemy you came. As an act of bravery, counting coup was regarded as greater than killing an enemy in single combat, greater than taking a scalp or horses or any prize. Counting coup was an act of almost abstract courage, of pure playfulness taken to the most daring extreme. Very likely, to do it and survive brought an exhilaration to which nothing could compare. In an ancient sense which her Oglala kin could recognize, SuAnne counted coup on the hecklers at Lead.

And yet this coup was an act not of war but of peace. SuAnne's coup strike was an offering, an invitation. It took the hecklers at the best interpretation, as if their silly mocking chants were meant only in goodwill. It showed that their fake Indian songs were just that—fake—and that the real thing was better, as real things usually are. We Lakota have been dancing like this for centuries, the dance said; we've been doing the shawl dance since long before you came, before you had gotten on the boat in Glasgow or Bremerhaven, before you stole this land, and we're still doing it today; and isn't it pretty, when you see how it's supposed to be done? Because finally what SuAnne proposed was to invite us—us onlookers in the stands, which is the non-Lakota rest of this country—to dance, too. She was in the Lead gym to play, and she invited us all to play. The symbol she used to include us was the warm-up jacket. Everyone in America has a warm-up jacket. I've got one, probably so do you, so did (no doubt) many of the fans at Lead. By using the warm-up jacket as a shawl in her impromptu shawl dance, she made Lakota relatives of us all.

"It was funny," Doni De Cory said, "but after that game the relationship between Lead and us was tremendous. When we played Lead again, the games were really good, and we got to know some of the girls on the team. Later, when we went to a tournament and Lead was there, we were hanging out with the Lead girls and eating pizza with them. We got to know some of their parents, too. What SuAnne did made a big impression and changed the whole situation with us and Lead. We found out there are some really good people in Lead."

America is a leap of the imagination. From its beginning, people had only a persistent idea of what a good country should be. The idea involved freedom, equality, justice, and the pursuit of happiness; nowadays most of us probably could not describe it a lot more clearly than that. The truth is, it always has been a bit of a guess. No one has ever known for sure whether a country based on such an idea is really possible, but again and again, we have leaped toward the idea and hoped. What SuAnne Big Crow demonstrated in the Lead high school gym is that making the leap is the whole point. The idea does not truly live unless it is expressed by an act; the country does not live unless we make the leap from our tribe or focus group or gated community or demographic, and land on the shaky platform of that idea of a good country which all kinds of different people share.

This leap is made in public, and it's made for free. It's not a product or a service that anyone will pay you for. You do it for reasons unexplainable by economics—for ambition, out of conviction, for the heck of it, in playfulness, for love. It's done in public spaces, face-to-face, where anyone is free to go. It's not done on television, on the Internet, or over the telephone; our electronic systems can only tell us if the leap made elsewhere has succeeded or failed. The places you'll see it are high school gyms, city sidewalks, the subway, bus stations, public parks, parking lots, and wherever people gather during natural disasters. In those places and others like them, the leaps that continue to invent and knit the country continue to be made. When the leap fails, it looks like the L.A. riots, or Sherman's March through Georgia. When it succeeds, it looks like the New York City Bicentennial Celebration in July 1976, or the Civil Rights March on Washington in 1963. On that scale, whether it succeeds or fails, it's always something to see. The leap requires physical presence and physical risk. But the payoff—in terms of dreams realized, of understanding, of people getting along—can be so glorious as to make the risk seem minuscule.

I find all this hopefulness, and more, in SuAnne's dance in the gym in Lead. My high school football coach used to show us films of our previous game every Monday after practice, and whenever he liked a particular play, he would run it over and over again. If I had a film of SuAnne at Lead (as far as I know, no such film or video exists), I would study it in slow motion frame by frame. There's a magic in what she did, along with the promise that public acts of courage are still alive out there somewhere. Mostly, I would run the film of SuAnne again and again for my own braveheart song. I refer to her, as I do to Crazy Horse, for proof that it's a public service to be brave.

CHAPTER

13

Doni De Cory is a big, light-brown woman with vivid dark eyes and big hair. Or, as she puts it, "huge hair." "I had the hugest hair in Pine Ridge High School," she says. Immaculately done, ginger-tinted, and huge, her hair can make most other kinds of hair look bedraggled and not-well-thought-out by comparison. Besides being a basketball star, she was three times South Dakota state champion in the shot put, and an all-American in the event her junior and senior years, and she walks with the grace and control of someone who can do just about anything physical she chooses to do. When Chick Big Crow called her on the phone and told her that I was at the SuAnne Center and that I wanted to talk about SuAnne, Doni De Cory came over right away. She was wearing black pants and a black blazer with a white blouse, her long nails were manicured a light purple shade, and she had on high heels and big silver earrings. In a nondescript shirt and slacks, I felt disrespectfully underdressed.

She had clearly been waiting for someone like me to show up and ask her about SuAnne. She spoke with intensity, in a quiet rush, talking not so much to any one person as to listeners in general. From time to time she elegantly changed how she was sitting, recrossing her legs. "I was three years older than SuAnne, but it didn't seem like it," she said. "Even when she was little it was like we were the same age. SuAnne never hung out with her own age group—she hung with us older girls, and in sports she could keep up with anything we did. She and I were really close and shared everything and talked all the time—almost every day, even after I went away to college. We played on I don't know how many teams together, from when we were kids, and I had so much confidence in her. I always put pressure on her because I always knew she could do it. In basketball, SuAnne and me were one of the best fast-break teams ever to come out of the state. And it didn't matter how far down we'd get in a game, we never gave up. Even when we were forty points down we kept playin' hard, because we had that confidence in each other.

"I just love my tribe to death, and SuAnne felt the same. That was something else in common. We used to talk about all the good that's here, and about how we were gonna come back after college and make this a better place. She was really proud of bein' from Pine Ridge. Anywhere we went, for basketball or volleyball games, or for cheerleading competitions, she would tell people, 'We're from an Indian reservation in the middle of the country, we're from Pine Ridge, South Dakota.' Then sometimes she'd throw back her head and yell, 'We're Oglala Sioooooooooux!'

"SuAnne and me always went out of our comfort zone, wherever we traveled. A lot of times the other girls would just want to stay in the hotel, but we were always outspoken and outgoing and adventurous. When we went to Hawaii to be in the half-time show at the Aloha Bowl—our cheerleading squad won a national cheerleading contest in Rock Springs, Wyoming, that's how we got picked to go—we walked all over the island, it seemed like. We snuck into the Hard Rock Café, we weren't even eighteen years old. We had to rehearse for the half-time show five or six hours a day, and we got to meet the Osmond Brothers singing group. They were the main half-time act, these little, cute boys. We met them at a banquet where there was nothing to eat but stuff like octopus and shark, and afterward SuAnne and me came out of there *starving* for some McDonald's food, and we took off our high heels and walked two miles in our bare feet to the only McDonald's on the island and stood in line for an hour and a half to pay about twice what it costs in South Dakota. SuAnne didn't care, though. She loved McDonald's.

"The woman could *eat*. Four Big Macs and four large fries was nothin' to her. She'd finish all that and then come around to see if you had anything you didn't want to eat that was left over. The seven-dollar meal allowance did not begin to be enough for her. She'd stay at our house sometimes, and she could eat four big platefuls of carbo meals like spaghetti, no problem at all. She could eat a whole commod pie by herself—that's a big casserole made with canned commodity foods like meatball stew. When it came to eating in the school cafeteria, SuAnne could keep up with the guys. She was good at blowing bubble-gum bubbles, too. She'd throw a whole pack of that Hubba Bubba bubble gum in her mouth and blow bubbles one inside the other. She always won the bubble gum–blowing contests at pep rallies.

"One thing I know I helped her with was in how to make herself look good, how to do her makeup and her hair. She was always the center of attention when she walked into a room, but before she was fourteen or fifteen she had never tried to beautify herself. I mean, here she was in high school and didn't even know how to use a curling iron! Before our cheerleading picture one time I made her hair huge like mine, and streaked it with lemon juice and put a whole bunch of mousse in it. After that, when she would get dressed up for something, she would always ask me or Jeanne Horse, our cheerleading coach, how she looked. She was really pretty, and by the time she was elected Homecoming Queen her senior year, she knew it, and she knew how to take advantage of it.

"She was just a big personality, a big person. She cared so much about Pine Ridge. She wanted there to be more opportunities here. Sometimes we talked about how to provide for the tribe's future, for seven generations ahead, the way Chief Red Cloud and them said you should do. She always paid attention to anybody who wanted something from her. No one knows what she went through makin' everybody happy. Anybody who came to her door hungry, she gave 'em something from the cupboard—Chick finally had to tell her to stop givin' their food away. A lot of kids who are grown up now will tell you, 'She used to pump me home on her bicycle'—if she saw a kid walkin' when she was on her bike, she'd tell him to get on behind, and she'd pedal and give him a ride home. She had what she called her giveaway bag in her closet filled with stuff she'd brought back from her team trips, little souvenirs and stuff like that, and any time you went to her house she'd give you something to take with you when you left. Mainly, she helped people open their eyes to the good things that were right in front of them. She saw so much good in life herself. Everything was . . . *revealing* to her. Everything was revealing."

Doni De Cory said a lot more about SuAnne—about her ambition to be an optometrist, about her sadness at the jealousy on the reservation, about her horrible singing voice, about her collection of sweatshirts from many different colleges, about how hard she worked, about how SuAnne and Doni and a boy cousin once beat the best all-guy basketball teams on the reservation during a three-man basketball tournament in the town of Kyle. Doni also talked a lot about when SuAnne died—about the ugly feeling that came over her out of nowhere as she was doing her laundry at the time of the crash, and about the red light on her answering machine jumping out at her after her father had called to tell her the news.

"For some reason, when I think of SuAnne, the first thing that always comes to mind is her hands," Doni said. "I could do an exact description of her hands. There was the lump on her middle finger where she held a pencil, and her calluses from playin' ball, and her fingernails, which she always chewed. She had these real, real low fingernails, probably because you can't have very long fingernails and handle a basketball. Her fingernails were always so low they looked like they hurt."

Many people, I discovered, wanted to talk about SuAnne. All these years after she died she's still on people's minds. Some people dream about her. Many I talked to would recommend others for me to talk to, who would recommend others, and so on. Here's some of what they said:

Rol Bradford, teacher and coach: "When I was coaching boys' basketball at Pine Ridge, SuAnne was my student manager—she did that along with cheerleading—and I used to put her in scrimmages during practice sometimes. When she was playing, unless you looked close, you would never know there was a girl out there. She was just as good as a lot of the boys and better than some, and she could run with 'em perfectly easy, and the level of play didn't go down at all. If anything, it improved. For fun in gym class once in a while we used to play this game called Mob Basketball. It's basketball but with no fouls. Anything goes in Mob Basketball except bitin', kickin', and scratchin'. Well, once SuAnne and I went for a loose ball at the same time and we both got our arms around it, and we're down on the court rollin' around, and she would not let *go*. I could not believe she was so tremendously strong. I'm a rodeo cowboy in the summers, I rassle steers—and I really had to scrap to get that ball away. And I was exhausted when I finally did, too."

Gordon Bergquist, one of the most successful basketball coaches in South Dakota history, whose team SuAnne's team beat in the state finals: "Anytime I ran into SuAnne, she always said hello and talked to me without any hesitation at all. Now, I'm not making generalizations, but Native American kids very rarely do that. I'm an adult, I'm blond, I'm 'Euro,' and . . . well, Indian kids just don't usually go out of their way to talk to me. But when I ran into SuAnne in the Kmart in Watertown one time we visited for quite a while, leaning up against the clothes racks. She was telling me where she was thinking about going to college, how she wanted to do something for her people.

"What impressed me maybe the most about SuAnne was how she could play so hard, right at the top of her intensity, and never show the least bit of impatience or anger. She had such a pleasant disposition, and she didn't want to do anything except have a good time and win. I'll never forget when we played against her in a holiday tournament in Arlington in '91—I never saw a game in which one player dominated so much. She really took us apart. She scored forty-three points against us and Pine Ridge won, 87 to 53. If I hadn't been the opponent I'd've thoroughly enjoyed watching someone play that well. After the game I went over to her and kidded with her—I said, 'Are you gonna graduate pretty soon?' That was the last time I saw SuAnne Big Crow. I think about her more than you would expect to think about a kid you played against a long time ago."

Pigeon Big Crow, sister: "She had a funky laugh, this all-out laugh. There was a knock-knock joke she told for a whole summer—now I can't remember it, it'll come to me—and she'd laugh at it every time she told it, and you'd laugh at her laughin'. But after Magic Johnson got AIDS and there were those jokes about him goin' around, you could *not* say a Magic Johnson joke around her. She loved Magic Johnson and she would not hear a word against him.

"By the time SuAnne was a teenager she was in demand all the time, always with stuff goin' on. And yet somehow she was always there for my kids. If I needed someone to look after 'em, she found the time. Because of SuAnne, I never had to worry about my kids. I came home one time when Lyle was three months old and SuAnne had his legs propped way out and she was tryin' to get him to sit up. I said, 'SuAnne, what're you doin'?' She said, 'I'm trying to create equilibrium.' She got him sitting up, and she got him walking early, too."

Chick Big Crow, mother: "Don't start thinking that SuAnne was only an angel, though. She was mis-*chie*-vious, with a capital M. She was always testing how far she could go, what could and could not be done. She'd always push you. In our neighborhood we had a bootlegger who sold beer and wine from a drive-up window out of his house. The name he went by was Suitcase, and SuAnne used to harass and devil him. She used to yell, 'Hey, Soup-Face!' through the drive-up window at him, which for some reason he absolutely hated. He put SuAnne's name on a list of people he wouldn't allow on his property—SuAnne was blacklisted at Suitcase's along with a couple of the worst deadbeat drunks in town. One time she and another kid set a mattress on fire behind his house."

Yvonne "Tiny" De Cory, aunt: "I let her play on a girls' softball team I coached when she was only five or six years old. She wanted to so bad, I couldn't say no. The helmet couldn't fit her, it was way too big. I'd tell her all I wanted her to do when she went up to bat was draw a walk. I'd say, 'Now, SuAnne, you just stand there at the plate and *don't swing*.' She'd listen to every word I said, lookin' at me with her big raccoon eyes wide. Then she'd go up there—this was a twelve-year-old girl pitching to a six-year-old, remember—and she'd stand there, and first pitch she'd swing away. I'd call time out and bring her over and tell her again, 'Sue, I told you not to swing!' She'd look at me and listen and nod her head and say, 'Yeah, uh-huh, okay.' Then she go back up there and next pitch she'd swing again. Didn't matter what you told her, she was going to swing. She always went in there thinking maybe she'd hit a home run. Even at that young age, she wanted to make a statement with whatever she did. She was going to have her swings."

Jeanne Horse, Pine Ridge High School librarian; former cheerleading coach and sponsor: "I remember one time I went with the squad to a boys' basketball tournament at the Corn Palace in Mitchell, South Dakota, and I was in the ladies' room, and I heard some non-Indian girls in there say, 'SuAnne Big Crow is a cheerleader for Pine Ridge. Let's go watch her.' That cheerleading squad—Doni De Cory, Lisa Carlow, Robin Akers, Kellee Brewer, SuAnne and her sister Cee Cee— they were really achievers. I call it my dream team. I don't even know how many competitions we won, offhand. I was watching a football game at the University of Nebraska at Lincoln one time when Nebraska was the top college football team in the country and I saw their cheerleaders do a pinwheel stunt—bigger kids twirling in a circle at the center and some lighter girls, like spokes, flying out—and I said, 'Oh, let's try that!' We practiced and practiced the pinwheel, and we finally got it to work. Robin and Lisa were our lighter girls, and Doni and SuAnne were in the center, and it was really striking to see these high school kids do such a beautiful job on a difficult, college-level stunt. In cheerleading, I still compare everybody and everything to them."

Dennis Banks, AIM leader: "I was running the limo service in Rapid City when the Pine Ridge cheerleaders went to the Aloha Bowl. Jeanne Horse called me and asked if I'd drive the kids to the airport in my limo and I was happy to do it, door-to-door and for free. It's really exciting to see kids like that pushing and excelling, but with incredible allegiance to each other. For me as an AIM leader it was great the way SuAnne and them were against racial slurs, taking a stand on their own, letting it be known they weren't going to accept it. I became a big fan of Lady

Thorpes basketball and went to a lot of their games, and my daughter, Chubs, became their mascot. She was about five years old at the time. SuAnne and another girl made outfits for her. I truly, truly enjoyed being with the Lady Thorpes. Once just after they won a really close game, SuAnne saw me in the stands and yelled, 'Hey, Banks! How do you feel?' Holy cripes, I was still screaming, I was so excited."

Milo Yellow Hair, tribal vice-chairman: "One of our biggest problems as Oglala people is that we don't know how to take a compliment. If you single someone out for praise, it's a fine line not to embarrass 'em and make 'em uncomfortable with the unwanted publicity. For most of us, bein' a marquee character just is not in our capacity. SuAnne could be comfortable with a lot of attention, but at the same time she always understood that she was just a part of the whole. When she got a compliment, she always held back and allowed the other kids to get credit, too. She might have been the spirit at the center, but she didn't overwhelm you with her ego, she let the other kids rally around. She understood that was the essence of how things should be done."

Chick Big Crow: "She would never let me brag about her. She used to tell me, 'Mom, if you have to do that, I didn't earn it.' "

Wesley Bettelyoun, friend, second cousin; hospital maintenance man: "I grew up in the same neighborhood as SuAnne. She was three years older than me, and she used to bribe me to do stuff for her sometimes. Like, if her mom told her to pick up trash around the yard, SuAnne would tell me that if I did it she would ride bikes with me. A lot of kids liked her and wanted to do stuff with her. So I'd pick up the trash, and then we'd go speedin' around on our banana-seat bikes, racin' and goin' over jumps. Me and Butterball Littlebear, we were the chubby kids in the neighborhood, and she let us follow her around. When she was practicing jump shots or foul shots in the gym, we'd retrieve balls for her. SuAnne got me into sports, taught me about sportsmanship. When she was playin' sports she didn't ever get angry and she didn't ever cry. I played on the same hardball team with her one time and I was pretty little and they weren't putting me in the game, and she faked hurt so that I could play. That was cool of her—she grabbed her arm and fell down, and the coach sent me in for her at first base, and I played a lot after that. But no one besides me knew she wasn't really hurt, because when she really was hurt she didn't ever cry.

"One thing she did for me I'll always remember—I was a freshman at Pine Ridge High School when she was a senior, and back then at Pine Ridge they had this setup where all freshmen had to go through initiation. The way it worked, a senior would pick a freshman to initiate during initiation week, and then the senior would make the freshman do stuff like dress up in dresses (if the freshman was a guy), or wear weird makeup, or bring the senior cookies, or carry his books, or clean out his locker—stuff like that. Well, when SuAnne was a senior she had to pick a freshman to initiate, and I don't know why, but she picked me. And then she didn't make me do nothin'! All the other freshmen were doin' all these dumb initiation things, and I was walkin' around free with nothin' to do at all. Me and SuAnne were just laughin'. It made the other freshmen kind of mad. Pine Ridge outlawed initiations a few years after that.

"SuAnne always told me to be strong, to make my own way, and to look out for my family and friends. She said that if everybody on the rez did that, this place would be a paradise. She always treated people good herself. I never saw her disrespect anybody. She used to say, 'I want to go somewhere to college and then come back here and work.' She's always in my mind. I got pictures of her on the walls all over my room, they're the first thing I see every morning when I get up.

"Of course I loved her. I love her still."

SuAnne's freshman year, the year after her dance in the gym at Lead, the Lady Thorpes basketball team beat the team from Winner, South Dakota, in the regional play-offs. In the state tournament, Doni De Cory was sidelined with a sprained ankle, and Pine Ridge lost a key semifinal game and finished fourth. At the end of the season SuAnne promised Coach Zimiga that before she graduated, Pine Ridge would win the state championship. Zimiga thought they had a good chance. Pine Ridge had never won the championship before.

The season for girls' basketball in South Dakota lasts from September until late November. In the winter, SuAnne was a cheerleader for the boys' basketball team, and she played on the girls' volleyball team. In the spring, she ran sprints and relays on the girls' track team. She also paid attention to her studies; like her sisters and Doni De Cory, SuAnne usually got the best grades in her class. That summer she had a job at Big Bat's—thirty to forty hours a week at the register and the deli counter, making $3.85 an hour. In her spare time she ran the cross-country course for endurance and practiced basketball, working out perhaps harder than she ever had. Coach Zimiga found her in the school gym early and late, lifting weights in the weight room or shooting jump shots.

When school started again in the fall of 1989, SuAnne was a sophomore, fifteen years old. Many people in high school sports in South Dakota knew about her by then. They knew, too, that Doni De Cory had graduated. What they didn't know, Zimiga was sure, was how many other good girl basketball players Pine Ridge had. There was Rita Bad Bear, a senior, who at almost six feet was the team's center and leading rebounder; Mary Walking, a junior who had grown up way out in the country where there was nothing to do but practice three-point shots, which had made her an excellent shooter from outside; Dakota "Happy" Big Crow, a skilled ball handler; and Darla Janis, Toni Morton, Jodee Bettelyoun, and Kellee Brewer, versatile athletes who could fill in anywhere. For their part, the girls thought Zimiga was great. He is a slim, quiet man as intense as a migraine, from which he in fact suffers sometimes. His players all called him Charley, or "Char" for short.

A record of this 1989 team exists in videotapes of their games made by friends and family members. The crimson, black, and white of the Pine Ridge game uniforms go well with the girls' dark features. The girls look confident and strong, exchanging high-fives after a score, hanging their heads and breathing hard during a time-out, ambling to the bench and sitting down and wiping the sweat from their faces with a towel as they listen to Coach Zimiga. Each is different from the next—one is tall, one short, one movie-star lovely, one curly-headed, and so on—and one is SuAnne, even in an amateur video clearly the star. But most striking is how solid they appear as a team. At certain moments when they are standing together, their different-looking faces are all lit similarly from within, and they have a constant awareness of one another in their eyes.

Local newspapers covering girls' basketball that year sometimes called her "sophomore sensation SuAnne Big Crow," and she lived up to the billing. In a game against Lemmon, South Dakota, SuAnne scored sixty-seven points, setting a single-game scoring record for the state. Afterward the Lemmon coach asked Zimiga, "How many SuAnnes did you have out there, anyway?" She was averaging over thirty points a game on her way to setting another state record—761 points, the most ever by a player in a single season. Pine Ridge beat Custer, Spearfish, Lead. When the Lady Thorpes played in their home gym, it was always packed. People on the reservation who couldn't get to the games listened to them at home over KILI radio, which broadcast every game live. In mid-November Pine Ridge won an important match-up against their always-strong reservation rivals, the team from Red Cloud Indian School. SuAnne scored thirty-five points in that game.

Late in the season the Lady Thorpes went to Eagle Butte, South Dakota, on the Cheyenne River Indian Reservation, for an all-Indian girls' basketball tournament. Just before it, a medicine man took Chick Big Crow aside and told her that someone was trying to harm SuAnne. He knew this, the medicine man said, because he had seen blue sparks coming off her. He said he could do a ceremony to remove the danger but that it would require twelve medicine men, because there were so many angry spirits around. In the tournament game between Pine Ridge and Little Wound not long after, a Little Wound player ran up behind SuAnne when she was shooting a layup and slammed her into the wall. As SuAnne collapsed to the floor, the girl who had hit her threw her arms into the air in triumph and grinned at the crowd. SuAnne got up slowly, went to the sidelines, and then came back in and made both foul shots. She felt dizzy and had a bump on her head, and Chick took her to a hospital, where she was diagnosed with a mild concussion.

On the strength of their regular-season record (sixteen games won, four lost) and their victory over Red Cloud, Pine Ridge got a spot in the district championship play-off against the Bennett County Lady Warriors, from Martin, South Dakota. SuAnne had recovered enough from her injury to score twenty-eight points in the district game, and the Lady Thorpes won it easily. Next step was the regional play-off in late November against the team from Winner, whom Pine Ridge had met in the regionals the year before. At this level of competition, the referees again clamped down on the Pine Ridge defensive style, and the Lady Thorpes soon got into foul trouble. With the team behind in the fourth quarter, SuAnne fouled out. Rita Bad Bear, another stalwart, had to play gingerly because she was carrying four fouls. Zimiga turned to the players on his bench for reinforcements, and sent in Toni Morton and Jodee Bettelyoun. These girls hadn't played much in the post-season, and they were keyed up and shaking as Zimiga told them what he wanted them to do. On the court they calmed down, and ran a complicated trapping defense so expertly that they turned the game around. Pine Ridge beat Winner in overtime 54–52. SuAnne had seventeen points in the game, but this time Toni Morton and Jodee Bettelyoun were the stars.

By coincidence, the same week that the Lady Thorpes won the regionals, Pine Ridge was once again in the national news. A crew from the NBC *Nightly News* had visited the reservation and interviewed people and shot a lot of footage for a multipart report titled *Tragedy at Pine Ridge*. When people came home the evening of November 20, and when the girls sat down to dinner after basketball practice, the first part of *Tragedy at Pine Ridge* was on TV. NBC anchorman Tom Brokaw announced, "This is Thanksgiving week, of course, but on the Pine Ridge Indian Reservation in South Dakota it's hard to find reason to give thanks, when tragedy is never out of season." There followed pictures of reservation poverty, statistics on unemployment and average yearly income, and interviews about the damage done by alcohol. The reporter, Betty Rollin, said, "The high point of life here, called Carnival Week, is the start of every month when the aid checks come in . . . almost everyone spends some, even all of the money, or barters food or sells cans for alcohol." (Chick Big Crow and her daughters found this surprising; they had never heard of the term "Carnival Week.") The segment ended with Rollin's observation that people here find it hard to

leave because the reservation has not equipped them to live anyplace
else, and that those who do leave usually come back and "succumb
again to the ways of Pine Ridge—idleness and alcohol." The reports
that followed over the next two nights were variations on this theme.

The success of the Pine Ridge High School girls' basketball team,
the fact that one of its players had set state records that fall, the fact
that the team was going to the state tournament—these all escaped the
notice of NBC News. Indeed, from the beginning of the report to the
end, NBC did not find one good thing to say; the "bleakness" story is a
rigorous form, with little room for extraneous details. Undeniably, many
sad facts of the reservation can be told with bleakness as the text. But
the NBC story irritated people on Pine Ridge no end, especially
SuAnne. She talked to anyone who would listen about all the good on
the reservation that NBC had overlooked, and about the unfairness of
showing only the suffering and apparently hopeless side. She went
around saying "Carnival Week!" and *Tragedy at Pine Ridge!* in a derisive snort. Years later she would still complain about how stupid
Tragedy at Pine Ridge was.

That year the state tournament for class A schools (those with enrollment under four hundred) was held in an arena in Sioux Falls, about
300 miles east of Pine Ridge. People in South Dakota sometimes divide
the state into East River and West River when speaking of it; the Missouri River crosses South Dakota from south to north and cuts it more
or less in half. East River gets more rain, and its grasses grow higher,
and the landscape looks more like green Minnesota than like the tawny
short-grass plains of the West. To someone from Pine Ridge, East River
places like Sioux Falls can seem very far from home. The Lady Thorpes
set out for Sioux Falls and the tournament in their chartered bus on a
Wednesday morning with Coach Zimiga, and with Jeanne Horse as
chaperone. The bus had a tape player and a TV and VCR. The New
Kids on the Block Christmas tape was playing as they pulled out of
town, and everybody was in a festive mood. SuAnne was saying, "When
we come back with the trophy, then it'll really be 'Carnival Week'!"

They reached the city late in the afternoon and checked into the
Holiday Inn in downtown Sioux Falls. Jeanne Horse had a suite and the

girls hung out in it, ordering pizza and watching TV. The girls were high and happy, with no apparent fear at all. Zimiga wanted them to get to bed early because their first game was at eleven the next morning, but he saw they were having fun and he wasn't strict with them. He let them stay up a while, and a few went down and swam in the pool. They even got a kick out of the lobby and the elevators; some of the Pine Ridge kids had not spent much time in a high-rise hotel before.

To reach the finals Pine Ridge needed victories in the tournament's first two rounds. On Thursday morning they played the Flandreau Lady Knights, from the Flandreau Indian School just north of Sioux Falls. For this game the stands were mostly empty, the loud contingent of fans from Flandreau outnumbering a small Pine Ridge crowd. Throughout the game Pine Ridge kept building up big leads, but Flandreau kept fighting back. Pine Ridge was ten points ahead at the end of the first half. At the start of the second half, Flandreau pulled to within one. Pine Ridge was ahead by nine in the third quarter when Rita Bad Bear went out with an injury and Flandreau scored four unanswered points. Finally, in the fourth quarter, SuAnne scored thirteen points, giving her a total of thirty-six for the game, a tournament record. Pine Ridge won, 70–55.

In round two on Friday afternoon, Pine Ridge played the Parkston Trojans, a team with two tall sisters named Dawn and Staci Schulz. Zimiga countered their scoring threat by collapsing his defenders around them, but the game stayed close to the end, with Parkston just two points behind in the fourth quarter. A run of fourteen straight points for Pine Ridge then put the game out of reach, and Pine Ridge won, 62–47. SuAnne scored twenty-eight points, Mary Walking hit three three-point shots, and Rita Bad Bear and Darla Janis each scored ten. Both victories had been tougher for the Lady Thorpes than the final scores made it seem.

While Pine Ridge was advancing to the championship, so were the Lady Bulldogs, of Milbank High School. Milbank is a town of about 4,500, ten miles from the Minnesota border in the northeast part of the state. People in Milbank work in the granite quarries, for the coal-fired electric plant, in the cheese factory, or for two small insurance companies. Milbank's streets are tree-lined and quiet, and at noon on a summer day you can hear the sounds of many differents kinds of cuckoo clocks chiming from the well-kept houses. The town's big high school was built in 1978, and as at Pine Ridge High School, the bouncing of basketballs echoes from its gym on idle afternoons. The Milbank girls had won the state championship in 1987, and had been runners-up in 1988. For Milbank's coach, Gordon Bergquist (quoted earlier on the subject of SuAnne), his team's victory in the second round of this tournament had been his hundredth win in five years of coaching girls' basketball at Milbank High.

Pine Ridge met Milbank for the title game Saturday evening in the Sioux Falls Arena at eight o'clock. As it happened, this was the last game of the tournament (which also included bigger schools, in the AA division), because the bigger schools had played earlier in the day. Fans of girls' basketball had heard about SuAnne and they knew how tough Milbank was, and they expected a good contest. The arena was full and highly charged. A large group from Milbank filled a block in the center of the stands on one side. Across the way the Pine Ridge rooters made a smaller group, which was nonetheless impressive when you considered how far they'd had to drive. Chick Big Crow sat close to the aisle; she knew her nervousness would eventually cause her to get up and walk somewhere. As the public-address system announced the names of the Lady Thorpes one by one and the girls ran out from behind a curtain at an end of the arena, they were startled for a moment at the noise and the people in the cavernous hall. None had ever played in front of a crowd this large before. The Lady Thorpes formed two lines and gave each other high-fives with both hands, then gathered around Coach Zimiga for some final words as the Milbank team came out.

Zimiga's strategy for the first half was to try to keep the game close. In the front of his mind was a rule he had learned playing non-Indian schools east of the river: Don't foul. He told the girls to play cautiously, not to press on defense, and to be patient. Somehow beneath his anticipation he felt comfortable and calm. On the Milbank side, Coach Bergquist's plan involved maneuvering his tall girls, Kris White and Jolene Snaza, underneath the basket, where they could get rebounds. Mainly, he wanted to shut down SuAnne. He knew she liked to play close to the basket and he told his players to try to keep her farther outside.

I must imagine this game based on what people who were there told

me, on news stories, and on videotapes made by fans of Milbank or
Pine Ridge. My impressions of it are sort of jumpy, like images in a
hand-held video camera. The slap and squeak of rubber shoe soles on
the floor, the nervous drumming of the ball, the referee's whistle,
and the multiplied noises from people in the stands all crowded together in the brightly lit air above the game. The Pine Ridge girls
looked excited enough to run through walls. The effort it took to follow
their coach's instructions about patience and restraint showed in the
tentativeness of their offense at first, and in the way they sometimes
seemed to recoil from any contact with the Milbank girls. For Milbank's
part, the team moved up and down the floor deliberately and confidently; some of the Milbank players, of course, had been in a championship game before.

The collision of the two coaches' strategies made for a slow-scoring
and stiff first half. Milbank kept Pine Ridge away from the basket, and
Pine Ridge was hesitant to object. SuAnne got almost no close-in
chances. Whenever she took the ball, two or even three Lady Bulldogs
converged on her; she scored only five points the whole first half. Mary
Walking tried several three-point shots, but made none. Milbank's re-
bounding plan worked well, with Jolene Snaza taking the ball off the
boards and sometimes putting in missed shots; in the first quarter alone
she scored eight points. Kris White got eight of her own for the Bulldogs in the second quarter, mostly on offensive rebounds. If it hadn't
been for Rita Bad Bear, Pine Ridge would have ended the first half far
behind. Rita got rebounds and made follow-up shots and short jumpers,
to account for nine points in the half. Her performance was the more
remarkable because she was weak and faint from spells of morning sick-
ness that came and went in waves. She had recently discovered she was
pregnant, but told no one.

When time ran out at the end of the first half, Pine Ridge was behind, 22–18. The Lady Thorpes were dejected; they had not looked
flashy or strong, Milbank had stymied them. They went to their locker
room and lay on the floor, sat in chairs with their heads drooping to
their knees, or perched on stools and stared. Coach Zimiga stood at the
chalkboard and described the more aggressive defense they would use
later in the second half. He did not get mad or holler at them to listen
up. In fact, he was not unhappy with how the first half had gone. His

team had done as he asked—their careful play had kept them from collecting too many fouls, and the score was about as close as he had hoped it would be. He knew, too, that Milbank would be delighted at their success against SuAnne, and might get overconfident. He told the girls that they had played well, that they were definitely still in the game, and that they could win.

The start of the second half seemed to refute his optimism. Milbank's Kris White got a quick tap-in basket, and on their next possession Christi Wherry hit a shot from outside. Pine Ridge was now down by eight. At this point Dakota "Happy" Big Crow decided that since no one else on her team appeared to be hot, she would take a chance on her own. Starting far from the basket she drove through Milbank's defenses in a high-speed dribble, changing hands as she did, and scored. The dazzle of the move was itself a lift to the spirits of Pine Ridge. Next time Happy got the ball, she took a shot from outside and again hit, bringing her team back to within four. Christi Wherry then hit a shot, which was answered by a score from Rita Bad Bear. On the next Milbank possession, SuAnne stole a pass and sprinted away from everybody for an easy layup. Soon after, she hit a twenty-foot jump shot. Darla Janis, the team's worst foul shooter, then sank two foul shots. The referees had called Kris White for her fourth foul, and Coach Bergquist took her out of the game. A foul shot by Darla in the last second of the third quarter put Pine Ridge ahead, 31–30.

Starting the fourth quarter, SuAnne stole another pass and made the layup. Now it was Pine Ridge by three. Milbank then got two baskets in a row, and Rita Bad Bear hit a foul shot to tie, 34–34. On Milbank's next possession, Mary Walking committed an unnecessary foul, and after the second foul shot had been missed, she let the rebound slip from her grasp. Milbank grabbed it and put it up and in. Now Milbank was ahead by three. As the Lady Thorpes went back downcourt, Mary called to Happy Big Crow to give her the ball. Happy passed it to her, and Mary pulled up just outside the three-point line to the left of the basket, aimed, and shot. She had not hit a three-pointer all evening, and Zimiga said (quietly), *"No Mary no!"* as he saw what she was doing. But in the next instant the ball went in, and his last "no" became an astonished cheer.

Now Zimiga was sure they could win. He called a time-out and put in his team in a tight pressing defense. The tactic seemed to discomfit Milbank. Both teams traded foul shots, Pine Ridge getting the advantage by two. Now it was Pine Ridge, 40–38. Milbank's ball; another foul followed, the foul shot missed, and two rebound shots went wide. Then Milbank's Ginny Dohrer came up with the ball and fired an awkward, off-balance shot from about twenty feet away. It went in. Score: Pine Ridge 40, Milbank 40.

Eleven seconds now remained in the game. Zimiga took another time-out. The girls stood close around him listening as he explained a last-second play. SuAnne concentrated so closely, was so focused and attuned, her metabolism seemed to be going a hundred miles an hour. She stood almost on her tiptoes, her eyes scanning quickly from him to her teammates and back again; she hardly seemed to breathe. The ref calls time in. He blows his whistle for play to resume. The ball goes to SuAnne. She takes it fast all the way down the court, pulls up short of the basket, jumps, shoots. The ball caroms off the rim. Rita gets a hand on it, slaps it to Darla. There's a scramble, Milbank has it for an instant, loses it; and then, out of the chaos on the floor: order, in the form of SuAnne. She has the ball. She jumps, perfectly gathered, the ball in her hands overhead. Her face lifts toward the basket, her arched upper lip points at the basket above the turned-down O of her mouth, her dark eyes are ardent and wide open and completely seeing. The ball leaves her hand, her hand flops over at the wrist with fingers spread, the ball flies. She watches it go. It hits inside the hoop, at the back. It goes through the net. In the same instant, the final buzzer sounds.

Ginny Dohrer, the Milbank player who tied the game at 40 in the closing seconds, is now Ginny Dohrer Schulte. She lives with her husband, Calvin, and their two small children in Watertown, South Dakota. One evening they kindly agreed to watch their videotape of the game with me on the television in their living room. The video was made from the Milbank side, and at the moment of SuAnne's winning shot its perspective is from high up in the stands and includes the whole court. On the video, SuAnne makes the shot and then turns from the basket and throws her arms in the air. She waits for half a second, looking around to be sure that there are no fouls and that Pine Ridge has really won. When she realizes they have, she flings herself into the air and then leaps and bounds far down the court in ultimate cheerleader style, jack-knifing her head so far back and her heels so far up that they almost touch behind her, throwing her clenched fists out and up, covering the distance in a single bounding burst that hardly seems to touch the ground. She crosses the screen in a streak, like a bold signature written by a lighted pen. If you unfocus your eyes, she blurs into a vibrant beam of light.

The Schultes stopped the VCR and rewound the tape a little and played her victory run again. Calvin Schulte, a Milbank graduate who knew SuAnne only from watching his now-wife play against her, shook his head in quiet amazement as SuAnne leaped and ran. Then he said her name in the affectionate tones you might use about someone you had known your whole life. "SuAnne," Calvin said, shaking his head and smiling. "SuAnne."

The moment Pine Ridge won, a man from arena security came to Coach Zimiga and told him, "Charley, I don't want your people on the floor." Arena management was afraid of the Pine Ridge fans making a disturbance. After hugging in a toppling-over pile at center court, the Lady Thorpes shook hands with their Milbank opponents, then ran to Zimiga and lifted him onto their shoulders. The security guard told them to put him down. "We don't want no demonstrations," he said. "You're not gonna do any of that in here." Along the stands on the Pine Ridge side, security people stood and watched as the fans filed out. On the Milbank side, precautions were not so strict; Milbank fans came onto the court and wandered around and embraced the Milbank play-ers. TV coverage of the scene after the game showed mostly Milbank fans and players consoling each other, with only a few shots of players from the winning team. A half hour or so later, after the arena had emp-tied out, Zimiga returned with the championship trophy and ran his vic-tory lap around the dimmed court alone.

Outside Pine Ridge's locker room, several newspaper reporters were waiting for SuAnne. She answered their questions, and when they were done she told them, "Don't forget to call your story 'Tragedy at Sioux Falls.'"

Zimiga and Jeanne Horse and some other Pine Ridge people took the girls out to dinner at a Denny's restaurant. They stayed there late, then went back to the hotel. Rol Bradford and SuAnne and some of the other girls grabbed Zimiga to throw him in the hotel pool, giving him time first to remove his billfold and cowboy boots. Both he and the throwers ended up in the water. Everyone then gathered in Jeanne Horse's room and watched the video of him getting thrown in and talked about the game and made phone calls and accepted congratulations from well-wishers who stopped by and talked about the game some more.

Next morning they got on the bus for the long drive back to Pine Ridge. Most of the girls finally slept then. The bus stopped at a McDonald's someplace for a lunch break, and Jeanne Horse and the girls decorated the outside of the bus with streamers and slogans. The whole reservation knew about the victory by that time. In the most remote places, in houses and trailers scattered across the prairie, people had listened to the game on KILI radio, and at the end of it they had thrown open their doors and cheered themselves hoarse into the night. Rosebud Sioux police cars escorted the bus across the Rosebud Reservation. As soon as the bus crossed the eastern edge of the Pine Ridge Reservation at the Bennett County line (still over fifty miles from Pine Ridge village) carloads of fans began to fall into line behind. By the time the bus reached the Wounded Knee turnoff, hundreds of cars were waiting for it. Parents and kids and grandparents stood by the intersection peering east to catch the first glimpse of it. As the bus went by, they waved and cheered and ran to their cars to honk the horns, and then they joined the lengthening train. The cars had their headlights on in the late-autumn twilight, and the line of lights stretched behind the bus for miles. SuAnne and Coach Zimiga were standing by the front door of the bus on the steps looking out the window. At a place in the road where it curved, far into the distance she could see the line of lights following them. She said to Zimiga, "Oh, Char! Oh, Char! Oh, Char!"

Along the road approaching Pine Ridge village people had pulled their cars onto the shoulder on both sides facing perpendicular, and their headlights made a lit-up aisle. Hastily painted welcoming sign-boards lined the route. Horns were honking; pedestrians everywhere caused the bus and its entourage to go slower and slower. By the time the bus reached the four-way intersection in the middle of town, the crowds were too thick for it to move anymore. The sun had just gone down. SuAnne and the others came from the bus to loud cheering, and then several climbed onto the bus roof. They had promised each other that when they got to the four-way they would twirl on the streetlight, but now that they saw it they decided it was too high. A drum group had set up by the intersection and was drumming at top powwow volume as the singers' voices rose in a Lakota victory song. On the roof of the bus, SuAnne and the other girls danced.

People later said that it seemed as if everybody on the reservation was there. "It was the festival of festivals," recalled Dennis Banks, who had flown home early from a conference when he heard about the victory and had joined the procession behind the bus with his limousine. "Those girls *owned* that town," he said. People were carrying SuAnne and Rita and Mary and Darla and the other girls on their shoulders. As the drumbeats sounded, people threw their arms around each other's shoulders and formed a big circle and began a dance called the round dance. People outside the ring danced, too, stepping now this way, now that, shouting and singing. Kids from Pine Ridge High School and their rivals from Red Cloud, political enemies who hadn't spoken to each other in decades, country people who had supported AIM and village guys who had been goons, Dennis Banks and men who in 1973 might have been proud to shoot Dennis Banks—there on the pavement beneath the single streetlight at the four-way, everybody danced.

After a while the crowd went across the street to Billy Mills Hall for speeches and an honoring ceremony. Fans had decorated the hall with crepe paper and posters, and a big banner at one end of the hall proclaimed the words that had become a kind of slogan of the victory: "Tragedy at Sioux Falls!" Folding tables against the walls held trays of food and urns of coffee, and there were big single-layer cakes for each girl on the team, each cake with the player's name written on it in frosting. The drum group sang, tribal officials spoke in praise of the team, and Charles Zimiga said a few words. Light spilled from the doors into the night as people came and went; the crowd was almost more than the hall could comfortably hold. To the girls it seemed as if they had talked to everybody they had ever known. At about ten in the evening people started to go home.

Coach Zimiga lives across the street from the high school. When he awoke the next morning, he could hardly see his house for all the decorations heaped upon it. There were streamers and congratulatory posters and banners and artificial flowers and real flowers and plastic butterflies and wreaths and even a stuffed animal or two—the most thorough job of decorating he had ever seen. In the days after, he and his team got fan letters from all over the state. Grade school classes wrote to them, and little girls from tiny towns like Dupree and Timber Lake, and kids at Indian community colleges. South Dakota governor George Mickelson sent his congratulations, and thanked the team for the reconciliation and understanding they had helped to bring about. For SuAnne Big Crow, the victory meant statewide fame and more. A week or two after girls' basketball season ended, national organizations began to compile their high school all-American teams. The newspaper *USA Today* included SuAnne on its all-American roster, a remarkable honor for a sophomore from a small school in a prairie state. Soon, college recruiters would begin to call. SuAnne and the Lady Thorpes basketball team had made the biggest noise to come out of Pine Ridge in a long time.

CHAPTER

14

Small-town glory is like no other kind. It's so big you can hardly see around it, yet intimate at the same time. When you're fifteen years old, it's as much of glory as you can easily comprehend; praise from faraway strangers seems a bit unreal compared to praise from friends and neighbors you grew up with and run into every day. A small town, and even more a village like Pine Ridge, has for its citizens no very solid boundaries between inside and outside. If you were raised in Pine Ridge you know the inside of lots of houses there, and when you leave your house and walk the village streets you know almost everyone you see outside. Sometimes the warmth of this familiarity can give you an idea of why people decided to live in villages to begin with. And when you're fifteen years old and the people you see in your village greet you not only familiarly but with shouts of praise—well, for a moment then your happiness wraps around you a full three hundred and sixty degrees.

After basketball season, SuAnne's year proceeded like the one before it. Christmas was the usual big production in the Big Crow household, and SuAnne and her friends went around the village looking at the lights and arguing about which house had the best display. In the winter there was volleyball and cheerleading for boys' basketball. That season SuAnne won an individual cheerleading trophy at the boys' all-

Indian basketball tournament. In the spring she ran on the track team. She tended to her schoolwork and worked out in the gym and did errands for her mother on her bicycle just as before. Now, though, SuAnne was really *somebody*. Her school and her town had no bigger star. Little kids copied her, parents paid her to hang out with their kids, old women stopped her in the grocery store to tell her they hoped their grandchildren would grow up to be like her. As is only natural—indeed, as the dark Pine Ridge night follows day—SuAnne acquired rivals, and reservation jealousy began to watch her out of the corner of its eye.

A national Indian organization called Chick that year and said they were putting together the first-ever European tour of a Native American all-star girls' basketball team, to play exhibition games against teams in Finland and Russia. The tour would be that summer, and they wanted SuAnne to join it. Chick was agreeable and SuAnne liked the idea, so to come up with the expense money she and Chick and Pigeon held bake sales and sold raffle tickets and made snacks to sell at local bingo nights. The tribe chipped in some money, and an article in the newspaper brought in a few more donations. By midsummer they had raised enough, and SuAnne had gotten her shots and her passport. Chick drove her to Bismarck, North Dakota, for a few days of practice with the rest of the team. SuAnne later told her that she felt so scared just after she dropped her off that if Chick had come back she would have jumped in the car and gone home. But she stayed, drove with the team to the airport in Minneapolis, and went on to Europe.

Chick had a vision after SuAnne left that made her fear the plane had crashed or something else bad had happened to SuAnne. Both Chick's and SuAnne's misgivings turned out to be partly justified. The Finland leg of the trip went well, but then the team was not allowed to enter Russia, due to visa problems. They had to settle for playing teams in Lithuania; videotape of those games shows SuAnne zipping around the taller and slower Lithuanian girls. In Lithuania SuAnne came down with a stomach illness. On the other side of the globe Chick sensed that SuAnne was sick and prayed her daughter would get back safely. When Chick met the returning team in Mitchell, South Dakota, at the end of the summer she was shocked at SuAnne's appearance. SuAnne had taken on a sickly yellowish color and had lost eleven pounds.

Most likely SuAnne did not know that she was participating in another Native American tradition: since Columbus's time and through the days of the Wild West Shows, Indians have been going to Europe and getting sick there. For Pocahontas and many others, the trip proved fatal. After SuAnne got home she went to several doctors, but none could give her a definite diagnosis. Chick thought it might be a kind of hepatitis. Whatever the ailment was—an unknown virus, travel strangeness, a strong constitution's first intimations of mortality, or some combination of these—it lingered for a long time. SuAnne was tired and couldn't keep food down and some days could hardly move. In a span of two or three months she ended up losing over twenty pounds. She couldn't attend early basketball practice, and during basketball season her junior year she missed more than half the games. To keep up with her schoolwork she went to her classes once or twice a week just to get her assignments, then finished them at home. Her friends and teachers found it strange suddenly not to have her around. Once Jeanne Horse called her to find out how she was doing; she wasn't even sure SuAnne would answer the phone. But SuAnne did, sounding weak. She said she wasn't sure what was wrong with her and hoped to be back in school soon.

By the time SuAnne had recovered enough to return to the team, the Lady Thorpes had lost a lot of games. She played well in several games toward the end of the fall and again was selected for the all–South Dakota team; but this year Red Cloud beat Pine Ridge, and the Lady Thorpes did not advance to the play-offs.

With SuAnne's illness, a certain darkness enters her story. Chick has said that she does not think SuAnne was ever a hundred percent well again. This darkness often lifted, and SuAnne went on to other triumphs; but somehow from then on it was always there. At a distance, one can understand why SuAnne might have been a bit unhappy and confused at this point in her life. After the excitement of the championship had worn off, her fame perhaps became as uncomfortable for her as it was large. People who remember her often talk about how down-to-earth and unassuming SuAnne always was—how she took time for the younger kids who followed her around, how she acted no differently than she ever had, how she hung out with her friends just as before. Perhaps such self-effacement was a strain sometimes. No society is more egalitarian than the Oglala, and SuAnne had encountered one of its contradictions: how can a person always act just like everybody else when, as it happens, she's not?

Until then SuAnne had always been the kid sister, the youngster on the team. With the departure of senior stars like Doni De Cory and Rita Bad Bear, she became the leader looked up to by the younger girls. Perhaps as she got older and observed the Pine Ridge world from the higher vantage point of her fame, she could see just how big were the divisions she had miraculously bridged. Reservation enmities generations old had been set aside in admiration of her; what if people expected her to accomplish this reconciliation again and again? Also, she certainly had heard the old people say that no Pine Ridge basketball star had ever gone on to any big-time success in the sport beyond high school, and that she, SuAnne, would finally be the one. Such pressures might rattle anybody, let alone a sixteen-year-old girl.

As I went around talking to people about SuAnne, I sometimes stopped at Aurelia's house to see my friend Le, or I passed him along the highway and gave him a ride. My interest in SuAnne, when I mentioned it to him, seemed to make him morose and sour. He said a few disparaging things about Chick Big Crow and the SuAnne Big Crow Center, but I paid them little mind. Then one day when I visited him he was about three-quarters' drunk and he quickly cut short my latest revelation about SuAnne. "You know, that SuAnne Big Crow was a big hypocrite," he said. "All that stuff about how she didn't touch drugs or alcohol was a lie. She was a wild kid and she loved to party, and she drank whiskey and smoked marijuana all the time. That whole Big Crow Center is built on a lie." I asked him how he knew this, and he said a niece of his had gone to school with SuAnne and had often told him that she had seen SuAnne partying and that this niece had partied with her herself.

The news depressed me to a standstill. I left Le at Aurelia's house and drove away dejectedly. I didn't know whether to believe him, as I often don't, but I hated to hear him say this all the same. I remained in the dumps for a while. In Pine Ridge one afternoon I happened to run into the niece he had referred to, and I told her what Le had said. She said, "Where does Leonard *get* that stuff? I didn't go to school with SuAnne—I'm five years older than she was—and I never saw her drink or do drugs, and no one ever told me that she did. I didn't even know SuAnne. Why does Leonard say stuff like that about me?"

When SuAnne talked about the reservation, people recall, she sometimes used the metaphor of the basket of crabs. It's a common metaphor on Pine Ridge. She said that the reservation is like a bunch of crabs reaching and struggling to get out of the bottom of a basket, and whenever one of them manages to get a hold and pull himself up the side, the other crabs in their reaching and struggling grab him and pull him back down. The metaphor could apply, no doubt, to many places nearly as poor and lacking in opportunity as Pine Ridge. But somehow it seems even more true here—Oglala society is at once infatuated by and deeply at odds with fame. It creates heroes and tears them down almost simultaneously, as leaders from Red Cloud to Dick Wilson have learned. Perhaps the explanation for this has to do with the Oglala's free-and-equal view of how people are supposed to be, combined with the general distress the culture has undergone. But if the cause is unknowable, the result is usually quite clear: the Pine Ridge Reservation is not a comfortable place to be famous in for longer than a week or two.

The question of where SuAnne would go to college loomed. One of her life's ambitions was to play college basketball at a Division I school. Lots of colleges wanted her, and she had begun to hear from them even before her junior year. As a star athlete and the best student in her class, she qualified for full scholarship assistance at many places. Columbia University in New York City pursued her, offering to fly her and her mother there so she could see the school and meet the coaches. The Air Force Academy, the University of Montana, Penn State, the University of Colorado—sometimes two or three coaches called her house in an evening. SuAnne did most of the negotiating herself. She would put one coach on hold and then talk to the next; she seemed to enjoy bantering with them and asking what they could offer her. Big manila envelopes of promotional material from college sports programs began arriving in the mail. In the end she never actually got around to visiting any faraway schools, though, because the more she thought about it, the less she was sure that she wanted to be so far from home. She often talked on the telephone to Doni De Cory about what she should do. Doni was at Brigham Young University in Utah and feeling homesick herself. Chick inclined toward advising SuAnne to choose a school close by. SuAnne told Coach Zimiga that she couldn't imagine playing basketball where her mother and sisters and friends couldn't always watch her play. She asked him what people would think if she decided to go to college in South Dakota. He said she should not worry about what people thought, she should worry what she thought.

She was seventeen years old and still had not gone out on a date. Evenings when she wasn't at some sport or activity she spent at home, doing schoolwork or playing board games with her family. A group that wanted to stop kids on the reservation from using drugs and alcohol paid for her to go to Chicago and make a video to be shown on local TV. SuAnne had never given a speech to a camera before, and as she argued her anti-drug and -alcohol views, her face appeared rigid and ill at ease, so unlike its vivacity in films where she did not notice she was being watched. For a similar campaign she made a film in which she pretended to be a drunk. This film, which was never finished, shows her sitting on a chunk of rock before the Longhorn Saloon in Scenic swilling on a wine jug (empty) and saying, "I was once state champion!" In an outtake, she nearly falls over and then comes up giggling—the effect is of a death-defying kind of fooling around. Though the trip to Europe the year before must have been scary to remember, she again joined the Native American girls' all-star team the summer after her junior year. This time the team toured Australia and New Zealand, and she did not get sick there.

I know only a few details about the trouble SuAnne got from people on the reservation who didn't like her. Friends say that kids sometimes yelled insults at her and spread rumors and threatened to beat her up, and that two or three large families were very anti-SuAnne. This hostility saddened her; she didn't know what to do about it. Some of the problem seemed to come from the rivalry between the two high schools, Pine Ridge and Red Cloud. Some of her most persistent enemies were Red Cloud girls. In the early fall of SuAnne's senior year, a conflict with Red Cloud kids that had been going on for a while led to a fistfight that ended with several combatants, including SuAnne, in the tribal jail.

The fight started one Thursday evening by the gas pumps at Big Bat's. SuAnne's friend and cousin Angie Big Crow and a Red Cloud girl got into an argument, yelling back and forth, and then suddenly began to fight. They were punching hard and ripping at each other's clothes. Angie ripped off the other girl's shirt and the girl continued to fight just in her bra. Angie stopped fighting for a moment to let her put her shirt back on, and then they went to slugging each other again. Inside the store Chick saw the fight, and she and SuAnne ran to break it up. Other Red Cloud kids piled out of a pickup and started yelling stuff at Chick, and SuAnne went after them, and a general brawl ensued. The tribal police came and got into it, stopping one group of battlers only to have the fighting break out someplace else. The police arrested SuAnne and Angie and the kids they were fighting with and charged them all with disorderly conduct. (Chick later was also charged, with assaulting a minor.) They put the kids in jail, SuAnne and Angie in the same cell. The two had a long wait before their parents could get them out, so to kill time, they ran through their cheerleading cheers.

In the aftermath, nothing came of the fight. All the charges were dropped eventually, and no one had been seriously hurt. Angie Big Crow got a black eye, of which she was very proud the next morning in school. She later came to be on cordial terms with the girl she had fought. The girl told Angie that for such a skinny kid, she fought good. SuAnne showed no ill effects of the brawl when she appeared as her school's Homecoming Queen during half time at the football game a week or two later. She wore a ruffled red dress and a black sequinned top and a tiara in her hair as she stood smiling beside the Homecoming King, Charlie Campos, a longtime friend. Her fight, the only one she ever got into, can be dismissed as the kind of minor scuffle that tribal police deal with often. And yet it has endured as a marker on SuAnne's timeline: The Fight at Big Bat's. Like her illness, in retrospect it takes on the exaggerated darkness of a bad omen. To people for whom she was a hero, the fight was an unscripted event, out of character for SuAnne, one that should never have occurred.

SuAnne played a full season of basketball her senior year and did well. She averaged thirty-nine points a game and again made the all-state team, and Pine Ridge lost only twice. Unhappily, both those losses were to Red Cloud, who beat Pine Ridge by three points in the all-Indian tournament and again by three in the district play-offs. None of the starting players from Pine Ridge's '89 championship team besides SuAnne remained, and the Lady Thorpes no longer had as much depth as Red Cloud. Late in the season the team went to an invitational tournament, where they gave a drubbing to their old foe Milbank as SuAnne scored forty-three points. After that game, as Milbank's Coach Bergquist recalled, he had his last conversation with SuAnne.

Many memories people have of SuAnne her senior year involve "last times." For Christmas that year SuAnne gave presents to everyone she knew. Some of the presents were big and some small, but she made sure to include everyone, even if the present came from the dollar store. She gave her mother a necklace with three gold shoes for pendants, each shoe engraved with the name of her or her sisters and each set with the appropriate birthstone. Toward the end of her Christmas shopping she ran out of money and was hurrying from the house of one friend and another to borrow coupons for last-minute gifts from the grocery store. When people asked her about plans for the future, she often answered vaguely. Her mother asked if she would like a car for graduation, but SuAnne said she didn't think she'd need one. A chance came up for her to go to Spain the following year but she said she would not be going. If later circumstances had been different, remarks like these would have been forgotten.

Just before Christmas SuAnne received a letter from a medicine man who told her that she was a holy person of great importance to the future of her tribe. She told her mother what the letter said, and added that it upset her to think of herself that way. She tore the letter up and threw it out.

That year the Pine Ridge cheerleaders had been invited to take part in another half-time show at a college football bowl game—the Fiesta Bowl, in Tempe, Arizona, over New Year's. After Christmas the girls made the long drive from Pine Ridge in two cars with Jeanne Horse and Wes Whirlwind Horse, a Pine Ridge High School administrator. The traveling was long, the expense money tight, and the group uncongenial, and the trip did not succeed as well as the one a few years before to Hawaii. The kids had no opportunity to sightsee, and rehearsed or stayed in the hotel almost the whole time. In the show they joined a cast of hundreds doing dance routines in the background behind the main star, singer Merrill Osmond. (They thought it strange to be performing again with an Osmond Brother.) The show's theme was "The Year of the Child," and Merrill Osmond surrounded himself on the stage with elementary school kids of many races, including a lot of Indian kids from the Navajo reservation. SuAnne told Jeanne Horse that the way he used the kids, especially the Indian kids, gave her the creeps. On the way to a Fiesta Bowl banquet, SuAnne left one of the memorable images of herself on video. She is walking up some stairs in the hotel wearing a peach-colored silk dress. The camera (held by someone in the Pine Ridge party) is following close behind. All at once SuAnne stops, checks over her shoulder, flips up the back of her dress, and accurately moons the camera. Then she laughs goofily and continues up the stairs.

A teacher at Pine Ridge High School, Harvey Nelson, died unexpectedly of a heart attack that January. He was only in his forties and had been a popular teacher and was well liked in the town. The school held a memorial assembly for him. His death was a shock, and students and teachers talked a lot about it afterward. On the team bus coming back from a volleyball game in Edgemont, South Dakota, SuAnne and the other girls on the volleyball team were remembering him, discussing his death and his funeral. The talk turned to funerals in general, then to imagining what their own funerals would be like. SuAnne said that if she died everyone in town would go to her funeral, and that they'd announce her death on the radio, and that she would have a funeral procession through town that was hundreds of cars long. She wasn't sad as she said this—she seemed to get a kick out of picturing it, as teenagers in particular sometimes do. She said that if she died tomorrow she'd die a virgin and would be buried in a coffin of pure white.

In February, SuAnne and her mother planned to go to Huron, South Dakota, for the Miss Basketball in South Dakota award banquet. The award is the state's most prestigious for girls' basketball, and SuAnne was one of the nominees. The day before the banquet she talked to Doni De Cory on the telephone. She said again how sad she was about the jealousy on the reservation, how tired she was of it. Doni told her that nothing people could say could take away what she'd accomplished. Doni said she thought SuAnne would win the Miss Basketball award. SuAnne said she hoped she could come up with a good acceptance speech if she did. They talked a while longer, told each other they loved each other, and hung up.

SuAnne had her first-ever real date that evening, with a boy named Justin, the quarterback on the Pine Ridge High School football team. SuAnne usually never talked much about boys, but she had been mentioning Justin's name a lot since New Year's. He was a sophomore, two years younger than she. She asked her mother to cook something for her so she could have dinner beforehand; she said, "If he sees how much I eat, he'll never ask me out again." Justin picked her up at six and took her to dinner at Pizza Hut in Chadron, and then to a movie. SuAnne got home about eleven. Her mother was just leaving for her job at the tribal Department of Public Safety. Through a scheduling mix-up at Public Safety, Chick had to work the night shift at the police dispatch desk. She did not want to, knowing that she had to travel the next day, but agreed to relieve a dispatcher who had already put in three shifts straight. SuAnne was excited about her date and about the upcoming banquet, and she couldn't sleep. She called Chick at work; they talked at about two in the morning, and SuAnne didn't get to sleep until after that.

The day was Sunday, February 9, 1992. Chick came home from work, she and SuAnne had breakfast, and they set out on the 300-mile trip to Huron. A friend had told them he could drive them, but at the last minute he called to say that something had come up and he wouldn't be able to. SuAnne and Chick took Pigeon's car, a blue '91 Oldsmobile Cutlass Calais. Chick drove. They headed east from Pine Ridge on Highway 18 for about forty-five miles, then turned onto state Route 73 going north. At the town of Kadoka, Route 73 meets Interstate 90. Chick pulled over in Kadoka at a convenience store with a big statue of a bull out front and went in to get SuAnne a snack of chicken gizzards. SuAnne liked the gizzards at that place and said they always gave you a lot of them. She had been asleep, but when Chick returned she was sitting in the driver's seat. She told her mother she would drive and Chick could sleep now. SuAnne knew Chick was tired after working all night. Chick asked her if she was sure she wasn't too tired and SuAnne said she wasn't.

She turned onto the interstate eastbound. Chick pushed the passenger seat back into its reclining position and began to doze. She woke once or twice to see if SuAnne was getting tired, but SuAnne told her to go back to sleep, she was fine. They passed several exits for small South Dakota towns—Belvidere, Midland, Okaton. The road was straight and monotonous, unenlivened even by the billboards for Wall Drug that pester the westbound lanes. The sky was overcast, the weather calm. She was going about sixty miles an hour. About six miles past the exit for the town of Murdo, on a long, gradual upgrade, she apparently fell asleep. The car went off the road to the right and hit a delineator post. When SuAnne tried to correct the swerve and get back on the pavement, the car rolled over in the right-hand lane, then rolled a second time into the median strip. As per Pine Ridge custom, neither SuAnne nor her mother had her seat belt on. The driver's-side door came open as the car rolled, and SuAnne was flung from it. She landed in the median strip twenty or thirty feet from the upside-down car.

The accident occurred at about 11:40 in the morning. A state highway patrol car reached the scene seven minutes later, and ambulances arrived a few minutes after that. Chick had cuts and other minor injuries, but was conscious. She could hear people saying that she must be in shock, and she wanted to tell them that she wasn't, but somehow she couldn't talk. Paramedics were working on SuAnne. She had severe head injuries and was unconscious. The police told Chick they were taking SuAnne in the first ambulance and that the second one would carry her. Chick agreed to this, not really understanding what they meant. Both ambulances drove to St. Mary's Hospital in Pierre, about forty-five miles away. Doctors at St. Mary's examined SuAnne's injuries, then decided she should be flown immediately by helicopter to a bigger hospital in Sioux Falls. Before they could get her on the helicopter, at 3:35 that afternoon, she died.

I could try to describe the sorrow—the telephones ringing all across the reservation and across the state, the calls that poured in by the hundreds to KILI radio, the people driving disconsolately around Pine

Ridge village and stopping each other and having nothing to say, the weeping of men whom no one had ever seen weep before, the arrival of SuAnne's body in the early-morning hours of Monday at the Pine Ridge funeral parlor, the crowd that was there to meet it, the wake on Tuesday night in the Pine Ridge High School gym, the funeral the next morning, the basketball net Coach Zimiga put in her coffin, the military honors which a contingent of Pine Ridge war veterans awarded her, the farewell salute fired over her grave, and on and on—but knowing SuAnne's dislike for the tragedy-at-Pine-Ridge genre, I hesitate. The truth is, I can hardly bear to imagine it all.

As SuAnne had predicted just a week or two before, the line of cars in her funeral procession stretched for miles. People said there were more cars than had followed the bus into town after the '89 championship game. Also as she had predicted, her coffin was white. The governor of South Dakota sent his condolences, the state legislature held a moment of silence in her honor, and schools and tribal offices in Pine Ridge closed for the day. Lakota singers composed memorial songs, KILI radio played over five hundred requests in her honor. High school teams from the reservation and elsewhere that SuAnne had played against sent representatives. In a town that had seen too many funerals, nobody could recall a funeral as big as hers.

Jeanne Horse said later, "So much happened then, it was like a daze. I remember it in pieces. But I'll never forget that Monday morning, the morning after SuAnne died, when they got all the kids together in the high school gym for an assembly and a memorial. School attendance was almost perfect that day. When I arrived, the gym was already full, and what stays in my mind is the sound I heard as I walked in—the sound of all those kids in the gym crying."

Chick Big Crow never went back to work for the Department of Public Safety. Aside from attending the funeral, she stayed in her house day after day. Family members and friends took turns staying with her, because they did not want her to be by herself. She said little and emotionally more or less shut down. She had been raised a Catholic but could not see much purpose to her faith now. When she thought of it, she also remembered the hostility people harbored for SuAnne at the

Catholic Red Cloud School. Soon after SuAnne's death, medicine men started coming by to visit Chick. One in particular, Chauncy Yellow Horse, told her that the spirits had told him that it would be his job to comfort her. Chauncy Yellow Horse was living in a remote part of the reservation, but he said that she should not give him tobacco or blankets or even gas money, because his reward would come from the spirits.

Chauncy told her that in her grief she would often feel her soul start to slide away. Each time it did that, he said, the spirits would help it to return. He talked a lot about SuAnne, and what her purpose had been, and how her spirit had been with the tribe since a time far in the past. He said there was a purpose to her leaving and to Chick still being here. He took Chick to a traditional honoring ceremony called the Wiping of the Tears, held in a school gym in the little community of Cherry Creek. Chick resisted going and finally did only on impulse and at the last minute. The gym was packed with people, most of whom she didn't know. They sang honoring songs for SuAnne and for her, and they gave her gifts, and the elders whispered words of comfort and advice in her ear. Chick said later that if it hadn't been for Chauncy Yellow Horse she might have lain down and never gotten up again.

She wondered whether it made any sense to stay on in Pine Ridge. When she thought of the sadness here, and of the meanness and jealousy of so many people on the reservation, she considered packing up and moving away. She had no place in particular that she wanted to go—just away. Then one day something happened to change her mind. She tells the story often: "About a week after the funeral I was sitting in my kitchen in the afternoon. I was alone, for a change. I wasn't reading or watching TV or listening to the radio—just sitting there. It got to be late afternoon and darker outside, and I didn't even bother to stand up and turn on the light. Pretty soon it was almost completely dark. I heard someone knock on the door and I didn't care to answer it. The knock came again, and then two girls opened the door and walked in and came over to where I was. I remember what the girls looked like, but I'd never seen them before, and I've never seen them since that day. I had my head down on the kitchen table. I could feel their grief as they gave me a hug, and then they opened up my hand and put something in it. Then they left. After a while I finally got up and turned on the light and looked at the paper in my hand. It was a valentine—Valentine's Day had just passed—and on it were the words 'SuAnne was our hero. We loved her and we love you too.' "

The next day Chick decided what she wanted to do. SuAnne had often talked of an ideal place she called Happytown, where kids could go and hang out and have fun and not get in trouble. As her cousin Angie recalled, "Someday she was going to build Happytown, where nobody would fight or be jealous, where it would be clean, have a mall and lots of places for good fun. She was always making plans for her Happytown." Remembering her vision, Chick decided to build a place like that in Pine Ridge. In a few hours she had written out a statement of mission and a description of the facilities a Happytown would require. She envisioned a sizable space with recreation rooms, video games, a snack bar, trophy room, library, game room, computer room, and offices. When she called Rol Bradford and Jeanne Horse to tell them her idea, it was as if they had just been waiting for her to call. They came over to her house right away to discuss the plans with her. A day or two later her friend Tom Grey brought her a set of blueprints already drawn. Within a month Chick had set up the Visions of SuAnne Big Crow, Inc., as a nonprofit corporation to benefit Native American youth. Its board of directors included AIM people like Dennis Banks, along with former goons—the unexpected Pine Ridge coalition that SuAnne's appeal had helped to bring about.

Chick called tribal councilman G. Wayne Tapio and asked if the tribe had a building it wasn't using. A few days later he called back and said that she could have the old doll factory, a 6,000-square-foot space full of miscellaneous junk and old machinery. The tribe would lease it to her corporation, he said, for a dollar a year. At first a Pine Ridge group contested the claim to the building, but by May, Chick and her friends had it free and clear. They began by cleaning it out. The former factory had made small plastic Indian dolls to sell with the moccasins from another Pine Ridge factory, and there were lots of doll parts lying around, and hundreds of fifty-pound sacks of plastic pellets, and eight three-ton machines for melting the plastic down and molding it. People came with pickups and carted the sacks of pellets to the dump. In a single day a group of volunteers tackled the machines, heaving and skidding them across the floor on slicks of motor oil until they toppled them out the loading-bay doors. The tribe later sold them, and they were hauled away.

All summer, guys with carpentry skills donated their time to the Big Crow Center (as it was now being called), working mostly in the evenings and on weekends, putting up walls and remodeling the inside. People brought casseroles and hot dogs and crockpots full of beans for the workers. There was activity in the building at all hours, and electric saws buzzing at four-thirty in the morning sometimes. For Chick, the enthusiasm and the camaraderie were renewing. By mid-August most of the essential carpentry had been done.

Chick knew that the small donations that had carried the project so far would dwindle eventually and that she could expect no funding from the tribe. To succeed, the center would have to be able to support itself. Since the renovation began, there had always been food at the center; she and her sisters were good cooks; she decided that it made sense for the center to support itself with a restaurant. In those start-up days people joked that all Chick had to do when she needed something was reach up and pull it out of the air. Once, she mentioned in a meeting of the board that the center needed a hot water heater, and when they stepped out in the parking lot a local contractor was unloading a hot water heater for them from the back of his truck. Chick wanted a soda fountain for the restaurant and by chance came across a used one from an old drugstore at a small local auction. The auctioneer was trying to get rid of it and he let her have it for five dollars. Other fortunate purchases produced a counter, stools, tables, a refrigerator, a grill. The center opened the restaurant on September 1, 1992, and sold its first hamburger. The restaurant has remained open six or seven days a week ever since, serving hamburgers, sodas, ice cream, and daily specials like chicken and dumplings or meat loaf or chicken-fried steak or lasagna. In the summer tourist season it does a brisk business at lunch hour. The restaurant provided the essential income to keep the center running during lean times when bills were piling up and the power company was threatening to turn off the electricity.

During that first year a representative of the Boys' and Girls' Clubs of America who was visiting Pine Ridge stopped by the center and looked at the building and the plans. He said that he thought the center would be perfect as a member club in his organization. The center's

board of directors liked the idea of a national affiliation, so they applied
for a Boys' and Girls' Club charter. The Boys' and Girls' Clubs provide
sports and recreation activities for kids six or seven to eighteen years
old during vacation months and after school, and most of the clubs are
in cities. About a year after applying, the Big Crow Center became the
first chartered Boys' and Girls' Club on an Indian reservation. It served
a membership of over a hundred kids its first year, and over three hundred kids the next. With mostly volunteer counselors it offered weekday
and weekend programs for grade school and high school kids—softball,
weightlifting, table tennis, crafts, games, and special events like Halloween hayrides and Christmas sing-alongs. Besides the regular members, many drop-ins came to the center, and it did not turn any
well-behaved kid away. Since 1992, the center has served thousands of
kids.

Early on, the center set down a strict set of rules for kids on the
premises: No fighting, no speaking disrespectfully to peers or counselors, no drugs or alcohol, and no gang colors. The prevailing difficulty
of the Pine Ridge surroundings has often slowed the center's progress. Although dues are fifteen dollars a year per member—a modest
amount, given what many parents routinely spend on their kids—most
parents of kids who attend pay no dues. (The notion that all services
should be free runs deep among people on Pine Ridge.) The prohibi-
tion against gang colors and the center's unwillingness to be a hang-out
spot for any one gang have limited to some extent the teens it can attract, because so many of the kids on Pine Ridge are in gangs. The no-
drugs-or-alcohol rule, which also applies to counselors on or off the job,
has made finding and keeping counselors and other workers much
harder. Sometimes the center has no teen programs scheduled, due to
lack of members or of counselors, or both. Teenage kids on Pine Ridge
get into scrapes and violence and car wrecks all the time, and the teen
suicides common on other reservations also occur far too frequently
here. Despite a desire to reach the kids who most need its help, the
center often does not succeed.

Yet the Big Crow Center, amazingly, has stayed in operation for
seven years now with almost no funding assistance from anywhere. Not
many people know that Pine Ridge has in fact produced a number of
sound economic ventures in recent years, all of them unusual in that

they received little or no help from the federal government or the tribe. Big Bat's Texaco is one; KILI Radio, the locally owned radio station, is another. *Indian Country Today*, an Indian-owned and -staffed newspaper with a national circulation and a reputation for good reporting and commentary out of Rapid City, began as *The Lakota Times* in Pine Ridge. The Big Crow Center, like these enterprises, has survived on its own against the daunting reservation odds.

"I've made many mistakes in what I've done here over the years," Chick Big Crow said to me recently. "I never followed up on a lot of ideas for improvements I had, I didn't acknowledge people who sent me donations, I let important matters slide sometimes. I tried to handle everything myself, from cooking in the restaurant to figuring out our computer system to managing the budget to mowing the softball field. I had a hard time delegating any job. Maybe I was trying to punish myself over guilt at SuAnne's death, maybe I was expressing a grief that I had never dealt with. I don't think I was really fitted to the job of running this place—I guess I had never even liked kids very much before. Looking back now, I see what I would have done differently, and what I'll do differently in the future. I've learned a lot—I've learned more from SuAnne than she did from me. But considering all my failings, I really believe it was the spirituality of this place that's kept it open, not me."

So much is so wrong on Pine Ridge. There's suffering and poverty and violence and alcoholism, and the aura of unstoppability that repeated misfortunes acquire. But beneath all that is something bigger and darker and harder to look at straight on. The only word for it, I'm afraid, is evil. News stories emphasizing the reservation's "bleakness" are actually using this as a circumlocution for that plain, terrible word. For journalistic reasons the news cannot say, "There is evil here." And beyond a doubt there is. A bloody history, bad luck, and deliberate malice have helped it along. Sometimes a sense of it comes over me so strongly that I want to run home to bed—for example, when I walk down the row of almost-new child-size bicycles in a local pawnshop, or when I see a bunch of people the police have recently evicted from White Clay staggering back to it, or when I'm driving on a deserted reservation road at night and there's a large object suddenly up ahead, and I skid to a stop a few feet from it, and it's the hulk of a car so completely incinerated that it has melted the asphalt around it; it's just sitting there with no warning, with no other cars on the scene, empty and destroyed and silent in the middle of nowhere. At such moments a sense of compound evil—that of the human heart, in league with the original darkness of this wild continent—curls around me like shoots of a fast-growing vine.

Good appears most vividly in resistance to its opposite; that's what heroism is about, after all. The more you see of Pine Ridge's bad side, the more you long for evidence of good, and the happier you are when you find it. Great good does exist here, too, in the lives of people who hold fast to it and serve their neighbors without much encouragement or reward, and in the steadfastness of the old Oglala culture that endures. Longing for the good here was what first drew me to SuAnne. You sense the good in the SuAnne Big Crow Center when you walk in the door. Usually the awareness takes a few minutes to register; it's like feeling the sun on your face when your eyes are closed, or suddenly realizing in a smoke-filled room that someone has opened a window somewhere.

Big Bat's Texaco welcomes strangers for commercial reasons, but the Big Crow Center welcomes them for spiritual ones. SuAnne's well-known openness to people in general has provided the model for an openhearted place. All kinds of people come wandering through the center; I often see passersby looking at the trophies and clippings on the walls and asking questions of the staff. Nowhere else in town do you see strangers in a contemplative mood. A life of bravery and generosity and victory and heroism was the founding inspiration here, and if SuAnne's death was a terrible sorrow, it also had the effect of holding the good she represented fixed and unchanged. SuAnne Big Crow, though gone forever, is unmistakably still around. The good of her life sustains this place with a power as intangible as gravity, and as real.

A while ago I visited the site on Interstate 90 where SuAnne and Chick's car accident occurred. I would not have taken the interstate otherwise; I was driving from Pine Ridge to Minneapolis and in no rush for time. The interstate highways that cross the plains do indeed have many monotonous stretches. The Plains were not meant to be seen this way—through a speeding windshield heading east or west—no matter how much the wide-open geography tempts you to think in terms of the farthest horizon and the straightest line. Droning along on the interstate you forget sometimes that you're on the Plains, or on a highway, or anywhere at all.

As I got closer to the crash site, I could easily imagine the danger of falling asleep at the wheel. In this part of the state the prairie is rolling, but the interstate travels a roadbed that is raised above the low places and so stays essentially level all the time. I had the state Department of Transportation accident report with me, and it said that the wreck had been at four-tenths of a mile west of the milepost numbered 200. After I passed the Murdo exit I began to look for the mileposts. The time of the year was June and the hour midday; the heat above the road was hazy with traffic exhaust. I went as slowly as I could get away with as trucks and cars came up behind me and whizzed by. About seven miles past Murdo I spotted the 199 post. Six-tenths of a mile beyond it I saw the fatality marker erected by the state. The right-hand shoulder descends in a long, rather steep grade here, and the fatality marker looked small down at the bottom of it next to the fence that runs along the highway. If I had been in the passing lane I could not have seen the marker at all, nor if I had been on the westbound side. Even going as slowly as I was, in a second it had disappeared behind me.

I understood better now how the accident might have occurred. SuAnne, waking when her drifting car hit the delineator post at the roadside, looked to her right and saw that long and steep decline. She then probably turned the wheel violently to avoid going down it, and the suddenness of her correction caused the car to overturn. As the accident site receded in my rearview, I wondered how I could get back to it. Then I noticed a small dirt lane running just the other side of the highway fence. I turned off the interstate at the next exit, found the lane, and went bumping slowly back along it in the direction I had come. It dead-ended at a little hollow filled with brush. I left the car and walked through tall grass along the highway fence to the fatality marker.

I had never visited a historic site on an interstate highway before. I climbed over the fence and examined the marker. Its grim slogans—X MARKS THE SPOT and DRIVE SAFELY and WHY DIE?—looked new, their lettering still unfaded by the sun. It was, of course, a distance from here to the pavement and median strip, the actual site of the crash. From the marker I walked up the long incline to the shoulder beside the eastbound lanes, where the continuous traffic was going by like a loud, sooty wind. The cars made a humming that expanded in the ear as they passed, and the trucks gave off a rising and falling whine. I walked along the shoulder trying to imagine: The car would have hit the post here, it would have rolled there, it would have ended up there. In a momentary break in the traffic I could almost see it—but then the cars and trucks again came rushing by. Each passing vehicle was like the swoop of an eraser on a blackboard, and millions of them, probably, had gone across this piece of highway since SuAnne died.

Occasionally a passing driver quickly turned his head to look at me. I wasn't hitchhiking, I wasn't walking, and no disabled car waited nearby, so my presence could not be explained. This simply was not a place for a person to be standing around. After a few minutes I walked back down the incline to the fatality marker and sat beside it in the grass out of sight of traffic. When I did, I noticed wildflowers—little megaphone-shaped blossoms of pale lavender on a ground vine, called creeping jenny hereabouts, and a three-petaled flower called spiderwort, with a long stem and long, narrow leaves. The spiderwort flowers were a deep royal blue. I had read that in former times the Sioux crushed spiderwort petals to make a blue jelly-like paint used to color moccasins. Mid-June must be these flowers' peak season; among the roadside grasses, lost hubcaps, and scattered gravel, the spiderwort and creeping jenny grew abundantly.

There are no historic markers by the sides of interstate highways. You find them by two-lane roads, but almost never by any roads that are bigger. Evidently history cannot exist at speeds above 55 miles an hour. Because I knew that no historic marker here would ever tell about SuAnne, I began to compose one in my head:

SUANNE BIG CROW

SuAnne Marie Big Crow, a star basketball player for Pine Ridge High School on the Pine Ridge Indian Reservation, died as a result of a car accident that occurred at this spot on February 9, 1992. Born in Pine Ridge village on March 15, 1974, she was a talented athlete who took up basketball as a young girl.

During her high school career she set two South Dakota high school records and was named to the state all-star team four years in a row. In 1989 she led Pine Ridge to the state Class A championship, scoring the winning basket in the last second of play. Known for her humor, determination, sportsmanship, and generosity, as well as for the quickness and grace of her game, SuAnne carried the pride of her Oglala tribe to basketball courts all around the state, and beyond. She is a daughter this state of South Dakota and this country are proud to claim.

On down the slope, across the corner of a wheatfield, was a grove of cottonwood trees. I climbed back over the highway fence and walked to it. Perhaps because of the rolling topography, I could hardly hear the traffic here. Just a couple of hundred yards away, the twenty-four-hour-a-day noise of the interstate had disappeared into its own dimension. The cottonwoods stood in a grove of eight or ten, all of them healthy and tall, around a small pool of clear water bordered with cattail reeds and dark-gray mud. Herons, ducks, raccoons, and deer had left their tracks in the mud not long before. From the cattails came the chirring song of red-winged blackbirds, a team whose colors no other team will ever improve on. Old crumpled orange-brown leaves covered the ground around the trees, and false morel mushrooms of a nearly identical shade grew in the crotches of the roots. The cottonwoods had appeared a deep green from the highway, but seen from underneath, their leaves were silvery against the blue sky. High above the trees bright white cumulus clouds piled one atop another. They went on and on, altitude upon altitude, getting smaller as they went, like knots on a rope ladder rising out of sight.

Pine Ridge was Pine Ridge still. Its hard times, sadly, seemed to have no end; by phone and occasional visits I kept up with the news. Twelve people died as a result of alcohol-related car accidents on the reservation's roads in 1996, and seven in 1997, and at least five in 1998. Among the victims were a longtime teacher at Wolf Creek School and his grandchild, killed when a drunk driver ran into their car. Someone robbed the Taco John's take-out restaurant in Pine Ridge, and not long after that it burned to the ground. The tribal treasurer caused a commotion by buying a small herd of prize cattle with $200,000 of the tribe's money that people said should have been used to house the homeless. Later he had to resign. Former tribal officials sued current ones for various violations and crimes. The roads deteriorated to such a point that they were causing accidents themselves. In Oglala, some local teenage gang members tortured and killed a neighbor boy; FBI agents came and took them off to jail. Other Pine Ridge teenagers killed themselves. The regional bureau of the Indian Health Service reported that diabetes now affected over 50 percent of the adults on Pine Ridge, and declared the disease an epidemic there.

To make things worse, in June of '99 a tornado hit Oglala. It destroyed 160 buildings in the town and killed one man and left scores of people without homes, living in temporary shelters or camping in tents on the lots where their houses used to be. Government agencies hurried to rebuild or replace the houses and compensate the sufferers. A number of people whose houses the tornado had not touched damaged their houses themselves in the hope of qualifying for aid. In Pine Ridge village a group of protesters including reunited AIM veterans Russell Means and Dennis Banks said the government should pay attention not just to the tornado damage but to the violence done to Indians every day. To dramatize their anger at recent unexplained deaths of tribal members along the reservation's border with Nebraska, they led a march to the town of White Clay, where rioting soon began. People looted a store and set fires in it and threw rocks at fire trucks coming to put them out. The protest leaders promised marches every week until the mystery of the deaths was solved, the killers punished, and the liquor stores in White Clay shut down.

The tornado and the protests put Pine Ridge once again in the national news. Not long after the tornado, President Clinton came to Pine Ridge as part of a trip he was making across the country to draw attention to problems of poverty. He visited a woman who told him she had twenty-eight people living in her shack and trailer home. Outside Pine Ridge High School the President told the Oglala and other tribal leaders in attendance that the federal government would support economic revival in Indian country by providing tax credits for new business development. People were impressed that he had come—no President since F.D.R. had visited an Indian reservation—but no one got too excited about what he had to say.

Meanwhile, the teachers went on teaching, the school buses ran, the tribal casino on the western boundary of the reservation stayed open round the clock, the graduating classes at Oglala Lakota College kept growing, the crowds of summer visitors arrived as always for the sun dances, Big Bat expanded his operation with new stores in Chadron and Hot Springs, the doctors at the hospital kept delivering babies, and the annual August powwow was bigger than the one the year before.

And what of my friend Le?

I did not see much of Le for a while. I guess we were still kind of mad at each other. I know I was exasperated with him. On a couple of trips to the reservation I looked for him but did not find him. One time his sister Florence told me that he was staying over in White Clay, and that she had seen him on the street there so drunk he was blank. Another time Aurelia told me that he had been thrown in jail for disrupting the singing of the National Anthem at the Calico Community powwow. When I heard these reports I figured it was just as well I hadn't run into him. On the few occasions when we did get together he told me stories that were so wild and unverifiable I didn't know what to say. Then he'd repeat them, as if I hadn't appreciated them enough the first time.

Once when I was home Le called me collect and said he was going to tell me a story that he had never told anyone before. Then he went into a long description of a *yuwipi* ceremony his grandfather had held for him as a boy, during which a loud growling and a rank smell came into the cabin as the ceremony was going on, and then the door flew open and a bear walked in and put his paw on Le's chest, imparting to him the bear's power. The story went on from there, but I didn't listen closely, because I had heard it before. I only said, as I often do, "Wow!" In the next breath Le asked me to wire him some money. I told him that I couldn't, that my credit cards were limited out—a lie, but he sounded drunk and strange, and I didn't want to send him anything. He was silent. Then he told me that when I came back to the reservation not to look for him, because he didn't want to see me, and not to go around to see his sisters, either. Then he said that he would be dead in a few weeks and that I would never see him again.

When I was in Oglala a few months later I looked him up anyway. I found him staying at the house of the Porcupine boys, Sam and Gilmore. He greeted me as cheerfully as if our last conversation had not taken place. Though fall had arrived and a cold wind was blowing, he was walking around in just his shirtsleeves. He explained that he had gotten into a fight with some guys on the top of a nearby butte and in the course of the fight had lost his coat. I skeptically drove him to the butte he indicated and up a steep but navigable track to the top. To my surprise we immediately found his reading glasses on the ground and his glasses case and some folded-up prescription papers from his doctor a short distance away. But though we searched all over as Le told me about a UFO that had once landed there, we found no coat. I offered to give him the down coat I was wearing—it was old, and I had another in the car—but when he put it on, the sleeves came up to his elbows.

The next day I went to a clothing store in Chadron and looked through coats by the dozen until I found one I thought might fit him. It was a fleece-lined brown canvas Carhart coat, size 46 tall. I bought it and drove over to Oglala and took it to him at the Porcupines'. He tried it on and it fit exactly. Little in life is as satisfying as buying someone an article of clothing that really fits. After he had zipped it and buttoned it and shrugged the sleeves up and down for a while, he said, "You know, Wendy Cody and them were sayin' that you didn't want to see me that time we visited you, that you were tryin' to get rid of me. They said you never come around because you're not really my friend."

"Well, to be honest, Le, I wasn't very happy to see you that time. But that was mainly because you were drunk. I'm happy to see you otherwise."

"I can understand that. That's cool."

"And no matter what anybody says, I *am* your friend."

Over the following winter he and I talked often on the phone. He was staying at Bluch Fire Thunder's place out by the Oglala dam. He said someone had stolen his firewood, so he was burning old tires in his stove. When he went outside, he said, the chimney with the black smoke pouring from it looked like the smokestack of a train. I wired him money for firewood. In early spring he called with bad news: he had been diagnosed with prostate cancer. "I didn't react at all when the doctor told me," he said. "I just sort of shrugged and said, 'That's the way it goes, it's okay with me.' The doc was surprised; he said, 'You don't seem too upset.' I said, 'No, I'm actually glad. It gives me something to die of besides liver failure.' Those docs were all amazed at me. I had three different docs up there at the IHS hospital. One was a German woman, one was a Puerto Rican guy, and one was a Filipino guy. They had a conference with me, and I asked 'em, 'Tell me something—how come none of you doctors have American names?' They said, 'What do you mean, American names?' I said, 'You know, good American names, like Kills in Sight.' That made 'em laugh."

He said the doctors were sending him up to Rapid City Regional for a prostate biopsy, to be a hundred percent sure. I wired him money for the carfare. He could have been making all this up, but when he called me soon after, the details of the biopsy procedure he described were grisly and convincing. A few weeks after that he called to say he had received the biopsy results: they were negative. He didn't have prostate cancer after all. I shouted for joy.

In the late spring he told me I should come for the sun dance his younger sister Minerva planned to hold near Loneman. In July he announced that he would be one of the chefs at the big feast at the August powwow and that I should come down for that. But with work and family and summer company, I couldn't get away. I didn't have a chance to return to the reservation until that December, about two weeks before Christmas. I had never been to Pine Ridge around Christmas time. I wanted to see Le and Florence and Aurelia; also, Floyd John had just returned from a long stay at an alcohol rehab program in Wisconsin, and I hadn't seen him in almost two years. My wife bought a big ham for Florence and another one for Aurelia, and basketball-star Barbie dolls for Florence's granddaughters, and University of Montana T-shirts for her grandsons. I bought winter gloves for Le and Floyd John, and I supplied my wallet with twenties, always a useful denomination on the rez. The weather cooperated by being strangely warm and windy and clear. I loaded up the car and set out on an almost-hot afternoon.

I have visited the reservation in all seasons and in many personal moods, including foreboding, fear, and gloom. I know that the hopeful, big-sky feeling with which we often invest Western landscapes is at odds with the reality of life on Pine Ridge. And yet, despite the suffering there, again and again when I see the reservation it still looks grand to me. I came down Highway 79 from Rapid City early in the morning, noticing with surprise that this part of 79 had been widened to a more sensible four lanes. No longer did it give the impression that a serious wreck waited just up ahead; it was now well laid out and modern and safe. The eight crosses commemorating the Dismounts Thrice accident, however, still stood beside the road.

The sun had just come over the horizon as I turned off the highway at Hermosa and headed southeast on the two-lane road to Red Shirt Table and the reservation. The sky was a limpid blue, without a cloud. On the low buttes the shadows and the sunlight alternated like braiding, in long, horizontal sweeps. A pheasant stepped from the grass, set his white-ringed neck forward like a gearshift lever, and ran across the road. I passed the bridge over the Cheyenne River, the red-and-white sign with the Oglala flag announcing the boundary of the reservation, the village of Red Shirt. For some miles past Red Shirt the road was smooth and newly paved. Then, as it entered badland country, it got worse. The tribe had evidently torn up the pothole-riddled asphalt from before and simply graded over the rough surface beneath it. The morning sun left blue shadows in the washboard ruts.

Across the White River bridge and ahead on the horizon was the Loneman water tower. Then the elementary school, the tribal building, the intersection of Highway 18, and the wreath in memory of Wanda Kindle. I stopped and got out to look at it. Now it was decorated with Christmas ribbons and greenery, a large plastic snowflake, a white wooden cross, and a long-stemmed artificial red rose. I wanted to drop off the hams, so I swung by Florence's house—no one home. Then I decided to try Aurelia's, and on my way there I passed Le and Floyd John walking along the road. They didn't recognize me until I had pulled over and hit the brakes. I leaned across and opened the passenger door. Floyd John was wearing a black leather jacket, jeans, and cowboy boots. As he climbed into the back seat—accepting, as always, Le's natural right to the front—I asked how he was doing. He said, "How'm I doing? I'm myself, and I'm glad I am. I've got my self back. Been sober for ten months now." Le got in and shook my hand and closed the door. He had on an oil-stained brown down coat, jeans, tennis shoes, and a black felt cowboy hat with a bright red cord for a hatband. To my question, he replied, "Oh, I'm hangin' in there," as unsurprised as usual at seeing me.

I negotiated the long mud driveway to Aurelia's house almost without effort, remembering how challenging I used to find it. Now it seemed easy; I felt comfortable and oddly at home in this place I'd been to so often and thought so often about. Aurelia had left for her volunteer job at the Presbyterian child-care center, so Le led me into her house and we put the ham in her refrigerator. In her kitchen, I was suddenly so glad to see him I gave him a hug. It was kind of an awkward moment, but I think he was pleased. He said, "I'm glad to see you, too, bro." We got back in the car, and I told him and Floyd John that I'd never been to Pine Ridge at Christmas time before, that I'd wanted to see what the season was like here. "Seventy percent of the people on the reservation don't believe in Christmas," Le said. "I don't believe in it myself. It's something the priests wanted us to believe in, but we never did. Christmas ain't nothin' around here."

We were silent for a moment as we headed toward Oglala. Le told me to stop at the post office. As we pulled into the parking lot, Floyd John said, "Do you remember that song 'Grandmaw Got Run Over by a Reindeer'?" He began to sing:

> "Grandmaw got run over by a reindeer
> [something something something] Christmas Eve.
> You may say there's no such thing as Santa,
> But as for me and Grandpaw, we believe."

Le introduced me to the new postmaster, a young man named Kelly who asked me if Le was really as famous as he said he was. I said, "Oh, even more." Le checked his mailbox. It contained an eight-page newsprint circular for the Sioux Nation supermarket in Pine Ridge advertising holiday specials on baking supplies, self-basting turkeys, stuffing mix, and dinner rolls. He immediately threw it in the wastebasket, where it joined a growing pile. Floyd John opened his box and found a letter from a woman he knows in Germany and a Christmas card from a pawnshop in Hot Springs, South Dakota, thanking him for his patronage that year.

As it happened, Le and Floyd John had been on their way to another pawnshop that morning—the one in White Clay, where they planned to exchange Le's black felt cowboy hat and Floyd John's Walkman for money with which to buy a part they needed to repair Floyd John's car. Instead of going to White Clay, we now went directly to Pronto Auto Parts in Pine Ridge, where I exchanged two of my twenties for the part Floyd John needed and another part Le said he needed for a car of his and five quarts of transmission fluid. Outside, Le and Floyd John had a conversation in Sioux with an old man with a big nose and striped suspenders. They got back in the car laughing. "That was Raymond Pipe on Head," Le said. "Ray's a Korean War vet, and he's always kiddin' with Floyd John about the Army and him bein' in Vietnam. Just now Ray was sayin', 'I heard they had to discharge you from the service in Vietnam because you were eatin' up all the monkeys and snakes over there.' He told Floyd, 'When you started in on eatin' the *rare* and *endangered* ones, that's when they knew they had to get rid of you.' "

Floyd John's car, a Chevy Celebrity, was parked under the cottonwoods by Aurelia's place. We worked on it there all morning and into the afternoon. Le pointed out that I actually did not do much of the work myself, but I replied that I had watched so closely that I felt as if I had. The car's problem involved the right front axle. This axle, or transaxle, as it's called, connects to the transmission through a seal called the transaxle seal, a rubber-lined metal ring about two inches across which keeps the transmission fluid from leaking out. The Celebrity's transaxle seal had broken, causing a potentially disastrous leak. Le and Floyd John now had to jack up the car, remove the right front tire, remove the transaxle, remove the broken transaxle seal, install the new seal, and then put the transaxle and the wheel back on.

"We just replaced that transaxle a few days ago," Le said. "It give out when we were driving up in Rapid, so we hitched back down here, took a transaxle off a junker we knew about, put it in a rip-stop parachute bag of Floyd's, hitched back up to Rapid, took off the busted one, put in the good one, and drove the car back here. Only thing was, we didn't know that seal was shot, too. We had to keep stopping and putting in new transmission fluid. Between here and Rapid we went through twelve quarts.

"Our cousin Leon Long Soldier helped us with the mechanic work up in Rapid. Leon's pretty good at fixing cars. He had just gotten out of jail the day before. They had him down in Nebraska for vehicular homicide, but then they dropped the charges. What happened was, Leon was coming back from taking his dad to the doctor in Scottsbluff and he was driving really fast up Highway 87 between Rushville and White Clay, and all of a sudden he heard this *bump blam*—he run over something in the road. He thought he'd hit a deer, but when he went back to look he saw it was a man. He checked the guy and the guy was dead. So Leon came on to Pine Ridge and told the police, and they called the Dawes County sheriff in Nebraska, and the sheriff checked it out and found the dead guy, and then he came to Pine Ridge and arrested Leon. Leon was in jail for a few days before the highway patrol investigators went over the accident scene and found out that the guy had also been run over by someone else in the ditch beside the road.

They asked the coroner to determine the time of death, and it turned out the guy had been dead by the time Leon ran over him. I guess someone had run him over in the ditch, and then he had climbed up to the road and finally died there. But it ain't a crime to run over a dead body, so they had to let Leon go."

Floyd John borrowed the screw jack from my Blazer and got to work. He was under the car wrenching and hammering, while Le fetched tools and offered advice. They had to lift up the axle even farther to get some bolts out, and Le found a metal fence post to use as a lever. When it didn't work, he found a four-by-four wooden beam about six feet long, and that did the job. He was telling stories about his bull-riding days, such as the one about the bull nobody had ever ridden before—how he drew the bull in a big rodeo, and how he rode him for the full eight seconds and more, and how he finally jumped off, and how the bull then walked over to Le in front of the whole arena and bent his foreleg and bowed down to him. Le laughed. "I told that story the other day to a young guy and his girlfriend who gave me a ride from Pine Ridge. After I said that the bull bowed down to me, the guy asked, 'Did he *really?*' His girlfriend got mad at him and slugged him on the arm. She said, 'Don't you know Indian bullshit when you hear it?' "

At lunchtime Le went in the house and brought me out a sandwich made of a quarter-inch-thick slice of bologna on white bread with lots of mayonnaise. The sandwich had a few faint thumbprints of oil on it but was tasty anyway. I sat on an upended stove log in the sun and looked at the stuff in the yard—an armchair, a pink plastic bottle in the shape of a baby's shoe, a pile of shingles, an old-fashioned TV antenna, beer cans, a rusting John Deere swather. Across the open field to the east, a flock of pheasants flew low and almost in a straight line. I counted twelve of them. Le took a 12-volt auto battery from the trunk of the Celebrity and sat down cross-legged by it on the ground and began to clean the battery posts with a rag. On his back under the car, Floyd John wrenched and tapped. At the side of the house, Gunner, the dog, growled away at a section of deer ribs Le had thrown her. Two kittens, one yellow and one black, chased each other around. A warm wind blew. For a moment, we might have been sitting in front of a tipi in an Oglala camp along the North Platte River 150 years ago, braiding lariats and making arrows and gazing off across the Plains.

• • •

As usual, I spent the nights in a motel in Chadron, Nebraska. The thirty-two miles from Oglala to Chadron via the back road has become one of my favorite Western drives. The Budweiser cans and bottles and cases that sometimes litter it, and its occasional stretches of broken pavement, make it a road not to daydream on. But being alert helps you appreciate its scenery better, too. For miles its talc-colored track of dusty gravel stretches ahead through unfenced grasslands. I've seen many hawks on phone poles along the road or in the sky, and antelopes grazing, and a coyote loping across a field. The prairie grasses in winter turn a pale ginger-brown just the color of antelopes, and the leafless cottonwoods and willows in the creek bottoms are coyote-fur gray. The big cottonwoods standing here and there by themselves in the fields lose every leaf in winter, and then you can see how contorted their branches really are; they look as if they had decided never to grow leaves again and were tormented by the decision. Once, in the sky just west of the road I saw, two hundred or three hundred feet up, a bald eagle holding almost motionless. The white band of its tail was visible when it turned, and gently turned again. It flew offhandedly, with careless, recreational ease, the way a winged human might fly.

If I didn't take the back road but went the long way via Highways 18 and 385, I would pass the Prairie Wind Casino. The tribe built this casino on the reservation's western edge just thirteen miles from a highway—U.S. 385—which may someday be part of a major interstate running north and south to connect Interstates 80 and 90. If such an interstate is ever built, the tribe hopes it will bring lots of gamblers to this admittedly remote place. Sometimes when I went by Prairie Wind, its lights glowing in the empty Plains darkness reminded me of a military installation, or an oil-drilling rig from the former days of the energy boom. One night, out of curiosity, I stopped at the casino and played the nickel video-poker machines until nearly dawn. Until about midnight the casino was a mixed crowd of Indians and white-haired white people. Rumors of big payouts occasionally ran through the room. The slot machines were chiming their bells and their little signifying noises, with the frequent louder jingling of the *"Ahhh-le-luia!"* sound indicating a jackpot. A country-rock tape played hour after hour until it and the *"Ahhh-le-luia!"* sound chafed the mind.

By three in the morning I had lost twenty or thirty dollars in nickels. Besides me, only two other people were still gambling. Oglala employees in white shirts, black vests, and black bow ties idly dusted the tops of the slot machines. A young security guard hunched on a stool with his hands in his pockets and his heels hooked on a middle rung. At about 4:30 I went out in the parking lot and sat in my car. My hands smelled like coins, and cigarette smoke saturated my clothes. The prairie wind—the actual version—made the light poles shudder and caused shadows to shudder on the gravelly ground. Two reservation dogs came sore-footing along and got up on their hind legs to check the trash barrels by the casino's main entrance. A truck from a uniform and linen supply place pulled up, and the dogs sore-footed away. Beyond the casino's lighted oasis, no lights were visible anywhere.

Also as usual, at the first opportunity I stopped in at the Big Crow Center. What with all the time I'd spent there, Chick Big Crow and I had gotten to know each other and had become friends. I like her a lot, and I like her sisters and her daughters and her nieces. Chick talks in a small, quiet, and reasonable voice that can sometimes really make me laugh. Once she was talking about Dennis Banks and another Indian leader, and she said, in her quiet and reasonable voice, "Dennis Banks is a serious person who really cares about the Native community, but [So-and-so] is apparently just a stark raving lunatic." I laughed at this for about half an hour.

I found Chick sitting at her desk in her office and talking to her sister Mary Iron Cloud. Chick's hair was in a new shag cut with reddish tints and she had on a white blouse and a holly-leaf lapel pin. Someone had given her a talking Christmas tree about a foot and a half high which sometimes threw back its top to reveal a large mouth that said, "Merry Christmas! Ho ho ho!" in a loud mechanical voice. This happened unpredictably, causing everybody to jump. Chick was in a good mood. A friend of the center who works for the Ford Motor Company in Detroit had persuaded his bosses to give the center a brand-new heavy-duty twelve-passenger van, and Chick was due to go to a Ford dealer in Rapid City and pick it up the following day.

Kids and parents and counselors came and went past Chick's open office door as we talked. Two young Mormon men in white shirts and narrow ties who were volunteering leaned in the door to tell Chick good night and that they would see her tomorrow. A hefty Oglala woman marched past, followed closely by a boy and three tall Oglala men, and Chick said, "Would you excuse me for a moment, please?" and hurried after them. A few minutes later the party marched back out, and Chick returned. "That little boy called one of the counselors here a bitch, and the counselor told him he had to leave, and the boy went home and told his family, and they came back here to beat up the counselor. I talked to them in a polite and calm way and explained the rules. Fortunately, they left without a fight. And after all that, I can tell you for sure that the boy will be back here tomorrow."

Chick and Mary Iron Cloud were talking about a cousin, Richard Big Crow, who had just died. They said that they would combine a memorial for him with the graveside memorial they had every Christmas time for SuAnne. Mary Iron Cloud went home. Chick said that she was going out to the cemetery to put up Christmas lights around SuAnne's grave, and asked if I would like to come with her and help. I said sure. We got in her green Pontiac Grand Am and drove east from Pine Ridge about seven miles, then turned off at a dirt road. The cemetery, St. Anne's, is about half a mile down the road, behind a white wooden fence with a gate. We opened the trunk of Chick's car and took out boxes and boxes of Christmas lights. Some were those new icicle lights, the kind with many little white bulbs on strands that hang down from a central line like teeth on a comb. They took a lot of untangling. We plugged strings of lights together and draped them on the cemetery's few small pines and duct-taped them to the sides of SuAnne's headstone and stapled them along the cemetery fence's top rail with a stapling gun. Lots of Big Crows were buried here. We moved gingerly among the graves with our lights and extension cords.

One grave was a mound of fresh earth covered with windblown floral wreaths and bouquets. Chick said that was Richard Big Crow's grave. Something in her and Mary's conversation had made me curious, so I asked, "Was he run over on the road between Rushville and White Clay?"

"Yes, someone beat him up outside a bar in Rushville, and then I think they later ran him over in the ditch beside the road. He was only nineteen years old."

I didn't mention the story Le had told me about his cousin Leon. Still, I thought about the coincidence, and about how entwined with each other people are here. When we had finished hanging all the lights, we plugged them into the main cable leading from a box on the phone pole across the road. They lit up in a widely distributed multitude, brilliant in the twilight. "I think we need more," Chick said after considering them for a while. "It seems to me we had more of them last year."

The red sunset made a black silhouette of the house on the rise to the west, and of the basketball backboard and post beside it. A white horse was grazing along the cemetery fence. Its teeth pulled up a tuft of weeds with a dull snapping noise. Chick crossed her arms and shrugged her jacket more closely around her against the evening breeze. "At least this year it wasn't ten below out here when we put the lights up, the way it's been sometimes. There's been Decembers when we could only do this for a few minutes at a time between spells of warming up in the car. One Christmas Eve I came out here by myself and sat on that little bench by SuAnne's grave, and I fell asleep, and when I woke up it was late at night. I got chilled clear through, and I caught pneumonia, and I was sick for weeks afterward."

I knew that Florence had dialysis treatments on Mondays, Wednesdays, and Fridays, so on a Tuesday morning I went to her house to drop off the Christmas presents and the ham. She was home, making fry bread to take to a church event that evening and minding her grandchildren. Her fifteen-year-old grandson, E.J., had the day off from Red Cloud School because one of his classmates had shot herself and today was the funeral. Florence's five-year-old granddaughter, RaeDawn, was waiting for a van to take her to preschool. Florence cleared some breakfast plates from the kitchen table and made me a place to sit, and she gave me a cup of black coffee. The Sioux word for coffee is *pejuta sapa*, which means black medicine, and most of the coffee I've had on the reservation fits the description. A few sips set my heart pounding. ·

As Florence worked she told me what she knew about the girl who had shot herself, and she gave me the latest news about her own health and especially about a kidney transplant she might possibly receive from her son Willie, who's in prison. She also talked about her grandfather Woz'aglai, and how much he hated to see people drinking, and how he used to whack her father, Asa, with his cane when Asa came home drunk, and how Woz'aglai used to say, "Don't go near that town of Pine Ridge, it'll get you drunk! All you have to do is stand on the hill over Pine Ridge and breathe that Pine Ridge air, and you'll get drunk!" Meanwhile, she made a lot of fry bread. Fry bread is sort of like a glazed doughnut without the hole in the middle or the sugar glaze. Florence had a big blue plastic tub of dough beside her; first she took a double handful of dough, rolled it flat with a rolling pin on a floured place on the Formica countertop, cut it into trapezoidal pieces about the size of a small paperback, scored each piece in the middle with a knife, and dropped the pieces into an iron skillet full of bubbling lard. After the pieces had been in the skillet for a minute or two, she turned them with a long-handled fork. They puffed up and soon got golden brown on both sides. One at a time she took the pieces out and set them in an enamel colander to drain, and then she took the pieces from the colander and laid them gently one atop another in a big cardboard box. She gave me some fry bread to try. Freshly made fry bread and black coffee is the most delicious breakfast you can have. Fry bread cooked in lard tastes even better than it is bad for you, which is saying a lot.

RaeDawn, a sturdy little girl with quick, dark-brown eyes, came over to me and asked my name. I said, "RaeDawn, when I first saw you, you were just a little baby doing somersaults on the floor."

She said, "I'm five now. I just had my birthday on December 7th."

"You used to run around in those little plastic jellies—remember those green sandals you used to wear?"

"My little brother has those now."

"Well, you sure talk more than you used to. You talk really well, RaeDawn."

"Yes, but John won't let me answer the phone, because he says I get the messages all mixed up."

Florence explained that her son John, RaeDawn's uncle, gets a lot of calls there and doesn't like RaeDawn to answer them and talk so much to everybody, the way she does. Carefully Florence added another layer of fry bread to the cardboard box. I finished my coffee and stood up to leave. Florence went to the living room and returned with a large shopping bag containing a star quilt she and her daughter Flora had made for me. I took a look at the quilt and exclaimed over it and thanked her. It was lavender, with olive and brown and dark purple patterns on it. At the door I could not resist picking up RaeDawn and giving her a hug. I thought how much my own kids would like to play with her, and vice versa. For a mad moment I even thought of asking Florence if I could take her home with me.

Over at Aurelia's house, Le and Floyd John were drinking cups of *pejuta sapa* and sitting on the couch near the barrel stove. Their first attempt to repair the transaxle seal on Floyd John's car had not gone well. They had hammered and hammered at the seal trying to get it in, and in the process they had bent it. Now they were discussing what to do next. The job, they concluded, required an expert, and that expert was Chet Cross Dog. Chet is Florence's oldest son. He lives sometimes in Oglala and sometimes in Seattle, where he works for a big transmission-repair place and makes a thousand dollars or more a week. He has a degree from a transmission-repair school in Texas. Putting this seal in would be no problem for Chet.

First, though, we had to find him. Chet is a man much in demand on Pine Ridge. A skilled mechanic is always a useful person to know there, but a skilled mechanic who also happens to be a relative and who will work cheap or, out of the goodness of his heart, for free, is like an eminent old-time chief. Le and Floyd John had searched for Chet the day before with no success. Now we got in my car and set off to try again. I knew he wasn't at Florence's, so we didn't go there. We checked a couple of places between Oglala and Pine Ridge—no luck. In Pine Ridge Le and Floyd John got out at Pronto Auto Parts to pick up a new seal while I parked across the street at the BIA building and went in to use the restroom (*pejuta sapa*). When I came out Le and Floyd John were hurrying along the street and waving wildly at a passing car. The car pulled over.

Inside it were a young man named Jamie Yellow Horse; his wife, Cissy; their daughter, Julie; a young woman named Cory Spotted Elk; and, at the wheel, Chet. Le brought me over to introduce me. Then the conversation proceeded in Sioux. After a few minutes, Le stood up from the car window and reported, "Chet says he can do it, and he's got time to do it right now. He's only gonna charge us a case of beer." This was good news. We drove to White Clay, I provided the funding, and Jamie and Cissy went into the Jumping Eagle package store for the beer. Chet came over and leaned in the window of my car and took the transaxle seal from Floyd John and turned it this way and that in his hand. Chet is a round-faced man of about forty-five with slightly protruding eyes, a big chest, skinny legs, and a long, long black ponytail. He had on an Oglala Nation baseball cap. He talks very fast. He said, "Oh-yeah-okay-that's-a-seal-on-a-transaxle-intake, I-never-worked-on-one-when-the-tranny-was-still-in-the-car-the-way-yours-is, I-could-tap-it-in-with-two-taps-of-a-hammer-if-the-tranny-was-out-of-the-car-but-I'm-sure-I-can-do-this-anyway . . ." all in about two breaths.

Jamie and Cissy came out of the package store with a shiny new red-white-and-blue case of Budweiser. Twenty minutes later we were piling out of our cars in Aurelia's yard. The beers were broken out and passed around. Chet took a big sip, handed the can to Cory Spotted Elk, and approached the ailing vehicle. The rest of us withdrew a step or two to give him room. Like a magician he produced an object in his right hand: a box cutter. From the yard's scattered miscellany he took an empty cardboard appliance carton, and with a few strokes of the box cutter detached from it a rectangular section. He carefully laid the piece of cardboard on the ground under the car to protect his new shirt—black, with a Native American pattern in neon shades—his immaculate pipe-stem jeans, and his cowboy boots of light brown and shiny green. Then he crawled under the car until only his boots and blue-jean legs could be seen.

The rest of us looked on and talked in expectant tones. Cory Spotted Elk paid no direct attention to what Chet was doing, and yet somehow she seemed to watch him all the time. Le had told me that she was related to the Crows, a local family, and at a moment when I was standing next to her I asked her if she was a Crow. She gave me a level look and said, "Do I look like a Crow?" She had a full-lipped mouth that went all the way across her face, smooth brown hair, smooth brown skin, wire-rim glasses, lavender eye shadow, and hazel eyes. Such wattage turned directly at me caused me to hem and haw self-consciously and turn away. Chet suddenly popped out from under the car. Some inner part not involved in this operation was hanging down on him and bumping him and annoying him. He searched the ground for a moment, found a piece of barbed wire, and clipped a section from it with another tool that came miraculously to his hand. A few more clips trimmed the barbs. Then he dove back under the car and wired the offending part up out of the way.

The seal just would not go in, it seemed. Sounds of frustration rose from under the car. Le and Floyd John leaned in and consulted with Chet, shifting this way and that to see him through the machinery. Aurelia came home from her volunteer job, a scarf tied around her hair and a sack of commodity goods in her arms. She looked at the gathering in her yard, said, "Oh, me . . . ." shook her head, and went inside. Tools were called for and then set down. The kittens chased each other up the side of a cottonwood. The little girl, Julie, went around digging in the ground with a screwdriver. Cissy Yellow Horse and Cory Spotted Elk began to shiver from the cold beer and the rising wind. Chet called for something to pound the seal into place. Le and Floyd John produced the six-foot-long wooden beam they had employed before. The beam was thrust into the car through the wheel well. Floyd John held it in position so it wouldn't fall on Chet, Le held it by the middle to keep it level, and Jamie Yellow Horse whacked on the end of the beam with the butt of an ax. *Whack whack whack.* "Hit it again." *Whack whack whack.* "Again." *Whack whack whack.* Long pause. "The goddam seal just fell out," Chet said.

He hopped up from under the car. He said, "I-know-this-is-gonna-work, I-know-I-can-get-the-sumbitch-in." He took a breath and spoke more slowly to us all. "In the tranny shop, sometimes guys'll get scared or lose their confidence when they're workin' on a complicated car like an Infiniti or something. I tell 'em I don't let *nothin'* scare me. My philosophy is, someone with a human mind thought of this machine, so you can use your own human mind to figure it out. The worst mistake you can make is thinking something is more complicated than it is." Then he dove back under the car, the hammering with the beam continued, and in two minutes he hopped up again triumphant, but not letting on. "Just needs a couple taps with a ball-peen," he said. Jamie Yellow Horse went under the car, made the final taps: job done. Chet turned to me. He said, "Well, you watched pretty close. Did you learn anything?" I said, "Yes, I learned that a six-foot-long wooden beam is an important automotive tool."

Chet opened his hand, and a beer appeared in it. He took a long pull, hooked his other hand in his jeans pocket, and strutted around. Cissy Yellow Horse yelled, "Chet, let's go! We're gettin' cold!" Le and Floyd John set about putting the transaxle and the wheel back on. Orrie Morris, their next-door neighbor, came over to help them, making the fifth Indian to work on this car in less than an hour. Le told again his story about the bull who bowed down to him, and Chet said that when he was a boy he used to watch Le ride in rodeos, and he was always amazed Le didn't get killed. Cissy started the car they had come in, and it began to idle with a deep bass throb. Chet opened that car's trunk and took out a jar of GoJo liquid hand cleaner and cleaned his hands carefully, digit by digit, wiping each individually with a rag. To look at him when he had finished, you would not guess he had just been lying on his back under a car. "Well, we'll see you guys later," he said. Then to Le he said, "I'll send you a bill for my services."

"*Tok' sha Paha Sapa,*" Le replied and everybody laughed.

("What did you just say?" I asked.)

"That's something Sioux people say all the time," Le told me. " '*Tok' sha Paha Sapa*'—it means, 'I'll pay you when I get my Black Hills money.' "

A lot more stuff happened. Unexpectedly, on this trip I had a great time. Part of the reason probably was that Floyd John's not drinking made it easier and more fun to be with him and Le. We sat around the stove in Aurelia's with cups of *pejuta sapa* talking about one thing and another—Le told stories about how he wrote hit songs for the Jefferson Starship and the Steve Miller Band during his years in California, and he recounted the entire plot of *Hombre,* one of his favorite movies. Floyd John showed me choker necklaces of deerskin and leather belts he was working on. We again went looking for Chet to do some more repairs on various cars. I rode with Le and Floyd John, in Floyd John's car for a change. Sitting in the back seat felt very different from driving. Due to a further problem with the transmission, the car refused to shift out of second gear. I enjoyed watching the Pine Ridge scenery go by at thirty miles an hour.

One evening I went to the cemetery east of Pine Ridge for the memorial service for Richard Big Crow and SuAnne. About thirty-five of us assembled in an open part of the cemetery among the Christmas lights, under the needle-sharp stars. There were two Mennonite volunteers from the Big Crow Center; Rick and Ann Abdoo, the Michigan couple who had arranged for Ford Motors to contribute the van; a Pentecostal preacher and Oglala tribal member named Leon Matthews; Richard Big Crow's family; and other family members, teenagers, little kids, and friends. Tiny De Cory had us stand in a circle holding hands. She said that every circle of people is sacred and unique, because the same people will never stand in this exact same circle again. Leon Matthews gave a speech and led a prayer, and many talked of their love and support for the family of Richard Big Crow. Some people were crying. Occasionally little kids keeping warm in the idling cars honked the car horns, jarringly. Together we sang "Silent Night," but faltered at the second verse because nobody knew it, which caused some giggles.

Then a young man named Peta Catches, son of the famous Oglala medicine man Peter Catches, sang a traditional Lakota memorial song. Its words translated, "Where have you gone, departed ones? We are looking for you, we are not finding you." It was in a minor key, a descending series of notes, powerful and ancient-sounding in the Christmas-light glow on the dark prairie. The woman on my right kept dropping my hand to tend to a young child. I found myself squeezing the hand of the woman on my left harder and harder, and I quickly relaxed my grip so as not to seem weird. But soon I noticed that I was squeezing it hard again.

I knew I was almost done working on this book, and as I drove around the reservation or sat at Aurelia's or the Big Crow Center, I was tempted to draw conclusions. Books about Indians often end with an

analysis of Indian problems and advice from the author about what Indians could do to improve their lot. Certainly, I could imagine the
Oglala's lot improved. I could imagine the tribe growing in numbers
and prospering at new enterprises, at last; I could see them staying put
as the plains around them continue to lose population, and gaining
strength and importance in the region until in a hundred years or so
they regain their long-ago stature as a major power in the middle of the
continent. Maybe young leaders of SuAnne's generation and the ones
that follow will offer the tribe a vision that takes it beyond the hard
times of today. I recalled Angie Big Crow's description of SuAnne's
hoped-for Happytown, "where nobody would fight or be jealous, where
it would be clean, have a mall and lots of places for good fun." There
are worse dreams to work for. As to actual advice to the Oglala, however, I have none. Advice from authors and others—representatives of
the church, or officials in the government—usually has not worked out
too well in the past. Besides, no Oglala has ever asked me.

I do have a suggestion for the rest of us Americans. Back in the
1980s bills were introduced in Congress to return the federal lands in
the Black Hills to the Sioux. One of the bills was sponsored by Senator
Bill Bradley of New Jersey, who learned about the Sioux during a basketball clinic he held on Pine Ridge in his playing days. In 1987
Bradley's land-return bill died in committee, and no similar bill has
been introduced since. That the Black Hills were stolen is a fact on
which the Sioux and the government have been in essential agreement
for almost twenty years. The remaining disagreement is about how to
right the wrong. Perhaps now we could again consider the possibility of
returning some or all of the stolen federal lands.

One morning not long before Christmas it turned cold. An arctic front
arrived at about ten o'clock, and in fifteen minutes deep winter had
taken over the countryside. Snow crossed the ground and sky on winds
like an arctic express, never seeming to light anywhere. Tumbleweeds
invisible before were suddenly dashing before the wind—down dirt
roads, behind houses, along fences, across fields. Empty acres came
alive with the hither-and-thither panic of the tumbleweeds. Dark
clouds hunkered about a hundred feet overhead, blotting out the

tops of buttes and any trace of horizon. After the front's leading edge had passed, the winds decreased; by late afternoon eight inches of new snow had fallen. It was an airy, light powder snow in which each snowflake seemed unimpinged by the varied flakes resting lightly around it. The temperature had fallen to 2 degrees below zero.

As I drove to Oglala from Chadron on the back road the next morning I heard a disc jockey on KILI Radio say, "Okay, you Oglala carboys—it's time for you to get out there and warm up your cars, so your old ladies can get to work!" And indeed, every car I saw at that hour seemed to contain only a vexed-looking woman at the wheel. Black cows topped with snow stood breathing steam in the whitened fields while hawks sat in cottonwoods above, their feathers so fluffed out against the cold they looked like footballs. The dogs, too, looked bulky in their upraised fur, but unlike the other creatures, the dogs seemed to be having a good time, snuffling along in the drifts and checking things out and grinning companionably at passersby.

I could tell by the tire tracks in the snow of Aurelia's driveway that nobody would be home there. I found her neighbor Orrie Morris on a ladder repairing her windows. While unclogging a tube of caulk he told me that Le and Floyd John had gone to the commodities building in Pine Ridge. I drove to Pine Ridge, didn't find them, came back to Oglala, and spotted Le going into the post office. He told me he was on his way to Pine Ridge with some friends. I said I'd be glad to give him a ride, if he wanted. He said, "Sure. I love riding with you." With Le I drove back to Pine Ridge, where he did some business at the tribal building. Then we went to his sister Norma's house, where he gave her her mail; then over to White Clay. Then we drove around for a while. Le was drinking 24-ounce cans of Colt 45 extra malt.

He said, "Aurelia kicked me out of her house this morning. She says I can't stay there no more because I won't give her five hundred dollars. She's really an unpredictable person—she's got a Heckle and Jeckle personality. I'm gonna stay at Verna Yellow Horse's place tonight."

Eventually I drove him to Verna Yellow Horse's house across from the Catholic church in Oglala, and we sat in my car with the engine idling and the heater on. Le told me about police officers he had fought or intimidated (one in Grand Junction, Colorado, in particular), and he went on to revile and defy all immigrants to his country, and he said this was his land, and he said, *"I know who I am!"* He sang some Lakota songs. He said many times that he and I are brothers. He said that there is a deep spiritual bond between us. He took my hand in the "power" handshake—hands clasped upright, palm to palm—and held on to it for a long time. I was a bit uncomfortable, as I sometimes am with him. I disregarded a lot of what he said and reduced it in my mind to about 20 percent face value. But the part about us being brothers I did not discount. By different routes and for different reasons, our affections have ended up in the same place; being called Little Brother means a lot to me. Through the swerves in our relationship it took me years to discover this.

Le got out of the car and then leaned back in through the open door to say a lot more. He said that the part we had bought for his car some days previously needed a special socket in order to be properly installed, and the socket happened to be a rare one, and it cost twenty dollars. I gave him twenty. He said tomorrow we'd go way out in the badlands onto a butte called Cuny Table, and from there we'd drive on a little-known road to a place called the Stronghold, where the ghost dancers hid out after the massacre at Wounded Knee. He told me to give his love to my wife and kids, and said to drive safely, and that I'd find him here at Verna's tomorrow morning.

When I showed up at Verna's the next morning nobody knew anything about him. He hadn't slept there the night before. No one had seen him around. I went to Aurelia's and met Floyd John driving out her driveway. He hadn't seen Le either. He had some suggestions of where he might be, but the directions he gave were complicated and I decided not to look. Floyd John and I talked for a while through our open car windows while our engines idled loudly in the cold. Overnight the temperature had gone down to eighteen below. I could have hung around, but I wanted to start for home. I told Floyd John what a good time I'd had, and I thanked him, and I said that his quitting drinking was a wonderful thing. He said he would make me a choker necklace and send it to me. He checked in his billfold to make sure he still had my address. He said, "God bless you," and I said it back to him. Then he rolled up his window and spun his tires pulling out of the drive, and I started for home down the Red Shirt Table Road.

NOTES

CHAPTER 1

4   A description of the recalcitrance of Powhatan is found in *Linking Arms Together: American Indian Treaty Visions of Law and Peace, 1600–1800*, by Robert A. Williams, Jr. (1996), p. 31. The Englishmen wished Powhatan to come to them at Jamestown to receive his crown, and Powhatan objected, "Your father is to come to me, not I to him."

   John Smith, of the Jamestown Colony, was among the party who went to Powhatan's village to present the crown, and he recalled the ceremony in his *Captain John Smith's History of Virginia* (reprinted 1970), p. 69: "But a foul trouble it was to make him kneel to receive his crown; he neither knowing the majesty or meaning of a crown, nor bending of the knee, endured so many persuasions, examples and instructions as tired them all. At last, by leaning on his shoulders, he a little stooped, and three having the crown in their hands put it on his head."

4   Joseph Brant, a graduate of Dartmouth, also translated the Bible into Mohawk. On one of his visits to London he met James Boswell, who became a friend and interviewed him for *The London Magazine*. See *Life of Joseph Brant—Thayendanega*, by William L. Stone (1845), Vol. II, p. 251.

   Indians Abroad, 1493–1934, by Carolyn Thomas Foreman (1943), p. 96, says that the famous incident between Brant and the King and Queen took place during a visit Brant made in 1785.

4   There are a number of biographies of Red Cloud. The description of his trip to New York and Washington, D.C., and of his reception and speech in the capital, is in *Red Cloud and the Sioux Problem*, by James C. Olson (1965), pp. 103–5.

4   The Senate select committee went to Standing Rock Reservation in 1883 to investigate grievances there. The committee chairman tried to intimidate Sitting Bull with accusations that he was not a chief: "I do not know any difference between you and the other Indians at this agency." Sitting Bull replied, "I am here by the will of the Great Spirit, and by His will I am a chief. My heart is red and sweet, and I know it is sweet, because whatever passes near me puts out its tongue to me." The senator who told Sitting Bull that he had "no following, no power, no control, and no right to any control," and threatened to throw him into the guardhouse, was John A. Logan of Illinois. The Sioux called him "High Hat," because he wore one. See *Sitting Bull, Champion of the Sioux*, by Stanley Vestal (1957), pp. 241, 247.

5   Many twentieth-century Indian accounts describe the efforts of educators to break Indian students of speaking their native tongues. Among others, see *Sundance: The Robert Sundance Story*, by Robert Sundance with Mark Gaede (1994); *Lame Deer, Seeker of Visions*, by John Fire/Lame Deer and Richard Erdoes (1972); and the somewhat unreliable *Where White Men Fear to Tread: The Autobiography of Russell Means*, by Russell Means with Marvin J. Wolf (1995).

6   The quotation from the account of Amerigo Vespucci appears in "Americanizing the White Man," an essay by Felix S. Cohen collected in his *The Legal Conscience: Selected Papers of Felix S. Cohen*, edited by Lucy Kramer Cohen (1960), p. 324.

6   So widespread was the notion of the Indians' coming extinction that it served (for example) as the justification for the photographs of Indians taken by Edward S. Curtis at the turn of the century. These now-familiar pictures, of Chief Joseph and Geronimo and many other Indians famous and obscure, were done partly to record a race that would soon be gone, as Theodore Roosevelt pointed out in his foreword to Curtis's *The North American Indians: Being a Series of Volumes Picturing and Describing the Indians of the United States, and Alaska* (1907–9).

6   In February of 1891 Bill Nye wrote a column that attempted humor on the subject of the Ghost Dance and the Wounded Knee massacre:

> Standing Horse, who led the ghost dance, wore a United States wagon cover on his arrival, and also threw one corner of it over his departure; but when the dancing began he checked this outer wrap, and was discovered to be dressed lightly in a tiara of dickey bird's feet and a coat of shellac. He danced until utterly worn out and exhausted, when he fell to the ground, and a tidy was thrown over him by an attendant . . .

The column appeared in the Aberdeen (South Dakota) *Saturday Pioneer* of February 8, 1891. The *Saturday Pioneer*'s editor was L. Frank Baum, later the author of the "Wizard of Oz" books for children. Baum hated Indians, and days after Wounded Knee wrote in his editorial column: "The PIONEER has before declared that our only safety depends upon the total extirmination [sic] of the Indians. Having wronged them for centuries we had better, in order to protect our civilization, follow it up by one more wrong and wipe these untamed and untamable creatures from the face of the earth. In this lies future safety for our settlers . . ." Aberdeen *Saturday Pioneer*, January 3, 1891.

7   In 1996 the United Methodist Church apologized for the Sand Creek Massacre—Colonel John M. Chivington, who led the Colorado militiamen who attacked the Cheyenne at Sand Creek, was a Methodist lay preacher.

Laird Cometsevah, of Clinton, Oklahoma, is a spokesman for the descendants of Sand Creek survivors. He is the great-grandson of a survivor named Leg Calf.

7   Stories about the Mohican tribe's successful protest against Wal-Mart appeared in *The New York Times* of January 21, 1996 (XII-WC, 12:5), and February 16, 1996 (B, 6:1).

(The Mohican Tribe, known as the Stockbridge Munsee Community, whose reservation is in Bowler, Wisconsin, say that Fenimore Cooper got his orthography wrong, and that the Indians he had in mind were probably the Mohegans. Uncas was a chief of the Mohegans, not the Mohicans.)

7   Indian population figures come from newspaper articles on the U.S. Census (*The New York Times*, April 25, 1971, 61:2; October 20, 1971, 26:4; November 19, 1992, A, 20:4), and from *Killing the White Man's Indian: Reinventing Native Americans at the End of the Twentieth Century*, by Fergus M. Bordewich (1996), pp. 53–55.

7   Details about the genocidal policies of the state of California in the nineteenth century appeared in news stories in *Indian Country Today*, a nationwide newspaper published out of Rapid City, South Dakota (May 14–21, 1996, p. A6), and in *The New York Times* (May 7, 1996, A, 14:4).

7   The story of the Gnadenhutten massacre is in *A Century of Dishonor: A Sketch of the United States Government's Dealings with Some of the Indian Tribes*, by Helen Hunt Jackson (1881), pp. 317ff.

8   Nancy Bill, injury prevention specialist with the Indian Health Service in Window Rock, Arizona, told me about the high rate of traffic fatalities among the Navajo.

8   The contribution of American Indians to world agriculture is described in Cohen, p. 317. For a more extensive discussion of this subject, see *Indian Givers: How the Indians of the Americas Transformed the World*, by Jack Weatherford (1988), Chapters 4–6.

8   The first Europeans to record a sighting of the potato were Spaniards with the expedition led by Jiménez de Quesada to native villages in the Andes Mountains in what is now Colombia. The year was 1537. By 1590 the potato had appeared in England. See *The Potato: Evolution, Biodiversity, and Genetic Resources*, by J. G. Hawkes (1990), p. 10.

8   Cohen (pp. 321ff.) also describes the seminal contribution of the Iroquois to American democracy and constitutional government.

9   Besides Franklin and Jefferson, a number of others among the Founding Fathers—Adams, Madison, Thomas Paine—expressed admiration for Native American ways of government. A helpful book on the subject is *Indian Roots of American Democracy*, a collection of essays edited by José Barreiro (1992).

9   Cohen (p. 306) mentions the many thinkers of the Enlightenment who were inspired by the example of Indian liberty. Thomas More referred to the letters of Amerigo Vespucci in his *Utopia*, a work read throughout Europe, which incorporated Indian ideas of freedom and equality. See also Weatherford, Chapter 7.

10   General Howard's impatience with the Nez Perce is in Helen Hunt Jackson (p. 129). Her source is Howard's own account, which appeared in a magazine two years after the event. Chief Joseph remembered the encounter differently: he said that Howard "lost his temper, and said 'Shut up! I don't want to hear any more of such talk!' "

For more on the wrongs done to the Nez Perce, see *Let Me Be Free: The Nez Perce Tragedy*, by David Lavender (1992).

11   The preface to the *Lakota-English Dictionary*, by Rev. Eugene Buechel, S.J. (1970), has a concise description of the main tribal divisions among the Sioux.

In *Lame Deer, Seeker of Visions*, John Fire Lame Deer disagrees with recent tradition on the subject of the tribe's name. He says, "Our people don't call themselves Sioux or Dakota. That's white man talk. We call ourselves Ikce Wicasa— the natural humans, the free, wild common people. I am pleased to be called that" (p. 23).

12   For a history of the military campaigns of Chief Pontiac, see *The Conspiracy of Pontiac*, by Francis Parkman (reprinted as a Library of America edition, 1991), one of the classic works of American history. Two useful books on Chief Tecumseh are *Tecumseh and the Quest for Indian Leadership*, by David E. Edmunds (1984), and *God Gave Us This Country: Tekamthi and the First American Civil War*, by Bil Gilbert (1989).

12   For more on Protestant sectarianism in America, see my *Family* (1994), Chapters 3 and 13.

14   An interesting book, *Kill Devil Hill: Discovering the Secret of the Wright Brothers*, by Harry Combs with Martin Caidin (1979), has a photograph of Wilbur Wright flying around the Statue of Liberty in 1909.

14   I learned about new high-yield trees in an article in the Missoula, Montana, *Missoulian:* "Fast-growing Trees Have Power to Save the Planet," by Dennis T. Avery (August 19, 1997, p. A 4).

15   For details on the life of Crazy Horse, see my *Great Plains* (1989), pp. 96ff., and notes. The first full-scale biography of Crazy Horse, Mari Sandoz's *Crazy Horse: The Strange Man of the Oglalas* (1942), though flawed as history, remains a good place to begin when reading about the great Oglala warrior.

In *Red Cloud: Warrior-Statesman of the Lakota Sioux*, by Robert W. Larson (1997), Crazy Horse is described as belonging to the Hunkpatila band of the Oglala (pp. 64, 75). George E. Hyde, in his classic *Red Cloud's Folk: A History of the Oglala Sioux Indians* (1957), says that Crazy Horse belonged to the Bad Faces (Iteshicha). Some Oglala I have asked about this agree with Hyde. Charlotte Black Elk says he belonged to a band called the Oyukhpe.

17   The shooting of Clyde Bellecourt is mentioned in many accounts of the events at

Wounded Knee and after—e.g., *Wounded Knee II*, by Roland Dewing (1995), pp. 135–36. The *New York Times* story of the shooting appeared August 28, 1973 (36:5). The paper reported on September 13, 1973 (13:1), that Bellecourt had refused to press charges.

The item about Clyde Bellecourt's daughter working for her Gold Bar, "the highest achievement in Girl Scouts," was in *Indian Country Today* (April 28– May 5, 1997, p. C 7).

18 The firebomb on the subway exploded in the sixth car of a Brooklyn-bound number 4 train at the Fulton Street station in lower Manhattan during afternoon rush hour on December 21, 1994. The hero who said he was no hero was off-duty transit cop Denfield S. Otto, a fifty-four-year-old grandfather from Harlem. All the New York papers of December 22 covered this event.

18 Bil Gilbert's statement about Indians, Greeks, and heroes was in a *Life* magazine special issue on heroes (May 1997), p. 13.

CHAPTER 2

20 For more on my first meeting with Le War Lance, see my *Great Plains,* Chapter 6.

26 Jim Clark, twice world auto racing champion, died not at Indianapolis but in a crash of his Lotus Ford racer during a race at Hockenheim, West Germany, on April 7, 1968.

29 Sources on Indians in movies are: *The BFI Companion to the Western,* edited by Edward Buscombe (1988); *Movies: The History of an Art and an Institution,* by Richard Schickel (1964); *Western and Frontier Film and Television Credits 1903–1995,* by Harris M. Lentz III (1996); *American Film Institute Catalogue: Feature Films 1911–1920,* and *The Only Good Indian . . . The Hollywood Gospel,* by Ralph E. Friar and Natasha Friar (1972).

30 The Friars' book has the figures on movies about the Apache and the Sioux. The entry under *The Indian Wars* (Buffalo Bill Cody's movie) in the *American Film Institute Catalogue* goes into some detail about the making of the film, and about what happened to it. Apparently it was rather sympathetic to the Indians; this angered officials in Washington, and government pressure caused the film not to be widely released. Footage from this film was included in a number of films released after Cody's death in 1917.

31 Information about Indians and the Academy Awards appeared in an article about Indians and Hollywood in *Indian Country Today* (April 4, 1996; p. B 7).

Dan George, a Squamish Indian from the Berard Reserve outside Vancouver, British Columbia, who was memorable as the old Cheyenne chief in *Little Big Man,* lost to John Mills in *Ryan's Daughter.* Graham Greene, an Oneida from Ontario who played a Sioux medicine man in *Dances with Wolves,* lost to Joe Pesci in *Goodfellas.*

(Buffy Sainte-Marie, the lone winner, is a Cree. She is also from Canada.)

CHAPTER 3

35 The George Will column on the subject of sixties' era permissiveness and Jerry
Garcia was "About that 'Sixties Idealism' " (Newsweek, August 21, 1995, p. 72).

36 As I mention in Chapter 15, this section of Highway 79 has since been widened
to four lanes.

36 I learned Indian life-expectancy figures for the north-central Great Plains—
North Dakota, South Dakota, and including western Minnesota and eastern
Montana—from the offices of the Indian Health Service in Aberdeen, South
Dakota. The bulk of the Indian population here is in South Dakota, and the
figures are for 1992. In this region Indians of both sexes have a life expectancy
of 64.7 years, compared with a U.S. average of 75.8. Life expectancy for
males is 60.8 years (U.S. average is 72.3) and for females 69.3 (U.S. average
is 79.1).

37 Details about the car accident near Hermosa may be found in the Rapid City
Journal of June 28, 29, and 30, and July 1 and 2, 1986; and in the Sheridan
38–39 (Wyoming) Press, June 30, 1986.

For a good depiction of the shrinking of Sioux lands since 1851, see the maps in
Black Hills, White Justice: The Sioux Nation versus the United States, 1775 to
the Present, by Edward Lazarus (1991), pp. xviiff. The resistance of Red Cloud
and the Oglala to the idea of moving east to the Missouri is discussed in Olson,
Chapters 5–9.

39 By the terms of the Manypenny Agreement, ratified by Congress February 28,
1877, the Sioux received 900,000 acres of grazing land for the 7.3 million acres in
the western portion of the Great Sioux Reservation, a tract which included the
Black Hills. See Lazarus, p. 91.

39 The U.S. Court of Claims later ruled that only about 10 percent of the required
number of Sioux had signed the Manypenny Agreement.

Besides Pine Ridge, the other Sioux reservations within the former lands of
the Great Sioux Reservation are the Standing Rock Reservation in North and
South Dakota; and the Cheyenne River, Lower Brule, Rosebud, and Yankton
Reservations, all in South Dakota. See the map of the Great Sioux Reservation in
Lazarus; see also Discover Indian Reservations USA: A Visitors' Welcome Guide,
edited by Veronica E. Tiller (1992), p. 300.

39 The Oglala of the Great Sioux Nation (no author or date), an informational booklet on file in the Rapid City, South Dakota, Public Library, says that the original
land base of the Pine Ridge Reservation was 2,786,539 acres. Oglala Religion,
by William K. Powers (1977), gives almost the same figure, and says that Pine
Ridge is 4,353 square miles. Dewing says the original reservation holdings were
2,809,444 acres.

39 Any book that discusses federal Indian policy mentions the Dawes Act. For a good,
brief summary of the act and its consequences, see the entry under "Dawes Sever-
alty Act" in The Reader's Encyclopedia of the American West, edited by Howard R.

Lamar (1998). The entry says Indian lands were to be divided into "160-acre plots for heads of families, eighty acres for single persons over eighteen years of age, and forty acres for minors." (There were no provisions for the unborn.)

40   Dewing says that the loss of tribal lands on the Pine Ridge Reservation was over a million acres—of 2,804,444 acres, only 1,518,261 acres were still under Indian control in 1969 (p. 13). *The Oglala of the Great Sioux Nation* gives the distribution as follows: 2,786,539 acres in all; 835,917 owned by tribe; 24,095 owned by federal government; 930,083 allotted to tribal members (most of which is leased to non-Indian farmers and ranchers); and 996,444 owned by non-Indians.

40   Helen Hunt Jackson's *A Century of Dishonor* favored citizenship for Indians as a guarantee of their rights of property, so often cruelly abused. She wrote: "The utter absence of individual title to particular lands deprives every one among them of the chief incentive to labor and exertion—the very mainspring on which the prosperity of a people depends" (p. 341). Translated into law, this idea led to the Dawes Act, and allotment—an excellent example of good intentions leading to disastrous public policy.

40   The Red Shirt Table Road has been stripped, graded, and resurfaced various times since I first drove it. As of July 1999, it had been somewhat improved.

41   The closest interstate highway to the reservation is I-90, about ninety miles from Pine Ridge village (though closer to the reservation's less-populated northeastern part). The closest freight rail service is at Rushville, Nebraska, about 24 miles south of Pine Ridge village. There is no regular passenger rail service in this part of the Plains.

Although Pine Ridge residents travel to Rapid City, South Dakota, and other places for errands almost daily, no commercial bus lines serve the reservation.

41   In the mid-nineteenth century the Oglala ranged widely on the Central Plains— to the Powder River country, the Black Hills, and the Platte River country in present western Nebraska. They kept coming back to Fort Laramie, which was ideally located for them. A repeated request of Red Cloud's during negotiations with the government was that the Oglala be allowed to have their agency at Fort Laramie.

41   Many sources describe the government's desire to move the Sioux away from the route of the transcontinental railroad. *Our Indian Wards*, by George W. Manypenny (the official whose name is on the "agreement" by which the Sioux lost the Black Hills), published 1880, quotes the Act of Congress that created the 1867 treaty commission. Its purpose, the act said, was to move the Indians to a place where they would not "interfere with established highways of travel, and the contemplated railroads to the Pacific" (p. 194). On this subject, see also Olson, pp. 60ff., and Larson, pp. 106ff.

George Hyde (p. 161) says that the peace commissioners thought they were being clever when they gave such generous concessions with the Treaty of 1868: they were pretending to mollify the Indians as well as the Eastern supporters of peace while simultaneously pursuing the real agenda of moving the Indians away from the railroad. (The government would later regret its generosity when gold was discovered in the Black Hills.)

In 1876 the government had a plan to move the Oglala and other Sioux to Indian Territory (present Oklahoma), but it was thwarted by railroad interests who hoped for land grants there (Manypenny, p. 345). The railroads were indeed the behind-the-scenes power in the early reservation years of the Western Sioux.

42 James Naismith expressed his pleasure at seeing "basketball goals in some out of the way place" in his *Basketball: Its Origin and Development* (1905; reissued 1996), pp. 109–10.

CHAPTER 4

50 The traffic light at the four-way is no longer the only one on the reservation. Since my first visit to Pine Ridge, another has been installed, at an intersection on Highway 18 a short distance east of the four-way.

51 Long-time Pine Ridge resident Ben Irving used to sit by the four-way back in the fifties and tell stories to children and passersby. When Irving was three he went to England with the Wild West Show; the Queen liked the show so much that she kissed him. (See the *Sheridan County Star* of Rushville, Nebraska, August 14, 1958, p. 2.)

51 Baptiste "Big Bat" Pourier, the present Big Bat's ancestor, came West when he was seventeen and worked for the famous fur trader John Reeshaw. He also worked for the Army as a scout. He was an interpreter at the treaty council at Fort Laramie that produced the treaty of 1868, and the Red Cloud School has pictures of him at that council. His Oglala wife was a mixed-blood named Josephine Richards. (My thanks to Patty Pourier for supplying Pourier family data.)

In an interview with Judge Eli S. Ricker (included in the so-called Ricker Tablets, interviews on file in the Nebraska State Historical Society), Baptiste Pourier said that he was in the room with Crazy Horse all night on the night Crazy Horse died (Ricker Collection, series 2, tablet 13, p. 19).

53 The sun-dance controversy occupied the pages of *Indian Country Today* in July, August, and September of 1997. See particularly "The Selling of the Sun Dance: Spiritual Exploitation at Heart of Pine Ridge Controversy," *Indian Country Today,* July 28–August 4, 1997, p. A 1.

54–55 Many of Le's stories are hard to document. The death of Francis Slow Bear, however, was reported in the *Sheridan County Star,* December 8, 1960, p. 1:

PINE RIDGE MAN FREEZES TO DEATH

Funeral services for Francis Slow Bear, 28, of Pine Ridge, who froze to death in last week's blizzard, were held last week in Pine Ridge.

Slow Bear's body was found in an open pasture about 4½ miles northwest of Oglala on Friday. Floyd Clausen, who was herding cattle, found the body.

The dead man had last been seen on Saturday night, November 26, and said he was headed home when friends last saw him. He apparently got trapped in the blizzard of Sunday morning, November 27th.

An autopsy in Rapid City Saturday revealed no evidence of foul play.

57 *In the Spirit of Crazy Horse,* by Peter Matthiessen (1983), is the story of the Pine Ridge wars of the seventies, with emphasis on the shooting of the FBI agents and the capture and trial of Leonard Peltier.

59 The loss of the ancient tanned-hide star maps is mentioned in *Lakota Star Knowledge: Studies in Lakota Stellar Theology,* edited by Ronald Goodman (Rosebud, South Dakota: Sinte Gleska University Press, 1992), p. 18.

59 Books that discuss the Wounded Knee Massacre are too many to list. I recommend Hyde; *The Last Days of the Sioux Nation,* by Robert M. Utley (1963); and *Eyewitness at Wounded Knee,* by Richard E. Jensen, R. Eli Paul, and John E. Carter (1991). The last of these has a good summary of the massacre and events leading to it, as well as a selection of photographs taken at the time.

59 As with most casualty figures in combat, those from Wounded Knee are uncertain. One hundred and forty-six Indians are buried in the mass grave on the hill. Others died elsewhere. Including the Army casualties, the total was probably closer to 250 (see Jensen, Paul, and Carter, p. 20).

60 Among the many books about the Wounded Knee takeover in 1973, I have relied on *Like a Hurricane: The Indian Movement from Alcatraz to Wounded Knee,* by Paul Chaat Smith and Robert Allen Warrior (1996); Dewing; Matthiessen; and *Wounded Knee 1973: A Personal Account,* by Stanley David Lyman (1991).

The takeover was front-page news all over the country. I referred to newspaper accounts from *The Washington Post* and *The New York Times.*

62 The federal marshal, Lloyd Grimm, was wounded on March 26. On April 17, an occupier named Frank Clear or Frank Clearwater was hit during a firefight that followed a drop of supplies from airplanes over the occupiers' compound. He died soon after. On April 27, gunfire killed occupier Lawrence "Buddy" Lamont; his death prompted the occupiers to reach a negotiated solution.

68 David Carradine also says of Le, "I think he was not popular with his tribe because he was an inconsistent, emotional person. Also, he did not submit to the authority of his elders, not in the sense that he did anything bad, but in the sense that he ignored what they told him to do. He was a seeker, and he preferred to do his searching out there in the world." See *Endless Highway* (1995), p. 361.

Stories about the murder of taxicab driver George Aird, and about the arrests and trial that followed it, may be found in the *Los Angeles Times* of October 11, 1974, 1, p. 3; October 17, 1974, 1, p. 3; October 29, 1974, 1, p. 2; June 15, 1977, 2, p. 1; January 25, 1978, 1, p. 3; and May 25, 1978, 1, p. 1. See also *Blood of the Land: The Government and Corporate War against First Nations,* by Rex Weyler (1992), pp. 168–69 and 170–71.

CHAPTER 5

70　Much of the information in this chapter comes from newspaper reports over the last forty years. I will list only some of them.

　　A good comprehensive reference book on modern Indian reservations is *Discover Indian Reservations USA: A Visitors' Welcome Guide,* edited by Veronica E. Tiller (1992).

70　Before the casino boom, California's Agua Caliente tribe, which owns much of the land in Palm Springs, California, was sometimes referred to as the richest tribe in the United States. The Las Vegas Paiute tribe owns twelve acres of land in downtown Las Vegas.

71　The quarter-acre reservation belongs to the Paugussett Golden Hill, a state-recognized tribe in Connecticut. See *Discover Indian Reservations USA,* p. 92.

72　In February 1999, the federal government agreed to a return of over seven thousand acres of land in southeastern California to the Timbisha Shoshone; the tribe plans to use some of their new reservation for housing and commercial enterprises. See *Indian Country Today,* April 26–May 3, 1999, p. A 2.

74　Helen Hunt Jackson says (*Century of Dishonor,* p. 277) that Davy Crockett, the legendary frontiersman, "spoke warmly" against a bill for the removal of the Cherokee when he was a congressman from Tennessee. *David Crockett: The Man and the Legend,* by James Atkins Shackford (1981, p. 116–17), says that although a speech Crockett allegedly made against the removal was published in a volume of others on the subject, he in fact never made the speech. Crockett was no friend to Indians, Shackford says, and opposed the bill only as part of his larger campaign against President Andrew Jackson, whom he strongly disliked.

76　Historian Francis Parkman detailed the ferocity of the Iroquois with relish in his nine-volume masterwork, *France and England in North America* (1899). He thought the Iroquois were savages, and that to ascribe nobility to them was ridiculous; and yet he sometimes depicted them that way himself ("tall, stalwart figures, limbed like Greek statues"—Vol. IV, Part I, p. 82).

　　It was Parkman who mentioned Benjamin West's comment on seeing the Apollo Belvedere. See Parkman, *The Oregon Trail* (1849, reprinted 1982), p. 211.

77　The interest Karl Marx and Friedrich Engels had in Lewis Henry Morgan's writings on the Iroquois is mentioned in *Wasi'chu: The Continuing Indian Wars,* by Bruce Johansen and Roberto Maestas (1979), pp. 37–38. See also *The Origin of the Family, Private Property, and the State, in Light of the Researches of Lewis H. Morgan,* by Friedrich Engels (Alec West, trans.; 1884, reprinted 1972).

77　The St. Regis Mohawk Reservation, in upstate New York on the U.S.–Canadian border, includes almost 24,000 acres in both countries, and predates the founding of either. See *Discover Indian Reservations USA,* p. 236.

77　The recent struggle between the Iroquois and the state of New York over the state's attempt to collect sales tax received extensive coverage in *The New York Times.* See in particular its stories of May 9, 12, 19, 20, 21, 23, and 24, 1997.

78　What seemed to nettle Robert Moses most of all about the Tuscarora land-grab controversy was the mention of it in *Apology to the Iroquois,* by Edmund Wilson (1960). Wilson strongly sympathized with the Tuscarora. Moses's pamphlet, *Tuscarora Fiction and Fact: A Reply to the Author of Memoirs of Hecate County,* is an eight-page pamphlet (on file at the New York Public Library) that attempts to rebut Wilson.

80 For an excellent portrait of the violence and alcoholism in towns that border Indian reservations, see *Bordertowns,* by Marc Gaede (1988), a collection of photographs made mostly in Gallup, New Mexico, and Winslow, Arizona. Gaede says, in the note accompanying his photo of the big tank in the Gallup jail, "With dimensions of 4,500 square feet, *Police Magazine* reports it to be the largest jail cell in the United States. It holds 500 people . . . uncomfortably. The heat generated by so many bodies creates a furnace effect, and there is a blast of hot air on approach to the entrance. At first glance, this image usually provokes accusations of injustice. But those interned will go home to their families the following day. Without protective custody, there would be an endless nightly series of beatings, stabbings, muggings, rapes, death by exposure and car accidents."

80 Information about the many fatalities on U.S. 666 from Gallup to the reservation, and about the effort to get streetlights installed, comes from Nancy Bill of the IHS in Window Rock, Arizona; as well as from newspaper accounts (e.g., *Indian Country Today,* April 23–30, 1996, p. C 1).

81 The story of the rise of Indian casinos deserves a book in itself. Beginning in about 1992, newspaper articles about Indian gambling enterprises became so many as to crowd out other news from Indian country. A look at gambling coverage as represented by listings in the indexes of major newspapers in the 1990s shows how the gambling phenomenon grew nationwide. For example, in *The New York Times Index* for 1991, the listings under "Gambling" were about four columns long; in 1993 they were six and a half columns; in 1997 they were nine and a half columns.

82 The involvement of the federal government in the oversight of tribal gambling operations has followed major decisions in the federal courts that gave wider scope to the tribes. In the 1980s, a federal court in Connecticut ruled that the Mashantucket tribe's bingo operations were exempt from state jackpot regulations, and the U.S. Supreme Court ruled that the state of California could not regulate the gambling business of the Cabazon Band of Mission Indians. The IGRA was passed largely as a result of these decisions.

In 1996 the Supreme Court ruled for the state of Florida in a suit brought by the Seminole tribe, saying in effect that if a state refused to negotiate gaming compacts with a tribe under the provisions of the IGRA, the tribe had no recourse, because a state is immune from suit and the federal government cannot take that immunity away. By apparently undercutting the legal basis for the IGRA, this decision left tribal gaming in a legal limbo region, where it has remained.

83 I surmise that much of the gambling boom is related to the aging of the population, corporate downsizing that encourages early retirement, and the transfer of

much of the discretionary income in the country to people over sixty-five. Today the average seventy-year-old spends 20 percent more than the average thirty-year-old; the elderly have a median per capita income 67 percent above that of the population as a whole. See *The Future of Capitalism,* by Lester C. Thurow (1996), Chapter 5.

83 Americans legally gambled about $250 billion in 1987 and $638 billion in 1997. Of course, the figure for the total amount gambled would be higher, because much of gambling remains illegal and unreported. (See *The New York Times,* November 8, 1998, IV, 3:1.)

85 The Navajo leader so opposed to casino gambling was tribal chairman Albert Hale. See *Indian Country Today,* May 7–14, 1996, p. C 1.

89 During the bombing of Yugoslavia in the spring of 1999, an eighth F-117-A Nighthawk Stealth fighter was destroyed—shot down by Serb gunners who were apparently firing antiaircraft missiles at it more or less blindly.

90 The Oglala census with the obscene names was published in 1994 by the Nebraska State Historical Society under the title *The Crazy Horse Surrender Ledger,* edited by Thomas R. Buecker and R. Eli Paul. It reproduces photographically the pages of a ledger book in which Army officials kept records of Indians at the Red Cloud Agency, including a list of the Crazy Horse band compiled after they came into the agency in May 1877. The obscene names look especially striking in the careful Victorian handwriting in which they are set down.

91 Red Cloud went in search of Crazy Horse in April 1877, when efforts were under way to get Crazy Horse to surrender. His letter from the field to an Army officer, dictated to a companion who could write:

A Pril 15, 1877
Sir My Dear I have met some Indians on the road and they say the Indians on bear lodge creek on the 16th april and I thought let you know it and I think I will let you know better after I get to the camp so I sent the young man with this letter he have been to the camp before his name is arme blown off.

RED CLOUD

(Hyde, p. 291)

CHAPTER 6

99 Le was reading Oates's *Abraham Lincoln: The Man Behind the Myth* (1984). For a thorough discussion of Lincoln and the Mankato hangings, see *Lincoln and the Indians: Civil War Policy and Politics,* by David A. Nichols (1978), Chapter 8.

CHAPTER 7

118   The book in which Charlotte Black Elk explains her theory of precession as it relates to the Black Hills is *Lakota Star Knowledge: Studies in Lakota Stellar Theology.* (See note for p. 59 above.) Gerald Clifford died in 2000.

124   *Indian Country Today* occasionally does stories about the liquor traffic in White Clay. See "Tribe Wants Bordertown Bars Closed" (November 17–24, 1997, p. C 1) and "White Clay Liquor Problem Still Unresolved" (April 6–13, 1998, p. C 1). Additional information comes from the Nebraska Department of Revenue and the Nebraska Liquor Control Commission.

129   For stories about the Rodriguez shooting, see *Indian Country Today,* January 4, 1996, p. B 9; and August 5–12, 1996, p. B 1.

129   The state traffic accident report describes Wanda Kindle's accident somewhat differently than Le and others did at the time. According to the report, her car was not on the Chadron road but just west of the accident site, at the junction of Highway 18 and BIA 41 (the road to Loneman). Apparently her car had missed a turn and skidded into the ditch. Skid marks on the highway near her body suggested a hit-and-run accident. The driver who hit her was not in a pickup truck but in a Pontiac Lemans. The report says that a police officer found her body eighteen minutes after the accident occurred.

CHAPTER 8

131   Bars and drinking are naturally subjects that come up often in nonfiction accounts of Indian life published in the last fifty years. The bars in this chapter are taken from a number of as-told-to reminiscences and autobiographies.

    A harrowing and interesting book mostly about drinking is *Sundance: The Robert Sundance Story* (see note for p. 5 above). It tells the story of a Sioux, born in 1927, through his many misadventures as an almost-lifelong alcoholic.

    For additional information on this subject and many others, I am indebted to Sundance's brother Pat McLaughlin, past tribal chairman of the Standing Rock Sioux.

132   Robert Sundance spent a lot of time in Casey's Golden Pheasant in Billings, and describes the bar as it was then in some detail.

133   Joseph Mitchell's "The Mohawks in High Steel" appeared in *The New Yorker* of September 17, 1949. It may also be found in his collected works, *Up in the Old Hotel* (1992).

134   Many Los Angeles bars are mentioned in *Where White Men Fear to Tread: The Autobiography of Russell Means.*

138   The connection between Anheuser-Busch breweries and imagery of the Custer battle is examined in "Anheuser-Busch and Custer's Last Stand," by John M. Carroll, an interesting article published in *Greasy Grass,* an annual magazine of the Custer Battlefield Historical & Museum Association (May 1987; p. 25). (My

thanks to Thomas Buecker of the Fort Robinson Museum near Crawford, Nebraska, for calling it to my attention.)

139 The whiskey trader who bemoaned the liquor trade was J. W. Schultz, in his *My Life as an Indian: The Story of a Red Woman and a White Man in the Lodges of the Blackfeet* (1906), p. 95.

140 Frank Fools Crow talked about alcohol and the Oglala in *Fools Crow*, by Thomas E. Mails (1979), pp. 147ff.

In *Sundance: The Robert Sundance Story*, the reformed alcoholic Robert Sundance said, "As long as Indians remain terminally drunk in the gutter, there will be no respect for them . . . American society thinks, 'Why not take their water rights, their mineral rights, their land, why not flood their sacred land with dams? They're just a bunch of goddam drunks.' " (pp. 279–80)

140 Wesley Whiteman's statement on the subject of Buffalo Gap and the sun dance is in *The Last Contrary: The Story of Wesley Whiteman (Black Bear)*, by Warren E. Schwartz (1988), p. 72.

140 Information about the town of Buffalo Gap and surrounding region may be found in these books, all at the public library in Custer, South Dakota: *Our Yesterdays*, by the Eastern Custer County Historical Society (1970); *Custer County History to 1976*, edited by Jessie Y. Sundstrom (1977); *Buffalo Gap: A French Ranch in Dakota*, by Le Baron E. de Mandat-Grancy (1889). See also "Fire Station Latest Addition to Buffalo Gap," in the Rapid City *Journal* (December 1, 1974).

143ff Dewing, in *Wounded Knee II*, describes the Bad Heart Bull stabbing and its aftermath in detail. Other information about the incident may be found in accounts of Darld Schmitz's trial in the Rapid City *Journal* of April 30, May 1, May 2, and May 3, 1973.

144 Amos Bad Heart Bull (1869–1913) was one of the most gifted Indian ledger-book artists of his day. See *A Pictographic History of the Oglala Sioux*, drawings by Amos Bad Heart Bull, with text by Helen H. Blish (1967).

147 The former district attorney who told me about the film of the Custer riot is Lynn A. Moran of Custer, S.D.

148 I have been unable to find a full text of Sacheen Littlefeather's speech at the Academy Awards. *The New York Times* gave only a general description of what she said, and called the speech "an emotional diatribe." (Later it printed a correction, saying both her demeanor and her statement were restrained.)

148 I followed the post–Wounded Knee careers of Dennis Banks and Russell Means through newspaper reports at the time, and from the account in Means's autobiography.

CHAPTER 9

153 Father Buechel's dictionary, published by the Red Cloud Indian School (605-867-5491), is available from the school's bookstore.

166   The photo of my car was in the *Billings Gazette* of Monday, February 26, 1996, p. B 1.

CHAPTER 10

169   Jan Hardy of the Wright & McGill Co. in Denver is the source for information about the company's operations in Pine Ridge. The hand-tied hooks are now made in Korea as well as in Mexico.

170   Population figures for Pine Ridge and surrounding towns may be found in the *1990 Census of Population and Housing: Population and Housing Unit Counts* (U.S. Department of Commerce, Economics and Statistics Administration, Bureau of the Census).

172   For more on the poverty of Shannon County and the Pine Ridge Reservation, see "Sad Distinction for the Sioux: Homeland Is No. 1 in Poverty," in *The New York Times*, September 20, 1992, I, p. 1:5.

172   *The Washington Post* announced the capital area's dominance of per capita income in an article, "Washington Peerless on List of Richest Areas" (March 1, 1990; E, 1:2).

CHAPTER 11

184   Turner Network Television's *Crazy Horse* first aired on July 7, 1996. *Indian Country Today* reported the objections of Lyman Red Cloud and others to the movie in its issue of July 15–22, 1996, p. A 1.

185   Sources on the life of Red Cloud are the biographies cited (Hyde, Olson, and Larson) and *The Autobiography of Red Cloud*, edited by R. Eli Paul (1997).

Among sources published during Red Cloud's lifetime is an article describing his 1870 visit to New York City in *Harper's Weekly* (June 18, 1870; Vol. XIV, no. 703, p. 385).

186   The serious charge that Red Cloud conspired against the life of Crazy Horse is substantiated most tellingly (to my mind) by the account of William Garnett, interpreter at Fort Robinson; Garnett says that Red Cloud and other chiefs met with an officer at the fort who offered $300 and a fast horse to the man who could kill Crazy Horse. See "Report of William Garnett, Interpreter, to Gen'l H. L. Scott and Major J. McLaughlin," a copy of a typescript, on file at the New York Public Library. (See also my *Great Plains,* Chapter 6 and notes.)

191   Information about the life of Felix S. Cohen may be found in newspaper obituaries; in the introduction to his *The Legal Conscience: Selected Papers of Felix S. Cohen* (See note for p. 6 above); in the *Dictionary of American Biography* (supplement 5, 1951–1955); and in the Felix S. Cohen file in the Morris R. Cohen Library at the College of the City of New York.

Also, I am grateful to Lucy M. Kramer Cohen for kindly answering questions about her late husband which I sent to her by mail.

194 The siblings of Leroy "Sunshine" Janis I interviewed were Aqualynn Janis and Wilbert Janis.

CHAPTER 12

207 The story of SuAnne at Lead appeared first in a two-page article, "A Salute of Love," by Eric Haase and Jerry Reynolds, in the *Lakota Times* of February 19, 1992 (pp. B4–5). In 1995, the story was retold in *Athletes* by Nathan Aaseng, a book in the American Indian Lives series.

For my version of the story, I relied on the above accounts, which I expanded with details from interviews with Doni De Cory and Charles Zimiga, who were there. When *On the Rez* came out in hardcover, Bill Harlan, a reporter from the *Rapid City Journal* (South Dakota) with relatives in Lead, talked to people there to find out what they knew about the story. From school records and box-score lineups he learned that Pine Ridge did not play at Lead in 1988, SuAnne's freshman year, but did play there in 1987, when she was in eighth grade. According to the lineup from 1987, both she and Doni De Cory were in that game, SuAnne scored five points, and Pine Ridge lost, 66–64. A short news item in the *Rapid City Journal* (October 11, 1987, p. F2) contains two sentences about the last-second victory and the leading scorers, plus the box score of the game.

Although people from Lead whom Mr. Harlan talked to said that some Lead fans could be rowdy and racist at school sports events, they also said that by no means all Lead fans were, and that no one had a recollection of fans misbehaving at this particular game. Neither did anyone remember SuAnne's shawl dance at center court. When Mr. Harlan called Doni De Cory, the main source for the story, she said that SuAnne's dance was a smaller-scale event than she had previously described. Charles Zimiga, according to Mr. Harlan, also apparently backed off from details he had told me.

Later, Doni De Cory insisted to me that the basic facts of the story were as she had told me originally. She said that the main offenders among the Lead fans were a bunch of boys, possibly a pep club, at one end of the bleachers, and that SuAnne did her dance in front of them. She added that the fans' challenge, SuAnne's happy and defiant response, and the silence and then cheering that followed was how the event appeared to her. Cee Cee Big Crow, SuAnne's big sister, who scored two points in that game, does not remember SuAnne dancing as Doni De Cory describes, but does remember her leading the team fearlessly in front of jeering fans during warmups. Cee Cee says that SuAnne often rallied her teammates and stood up for them with gestures like that.

SuAnne did a shawl dance at center court of a basketball gym on at least one other occasion, and there is even a video of her dancing in buckskin dress, moccasins, and fringed shawl in a gym on her Australia–New Zealand tour. The story of SuAnne at Lead is a heroic story, one of the most important to emerge in the modern West. It conveys the hope and endurance of a whole tribe, and it speaks to a reality larger than the particular basketball game it's about. I am grateful to Bill Harlan for bringing out Lead's side of the story; people he talked to in Lead confirmed Doni De Cory's statement that the two teams became friendlier after that game. (See also my exchange of letters with Bill Harlan on this subject in the *New York Review of Books,* May 11, 2000, p. 60.)

210 The Homestake Mine in Lead maintains a small historical museum; some of the information about the mine comes from there, and from *History of the Homestake Gold Mine*, a pamphlet published by the company.

210 The mining career of George Hearst is described in *The Hearsts: Family and Empire—The Later Years*, by Lindsay Chaney and Michael Cieply (1981). *William Randolph Hearst: His Role in American Progressivism*, by Roy Everett Littlefield III (1980), has details about W. R. Hearst at Harvard (pp. 3–5).

210 Sioux sources put the value of the gold taken from the Homestake Mine at $14 billion (*Indian Country Today*, June 18–25, 1996, p. A 1). The Homestake Mining Co. itself says it has produced 39 million ounces of gold. The price of gold fluctuates, of course. At present prices, which are low, that much gold would be worth about $10 billion.

210 Episcopal Bishop William H. Hare, head of a government commission to investigate problems at the Red Cloud Agency, wrote to President Grant of his displeasure at the planned Custer expedition (Olson, p. 173). Commissioner George W. Manypenny later called the Custer expedition "unlawful"; see Manypenny's *Our Indian Wards*, p. xxix. He and the other commissioners used the opportunity of the report that accompanied the Black Hills "agreement" to lecture the government on the wrongs it had done.

211 The course of the Sioux claim for the Black Hills through the Indian Claims Commission and the courts may be followed in newspaper stories—see *The New York Times* of July 1, 1980, p. 1:6; July 19, 1980, p. 5:1; May 27, 1981, p. 12:1; June 3, 1981, p. 18:5; January 19, 1982, p. 14:3; January 28, 1982, p. 14:6; December 11, 1983, I, p. 28:6; March 11, 1987, I, p. 23:1).

Lazarus (see note for p. 38) provides a good and readable account of the history of this complicated claim.

CHAPTER 13

For details about SuAnne Big Crow's high school basketball career I am indebted to Chick Big Crow, Rol Bradford, Charles Zimiga, Gordon Bergquist, Jeanne Horse, and Yvonne "Tiny" De Cory.

Interviews with members of the 1989 championship team—Rita Bad Bear, Mary Walking, Dakota "Happy" Big Crow, and Angie Big Crow Cournoyer —

also furnished valuable information. Ginny Dohrer Schulte and Coach Bergquist gave the perspective of the Milbank side in the championship game.

Additional facts may be found in the sports coverage of the *Lakota Times* (a reservation newspaper that later became *Indian Country Today*) in its issues of November 21, November 28, and December 5, 1989; and in the Grant County *Review* of Milbank, South Dakota, December 6, 1989.

226 Transcripts of the NBC *Nightly News* report on Pine Ridge that was broadcast on November 20, 21, and 22 of 1989 were obtained from Burrell's Information Services, Livingston, New Jersey.

234 Many people described the celebration in Pine Ridge after the victory. Dennis Banks, Charles Zimiga, Jeanne Horse, and the players on the championship team mentioned above were especially helpful.

CHAPTER 14

As with much of what I know about SuAnne, information in this chapter comes from interviews with her family, coaches, and friends, in particular Doni De Cory, Chick Big Crow, Wesley Bettleyoun, Jeanne Horse, and Charles Zimiga.

247ff For the details of SuAnne's car accident and her funeral I have relied on newspaper accounts (the Chadron [Nebraska] *Record* of February 14, 1992; the Rapid City *Journal*, February 10, 1992, p. 1; the *Lakota Times* [now *Indian Country Today*], February 12, 1992, p. 1; February 19, 1992, B 4–5); interviews with Chick Big Crow; and the South Dakota Department of Transportation accident report.

250 Along with Chick Big Crow, Rol Bradford described for me the early days of setting up the Big Crow Center.

CHAPTER 15

143ff My sources for statistics on alcohol-related vehicle fatalities on the reservation come from *Indian Country Today* (November 25–December 2, 1997, p. C1) and from the South Dakota Department of Transportation booklet, *Motor Vehicle Traffic Accident Summary* (1997, with additional data for 1998).

If one includes accidents involving alcohol not only on the reservation but near it, the figures are higher. *Indian Country Today*, citing the Pine Ridge Office of Environmental Health, reported (July 12–19, 1999, p. A1) that thirty-seven people died on or near the reservation in the preceding three years in alcohol-related crashes.

None of the people I know in Oglala suffered serious damage in the tornado. After the wreckage had been cleared away, much of the village had disappeared and neighborhoods were reduced to streets and driveways leading to nothing. The tribe says that Oglala will soon be rebuilt with two hundred new homes.

The protests in White Clay declined in size in the weeks following the riot, and no further violence occurred. The protesters had given the liquor stores in White Clay a deadline to shut down that came due about a month after the first march; the deadline passed unmarked. One of the store owners said business in White Clay had returned to normal.

President Clinton's visit to Pine Ridge was a major news story of July 8, 1999. See *The New York Times* of that date, p. A 12.

INDEX